THE HORN OF A

Hot Spots in Global Politics

Christoph Bluth, *Korea*
Alan Dowty, *Israel/Palestine*
Amalendu Misra, *Afghanistan*
Gareth Stansfield, *Iraq*
Jonathan Tonge, *Northern Ireland*
Thomas Turner, *Congo*

THE HORN OF AFRICA

Kidane Mengisteab

polity

First published in 2014 by Polity Press

Polity Press
65 Bridge Street
Cambridge CB2 1UR, UK

Polity Press
350 Main Street
Malden, MA 02148, USA

ISBN-13: 978-0-7456-5122-4(pb)
ISBN-13: 978-0-7456-5121-7

A catalogue record for this book is available from the British Library.

Typeset in 10.5 on 12 pt Sabon
by Toppan Best-set Premedia Limited
Printed and bound in Great Britain by T.J. International,
Padstow, Cornwall

The publisher has used its best endeavours to ensure that the URLs for external websites referred to in this book are correct and active at the time of going to press. However, the publisher has no responsibility for the websites and can make no guarantee that a site will remain live or that the content is or will remain appropriate.

Every effort has been made to trace all copyright holders, but if any have been inadvertently overlooked the publisher will be pleased to include any necessary credits in any subsequent reprint or edition.

For further information on Polity, visit our website:
www.politybooks.com

Contents

Abbreviations

ADF	Allied Democratic Forces
AFRICOM	Africa Command
AIAI	Al-Itihad al-Islamiya
ALF	Afar Liberation Front
AMISOM	African Union Mission in Somalia
APRM	African Peer Review Mechanism
ARDUF	Afar Revolutionary Democratic Union/Front
ARLS	Alliance for the Re-Liberation of Somalia
ARPCT	Alliance for the Restoration of Peace and Counter Terrorism
ASEAN/ARF	Association of Southeast Asian Nations (ASEAN Regional Forum)
AU	African Union
CEWARN	Conflict Early Warning and Response Mechanism
CFCs	Chlorofluorocarbons
CIA	Central Intelligence Agency
CJTF-HOA	Combined Joint Task Force – Horn of Africa
COW	Correlates of War
CUD	Coalition for Unity and Democracy
DMLEK	Democratic Movement for the Liberation of the Eritrean Kunama
DRC	Democratic Republic of the Congo
ECOWAS	Economic Community of West African States
EIJM	Eritrean Islamic Jihad Movement

ELF	Eritrean Liberation Front
EPLF	Eritrean People's Liberation Front
EPPLF	Ethiopian People's Patriotic Liberation Front
EPRDF	Ethiopian People's Revolutionary Democratic Front
EPRP	Ethiopian People's Revolutionary Party
ESF	Eritrean Salvation Front
FAO	Food and Agricultural Organization
FRUD	Front for the Restoration of Unity and Democracy
GDP	Gross Domestic Product
HDI	Human Development Index
ICC	International Criminal Court
IGAD	Intergovernmental Authority for Development
IGAD-ICPAT	IGAD Capacity Programme against Terrorism
IGASOM	IGAD Peace Support Mission to Somalia
ILRI	International Livestock Research Institute (Nairobi)
IPCC	Intergovernmental Panel on Climate Change
IUU	Illegal, Unreported and Unregulated (fishing)
JEM	Justice and Equality Movement
LRA	Lord's Resistance Army
MAAG	Military Assistance Advisory Group
MIO	Maritime Intercept Operation
MRC	Mombasa Republican Council
NALU	National Army for the Liberation of Uganda
NIF	National Islamic Front
NRM/A	National Resistance Movement/Army
OAU	Organization of African Unity
OEF	One Earth Future Foundation
OLF	Oromo Liberation Front
ONLF	Ogaden National Liberation Front
PAIC	Popular Arab and Islamic Congress
PPP	Purchasing power parity
RPP	People's Rally for Progress (Rassemblement Populaire pour Le Progrès)
RRA	Rahanwein Resistance Army

RSADO	Red Sea Afar Democratic Organization
SLM/A	Sudan Liberation Movement/Army
SNM	Somali National Movement
SPLM/A	Sudan People's Liberation Movement/Army
SPM	Somali Patriotic Movement
SNA	Somali National Alliance
SSDF	Somali Salvation Democratic Front
SSDM/A	South Sudan Democratic Movement/Army
SSF	Somali Salvation Front
SSLA	South Sudan Liberation Army
TFG	Transitional Federal Government
TLF	Tigray Liberation Front
TPLF	Tigray People's Liberation Front
UCDP	Uppsala Conflict Data Programme
UIC	Union of Islamic Courts
UNDP	United Nations Development Programme
UNEP	United Nations Environment Programme
UNICEF	United Nations Children's Fund
UNHCR	United Nations High Commissioner for Refugees
UNLA	Ugandan National Liberation Army
UNRF	Ugandan National Rescue Front
UPA	Uganda People's Army
UPDA	Uganda People's Democratic Army
USAID	United States Agency for International Development
USC/SNA	United Somali Congress/Somali National Alliance
USSR	Union of Soviet Socialist Republics
WNBF	West Nile Bank Front
WSLF	Western Somali Liberation Front

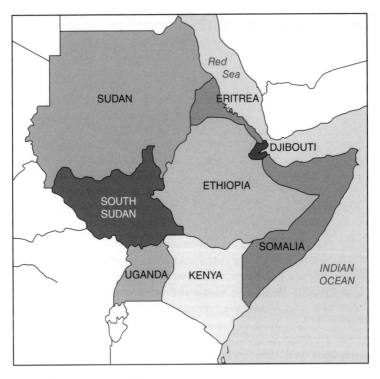

Map of the Horn of Africa

Acknowledgements ──────────────

I am grateful to the two anonymous reviewers of an earlier draft of the book. I benefited considerably from their insightful comments. I am responsible for all remaining shortcomings. This book is dedicated to all the victims of wars waged by brutal or irresponsible governments in the Greater Horn of Africa. How much it hurts when you realize how needless these devastating conflicts are and how thoughtlessly leaders drag their populations into them.

DKM, Semoo and Banci, this one is for you too.

Kidane Mengisteab

1   The Greater Horn of Africa: Hot Spot in the Global System

The Greater Horn of Africa is a region that contains one of the deadliest clusters of conflicts in the global system. It is also a region facing an alarming rate of environmental degradation, which has made it prone to humanitarian disasters, including sporadic droughts and famines. Moreover, without substantive changes in the political structures and institutional systems, the region is likely to remain one of the hottest spots in the global system for decades to come. Given this prognosis, this book grapples with two crucial tasks. One is to provide a comprehensive and yet concise analysis of the key factors which have engendered various levels of conflicts in the Greater Horn over the last sixty or so years and are likely to render the region prone to conflicts for some time to come. While key developments of the nineteenth century, which still impinge on contemporary conflicts, are examined briefly, the focus of this study is the post-decolonization era, which refers to the time period from the mid-1950s to the present.[1] Ethiopia, the largest country in the region, was not a colony and the concept of decolonization does not apply to it directly. However, decolonization has indirect relevance to Ethiopia since decolonization of neighbouring countries signified a new era in its regional as well as its internal relations. The second task is to explore rather briefly new political and institutional arrangements that may enable the region to transform the conflict factors and extricate itself from the devastations that have become its trade mark.

The conflicts that ravage the Greater Horn occur at multiple levels. Some of them are inter-state conflicts. Some are between the state and domestic armed entities that challenge it for various reasons, while others are among communities within the same country as well as across international boundaries. There are also one-sided conflicts where the state or rebel groups commit brutalities against civilian populations. The region has also seen some violent conflicts among armed groups, who, while fighting the state, also fight one another. Given such a variance in the nature of the region's conflicts, it is rather challenging to formulate a conceptual anchor that ties neatly together the factors that contribute to all the conflicts. One of the aims of this introductory chapter is to map out a workable conceptual framework that would help us in comprehending the complex set of factors that generate the region's various types of conflicts. A second task is to sketch the main objectives and tasks of each chapter in order to assist the reader in weaving though the various chapters and relate each one of them to the above identified two principal objectives of the book.

Conceptual Framework

The region's various types of conflicts are caused by a complex mix of interrelated factors. While difficult to capture all the factors in a single coherent framework, it is nevertheless, plausible to contend that most of the conflicts emanate from two core conditions that characterize the region. One is the failure of the internal political and institutional systems to accommodate and advance the interests of the disparate identity groups and to facilitate peaceful management of conflicts that arise between the state and identity groups and among identities and communities. The second is the failure of the existing institutions of regional governance to promote peaceful relations among the countries of the region by a timely management of boundary and territorial disputes and also by creating socioeconomic arrangements that advance mutual well-being and reduce the burden of ethnic groups that are partitioned by national boundaries. In other words, the factors for most of the region's conflicts are rooted in the failure of structures and institutions of domestic and regional governance. The failures in the two core areas identified, however, are to a large extent influenced by some contextual factors. One is the historical context, which left legacies that perpetuate the conflict-engendering conditions. Another is the existing global context, which often impinges on the region's ability to address the conflict-engendering conditions without external intervention. The environmental degradation the region has faced over the last several decades is another contextual factor that complicates governance and is exacerbated by poor governance.

Under this broad conceptual framework at least six categories of conflict-generating factors can be identified:

- One category of factors relates to the historical context and the manner in which the states in the region were formed and how the socioeconomic structures established during the formation of the states through the expansion of pre-colonial empires and colonization have impacted the interests of and relations among the various identity groups in the region. Pre-colonial empires, such as the Abyssinian empire and the Mahdiya state of Sudan have, for instance, altered and often poisoned inter-identity relations, as did the colonial state.

- A second category of factors relates to the nature of the post-colonial state, including the divergence of its economic and institutional systems from those adhered to by different segments of society, the structures of the state that hinder accountability within its component organizations, and the quality of its leadership. The societies in the Greater Horn, like those in the rest of the African continent, range from those who live under the traditional economies of peasants and pastoralists to those in the modern economic system that rapidly changes in complexity. The region's governments, regardless of their ideological or political orientations, operate under institutional systems that detach the state from large segments of its populations. Even in the rare cases where leaders might be relatively committed to advancing broad social interests, they lack the structural and institutional capacity and flexibility to manage the socioeconomic diversity and challenges of their societies. Moreover, they also lack the farsightedness and audacity to disengage from the existing dysfunctional structures and construct new political and institutional systems that reflect the socioeconomic realities and cultural values of their populations and coordinate policy and resources with broad social interests. The institutional detachment of the state from segments of the population implies that those segments of the population are largely excluded from the political process. The different organizations of the state also lack independence from the executive branch of the government and strongmen, who subordinate the state and thereby hinder its development. The upper echelons of the functionaries of the state are also often 'ethnocratic', as Ali Mazrui (1975) notes. As a result, the state often is viewed to be an expression of certain identity groups instead of one that promotes the interests of society at large. In other cases the leaders, whose primary preoccupation has been to preserve their monopoly of power, are simply self-serving. In some cases, such self-serving leaders may even perpetuate various conflicts as they find them to be instrumental in extending their tenure on power, by either diverting public opinion from domestic ills to external enemies or by using wars as a means of squashing popular demands for democratization of the political system. Political entrepreneurs often exploit diversity in their struggle for power and instigate inter-identity hostilities. Under such conditions state-building by developing institutions and infrastructures for effective governance has been impeded. Such a grand failure in state-building has, in turn, created conditions that foster conflicts.

• A related category of factors is the poor management of diversity and crisis in the process of nation-building, which entails integrating disparate social, ethnic, clan, religious or regional identities to form a community of citizens governed by a shared system of institutions. A state which lacks the structures that foster accountability and often represent ethnic identity, or fails to develop political structures and institutional systems that advance broad social interests, is unlikely to be effective in nation-building through effective management of diversity. Failure in diversity management is manifested by politicization of identity, power struggle among the elite of different identities and inter-communal conflicts over dwindling resources, which are exacerbated by a combination of environmental degradation and rapid population growth.

- A fourth category of factors which has generated conflicts and tensions among states is the absence of effective management of disputes over boundaries. Like the boundaries of most African countries, the international boundaries of the Greater Horn countries are not yet clearly demarcated on the ground. The countries of the region also lack effective institutional arrangements that would mitigate the effects of marginalization of ethnic groups who are split into several countries by national boundaries. In the absence of strong institutions of regional governance, such border disputes, along with weak or near absence of mechanisms for peaceful settlement of inter-state disputes, have led the states of the region to fight border wars and to intervene in each other's affairs and engage in proxy wars that destabilize the region and prevent regional cooperation. Religious zeal and intolerance between countries have also contributed to tense relations and conflicts among neighbouring states.

- A fifth category of factors relates to the global socioeconomic environment and different forms of intervention by various actors from outside the region. On a number of occasions external intervention has been life-saving and conflict-reducing. In many other cases, however, external intervention has contributed to initiate or to intensify conflicts in the region. In some cases, it has even changed the region's course of history. To fortify their grip on power, regimes in the countries of the region have often participated in advancing the agenda of external actors often at the expense of the region's stability and well-being. External intervention can under certain conditions help in mitigating conflicts as well as in advancing democratization. However, it can also adversely affect relations among the states of the region as well as inter-identity relations within countries. Since democracy entails self-determination in decision-making, external intervention, which tends to deliberately or inadvertently exert influence, can also undermine democratization and the development of indigenous political arrangements of conflict resolution and diversity management.

- A sixth category of factors is the alarming rate of environmental degradation, which has culminated in economic and social dislocations and widespread resource-based conflicts. Much of the Greater Horn region is arid or semi-arid and has over the last four or so decades faced a rapid rate of environmental degradation. No doubt, global climatic changes have contributed to this problem. However, local and regional factors are also major contributors. Rapid population growth, changes in land-use patterns and chronic conflicts are among the regional factors for environmental degradation, which is manifested by cyclical droughts, chronic food and water shortages and periodic famines. These conditions have exerted growing pressure on the region's populations, especially the peasants and nomads and have resulted in land and water-based communal conflicts.

The last two categories of factors may appear to be external to the identified conceptual framework since they do not entirely originate from the political and institutional systems in the region. On careful examination, however, it is clear that they are integral to the region's political and institutional systems as well as the conceptual framework. Competent domestic and regional governance systems do not allow destructive external intervention. The occurrence of self-serving external intervention is, thus, a clear indication of problems of domestic and regional governance. Similarly, environmental degradation becomes as destructive as it has been in the Greater Horn when the existing political and institutional arrangements are incapable of controlling its occurrence or in managing its impacts. Environmental degradation factors such as inappropriate land tenure systems, poor conservation measures and rapid demographic growth are largely problems of management, although the global factors of degradation, such as global warming, set the context within which the countries of the region have to operate.

Overview of the Book

The rest of the book consists of seven chapters. After briefly introducing the reader to the region's general socioeconomic characteristics, chapter 2 attempts to sort out the region's various conflicts into typologies and to provide a brief assessment of the socioeconomic costs of these conflicts. Chapter 3 examines the conflict-engendering contexts left behind by pre-colonial empires and kingdoms and the colonial state. Changes in inter-identity relations, fragmentation of economic and institutional systems and uneven development are some of the inherited contexts given special attention. Chapter 4 examines how and why the post-colonial state in the region continues to contribute to internal and external conflicts. To properly explain the role of the state, the chapter first conceptualizes the state and identifies the characteristics of a properly functioning and democracy-fostering state. The chapter then appraises the structures, institutions and quality of leadership of the Greater Horn's post-colonial state on the basis of the criteria of the properly functioning state. Chapter 5 examines how the state's failure in developing institutions of governance that accommodate the diverse groups of citizens has contributed in politicization of inter-identity relations and to the crisis of nation-building in the region. The sixth chapter examines the role of external intervention in fostering conflicts and instability in the region and in undermining its regional integration efforts. It also explains how lack of strong regional governance has exposed the region to a high level of external meddling. Chapter 7 explores how the environmental degradation that has ravaged the region has contributed to resource-based conflicts and general instability by threatening the viability of the peasant and pastoral economic systems that employ sizeable portions of the region's populations. The chapter also attempts to explain how poor management of resources has contributed to the alarming rate of environmental degradation the region has faced over the last several decades. Chapter 8 serves as a conclusion and explores political and institutional arrangements that can help the region transform the various conflict-engendering factors. One objective of this chapter is to explain how a contextualized and comprehensive democratization can adjust the institutional and political structures in the region so that they advance state-building and diversity management and nation-building. A second objective is to explore a system of institutions for more effective regional governance that (a) demarcates boundaries before they become sources of conflicts, (b) accommodates the social and cultural ties of identity groups split by national boundaries, (c) establishes mechanisms of regional cooperation to control proxy wars and harmful external intervention and (d) fosters regional economic development by taking advantage of the region's unrealized economic complementarities and by cooperating in environmental management.

Conflicts in the Greater Horn

Introduction

This chapter attempts to identify and categorize the key conflicts that have ravaged the region during the last half a century or so and to briefly outline some of the socioeconomic costs and implications of the conflicts. Before delving into these tasks, however, a brief description of the basic characteristics and socioeconomic conditions of the Greater Horn is provided in order to familiarize the reader with the region.

The region consists of eight countries with an estimated total population of about 226.9 million in 2012 and a total area of 5,209,975 sq km (see table 2.1 for details). The countries of the region include: Djibouti, Eritrea, Ethiopia, Kenya, Somalia, Sudan, South Sudan and Uganda, and they are all members of a regional integration, the Intergovernmental Authority for Development (IGAD), although Eritrea's membership in the regional body has been suspended since 2007.[2] Two of the youngest countries of the region, Eritrea and South Sudan, were formed through secessions from Ethiopia in 1993 and from Sudan in 2011, respectively. Somaliland has also declared its independence from Somalia but it has not yet obtained international recognition as an independent state.

A notable characteristic of the region is that it is a mosaic of cultures with considerable ethnic diversity both regionally

Table 2.1. Area of territory and size of population of the countries of the Horn of Africa

	Djibouti	Eritrea	Ethiopia	Kenya	Somalia	Sudan (N&S)	Uganda
Area of territory (sq km)	23,200	117,600	1,104,300	580,367	637,657	2,505,813	241,038
Population in 2012 (000s)	923.0	5,581.0	86,539.0	42,749.0	9,797.0	45,722.0*	35,621.0
Average annual pop. growth rate 1970–90 (%)	6.2	2.7	2.6	3.7	3.0	2.9	3.1
Average annual pop. growth rate 1990–2010 (%)	2.3	2.5	2.7	2.7	1.7	2.5	3.2
Projected average annual pop. growth rate 2010–30 (%)	1.8	2.3	1.8	2.4	2.8	2.1	2.9
Pop. in 1960 (in 000s)	85.0	1,424.0	23977.0	8105.0	2,819.0	11,562.0	6,788.0
Change of population 1960–2012 (%)	1,085.9	392.0	361.0	527.4	347.5	395.5	524.8
Population projections for 2030 (in 000s)	1,263.0	8,394.0	118,515.0	65,928.0	16,360.0	51,775.0**	55,846.0

* The population of South Sudan in 2012 is roughly 10,314,000. The projected population for 2030 is 15,082,000.
** This figure excludes South Sudan.

Sources: UNCTAD Stat, http://unctadstat.unctad.org/TableViewer/tableView.aspx?ReportId=97; UNICEF, http://www.unicef.org/infobycountry/; African Development Bank, *African Economic Outlook*, 2012; UNDP, *Human Development Report*, 2012; World Bank, *World Development Indicators*, 2012; and IGAD, *IGAD Environment and Natural Resources, Strategy*, April 2007.

and within countries. If language can serve as a proxy for ethnic identity, the region is said to be home to some 340 languages. Sudan (both north and south) is said to have 134 languages, followed by Ethiopia with eighty-nine languages, Kenya with sixty-two, Uganda with forty-three, Eritrea with nine and Djibouti with two local languages (Lewis, 2009). The countries of the region are also characterized by religious diversity with various denominations of Christianity and Islam coexisting, along with various forms of traditional religions. No doubt peaceful governance of the countries of the region requires effective strategies of management of diversity.

Many of the region's ethnic groups are also split across several countries by national boundaries established by colonialism. The Somali people, for example, live in Somalia, Djibouti, Ethiopia and Kenya. The Beja, Tigre and Rashaida live in Sudan and Eritrea. The Tigrigna speakers, the Kunama and Shaho live in Eritrea and northern Ethiopia; the Oromo live in Ethiopia and Kenya, the Afar live in Eritrea, Ethiopia and Djibouti. The Luo are spread over Kenya, Ethiopia, Sudan, Uganda, Tanzania and Eastern Congo, while the Luhya live in Kenya, Uganda and Tanzania (see table 2.2 for further examples).

The partition of ethnic groups into different countries often involves the disruption of social and cultural ties. A number of studies have also shown that partitioned ethnic identities tend to face relatively greater levels of marginalization, ethnic struggles and civil wars (Asiwaju, 1985; Dowden, 2008; Michalopoulos and Papaioannou, 2011; Wesseling, 1996). In the case of pastoral communities partition also implies disruption of economic process as it hinders the movements of groups who rely on regional ecosystems for survival (Samatar and Machaka, 2006). Addressing the challenges facing partitioned ethnic groups requires arrangements that enable such groups to maintain economic, social and cultural ties across national boundaries. While such arrangements would have wider benefits, they are particularly essential for pastoralist communities, whose economic system entails seasonal movements in search of pasture and water.

Table 2.2. Selected list of ethnic groups that are split into different countries

Ethnic group	Countries of habitation
Afar*	Djibouti, Eritrea, Ethiopia
Somali*	Somalia, Djibouti, Ethiopia, Kenya
Luo*	Kenya, Uganda, Sudan, Ethiopia, Tanzania
Luhya	Kenya, Uganda, Tanzania
Beja,* Rashaida, Tigre	Eritrea, Sudan
Tigrigna,* Kunama,* Shaho (Irob)	Eritrea, Ethiopia
Oromo*	Ethiopia, Kenya
Pokot, Teso	Kenya, Uganda
Kakwa, Sebei, Lugbwara, Madi, Ancholi,* Kaliko, Pojullo	Uganda, South Sudan
Anuak,* Nuer,* Bertha, Donyiro, Tirma, Shita, Gumuz, Murle, Kichepo, Wetawit	Ethiopia, Sudan
Daasanach	Ethiopia, Kenya, Sudan

*Identities that have engaged in violent protests or armed struggle against the state.

In the absence of such socioeconomic arrangements, the fragmentation of ethnic identities tends to become a source of instability and major conflicts as such groups often react by developing ethno-nationalist movements within their respective countries.

Another characteristic of the Greater Horn countries is the dichotomy of modes of production that govern their economies. The modes of production operating in the region range from a capitalist sector symbolized by emerging stock markets and relatively advanced financial systems to subsistence farming and pastoral economic systems, which are essentially non-capitalist. These parallel modes of production are associated with different economic, political and social institutions. Since institutions govern behaviour and social relations, parallel institutional systems represent different and often conflicting norms of behaviour and social relations.

Institutional clashes, such as conflicting land ownership systems between the customary (traditional/informal) and the state-sanctioned (formal) systems, easily become sources of social conflict and instability by creating parallel socioeconomic spaces. The parallel existence of modes of production and the resulting dichotomous institutional systems also create the challenge of crafting economic policy that accommodates the interests of the different segments of the population, who live under different institutional spaces. In the absence of transformation of the modes of production and reconciliation of the fragmented institutions, poor governance and social instability become hard to avoid. Institutions of democratic governance also become difficult to establish, as will be explained in chapter 5.

Socioeconomic Conditions

The Horn of Africa is one of the poorest regions of the world. All the countries of the region fall within the bottom 20 per cent of the UNDP's Human Development Index (HDI) (see table 2.3 for social data). Kenya, which has the highest level on the HDI in the region, with a score of 0.509 in 2011, is ranked 143rd of 187 countries. Ethiopia is ranked 174th while Somalia is no longer ranked.

The economy of the region is dominated by a subsistence sector in terms of employment. In 2011 roughly 80 per cent of the population in Eritrea, Ethiopia, Kenya and Uganda, and 62 per cent and 59 per cent in Somalia and Sudan respectively lived in rural areas (see table 2.4). The region also contains the largest cluster of pastoralists in the world, with roughly 17 per cent of the region's population engaged in pasture-based production systems. Excluding Somalia, livestock make up approximately 15 per cent of the GDP of the IGAD countries (Sandford and Ashley, 2008). The region as a whole contains roughly 68 million livestock units. Ethiopia and Sudan (before the secession of the South) have the highest livestock populations in Sub-Saharan Africa with 28.4 and 22.3 million respectively. Pastoralists also constitute 61 per cent of the region's poor.

Table 2.3. Selected indicators of socioeconomic conditions in Greater Horn countries

Indicator	Djibouti	Eritrea	Ethiopia	Kenya	Somalia	Sudan	Uganda
GDP (bn US$) based on PPP, 2011	2.198	4.018	113.729	79.720	–	97.850	57.451
GDP/capita (PPP) US$, 2011	2,427.0	742.0	1,342.0	1,916.0	–	2,192.0	1,665.0
Life expectancy at birth, 2011 (yrs)	57.9	61.6	59.3	57.1	51.0	61.5	54.1
Life expectancy at birth, 1970 (yrs)	43	43	43	52	40	45	50
Infant mortality/1,000 births, 2011	53.3	40.3	60.9	43.6	103.7	55.6	64.2
Adult (15 yrs +) literacy rate, 2005–10 (%)	67.9	67.8	42.7	87.4	37.8	71.8	76.8
Population below national poverty line, 2000–9 (%)	–	–	38.9	45.9	–	46.5*	24.5
Population living below US$1.25 2000–9 (% total)	18.8	–	39.0	19.7	–	–	28.7
HIV rate of total population (%)	3.1 (2007) 2.5 (2009)	1.3 (2007) 0.8 (2009)	2.1 (2007) –	6.7 (2003) 6.0 (2009)	0.5 (2007) –	1.4 (2007) 1.1 (2009)	5.4 (2007) 6.5 (2009)
HDI, 2011	0.430	0.349	0.363	0.509	N.A.	0.408	0.446

* Data are for 2009.

Sources: African Development Bank, *African Economic Outlook*, 2012; UNDP, *Human Development Report*, 2011; UNICEF, http://www.unicef.org/infobycountry/.

Table 2.4. Selected indicators of food insecurity and environmental problems in the Horn of Africa

	Djibouti	Eritrea	Ethiopia	Kenya	Somalia	Sudan	Uganda
Net food production index, 2007–9 (1999–2001 = 100)	–	125.7	143.3	130.0	104.0	119.0	110.0
Ratio of population living in rural areas, 2011	23.7	77.9	83.2	77.5	62.1	59.2	86.5
Ratio of pastoral population	71.0	–	5.9	–	76.0	20.0	–
Irrigated land (% total cropland), 2007–9	–	3.1	2.1	1.9	20.0	9.6	0.1
Net cereal imports kg/capita, 2007–9	–	27.0	17.0	38.0	–	–	11.0
Share of food aid to total consumption, 1990–2006 (%)	9.6	27.9*	6.3	2.6	N.A.	5.0	1.3
Proportion of undernourished % of total population, 2010–12	26.0	65.0	40.0	30.0	–	37.0**	22.0†
Proportion of undernourished % of total population, 1990–2006	44.8	66.7*	57.3	30.8	N.A.	24.3	18.3

* Data for Eritrea are for the 1993–2006 period.
** Data for 2007–9.
† Data for 2006–8.
Sources: World Bank, Africa Development Indicators, 2009; FAO, The State of Food Insecurity in the World, 2009, 2012; UNDP, Africa Human Development Report, 2012; FAO, The State of Food Insecurity in the World, 2012.

The Greater Horn has also been highly vulnerable to environmental degradation. Over the last half a century the region's temperature has shown a rising trend while rainfall has become increasingly erratic (Ouma, 2008). The rains have also become more stormy when they come, causing severe soil erosion. During the same time period large parts of the region, which are arid or semi-arid, have faced rapid rates of degradation, in the form of frequent occurrence of droughts, deforestation, loss of vegetation and biodiversity, increased soil erosion, desiccation and desertification. Rampant poverty, along with rapid environmental degradation, has also contributed to the region's instability. The impacts of environmental degradation are discussed in greater detail in chapter 7.

Food Shortages and Famines

Despite the fact that agriculture is the largest employer in all the countries of the region, most of them suffer from chronic food shortages, undernourishment and periodic famines. An IGAD official in 2010 described the region as 'the most critically food insecure region of the world'. The 2010 Global Hunger Index, for example, rates hunger severity of the countries of the region from 'extremely alarming' (Eritrea) to 'alarming' (Djibouti, Ethiopia and Sudan) and 'serious' (Kenya and Uganda) (Von Grebmer et al., 2010). The Maplecroft Food Security Risk Index of 2013 rates Eritrea, Ethiopia, Somalia and South Sudan as extreme (http://maplecroft.com/about/news/food_security_risk_index_2013.html). The countries of the Horn are also included in the FAO's 2013 list of low-income Food Deficit Countries. As shown in table 2.4, the region also contains a high ratio of malnourished people.

USAID's analysis of the region's food insecurity suggests that the root cause is unstable social and political environment that has precluded sustainable economic growth (http://www.usaid.gov/regions/Afr/Ghai/cycle/causes.html). Others attribute the food crisis to policies that neglect agriculture. Economic liberalization measures, which have been adopted in the continent since the mid-1980s, are said to be among such policies. Declining and erratic rainfall, along with a near total dependence on rain-fed agriculture, are among other contributing factors for the region's chronic food insecurity. As will be seen in chapter 7, with growing population and longer and more frequent droughts, shortages of quality pasture and overgrazing have become serious problems in many parts of the region. Poverty among pastoralists, who witness the depletion of their stock with every drought cycle, is relatively much higher than among other sectors of the population. Famines also generally strike pastoral communities more frequently, although pastoralists are by no means the only victims.

Despite their chronic food insecurity and frequent conflicts over land and water, some of the countries of the region have become major players in granting farmland concessions to foreign investors. A growing food market in the Middle East and Asia, rising food prices and a growing worldwide demand for bio-fuels are some of the factors that have stimulated investments in farmlands in the region, as in many other parts of Africa and the developing world. Middle Eastern countries, including Saudi Arabia, the United Arab Emirates, Qatar and Kuwait, along with China, India, South Korea and Egypt, are among the newcomers to investing in farmland in the Greater Horn region. Sudan, Ethiopia and Uganda, in particular, and Kenya to a lesser degree have become major targets.

The benefits and risks of granting land concessions to foreign investors, the magnitude of land concessions given and the institutional mechanisms which allow land-takings by the state from customary holders are discussed in greater detail in chapters 4 and 7. Here it suffices to point out the potential risks to pastoralists and peasant farmers. Some of the land concessions given to foreign investors by the Ethiopian government in the late 1960s resulted in alarming humanitarian crisis. The starvation of thousands of Ethiopia's Afar population in the early 1970s was to a large extent a result of the displacement of Afar pastoralists by land concessions granted to foreign investors. Thousands of Afar nomads in eastern Ethiopia starved following their eviction from the Awash River basin after the government gave their land to multinational corporations for cotton production (Bondestam, 1974; Harbeson, 1978). Pushed to the arid areas, the Afar first faced livestock starvation followed by mass human starvation. The starvation of the Afar, along with evictions of many peasants in several other parts of the country, contributed to conflicts and instability. The fall of the country's imperial regime in 1974 is at least in part attributable to the shock generated by the magnitude of the famine and the regime's attempts to hide it. If continued, the land concessions that are presently underway also have the potential to impose severe hardship upon the region's pastoralists and peasants, who face evictions from land they customarily hold unless careful provisions are put in place to prevent their victimization. Given the rapid population growth of the region, it is also possible that the land concessions, which are long term (usually ninety-nine years), have the potential to create severe land shortages and very high rates of unemployment in the future, unless a parallel transformation of the pastoral and peasant modes of production takes place.

Major Post-Independence Conflicts in the Region

Most of the countries of the Greater Horn have seen many wars and armed conflicts during the post-independence era, roughly between 1956, when Sudan became the first Sub-Saharan African country to win its independence, and the present. The region was by no means peaceful before the era of decolonization, as the discussion in chapter 3 shows. The period between roughly the mid-1800s and the era of decolonization, for example, saw many wars, which mostly revolved around state formation and empire-building, slave raids, control of resources and trade routs, colonization and resistance to colonialism, and liberation struggle. The objective of this chapter, however, is to identify the most important types of wars and armed conflicts of the post-independence era (roughly 1956–2012), with the aim of providing the reader a glimpse of the large number of wars and conflicts and the magnitude of their human and socioeconomic costs.

While interconnected and often with murky boundaries, the region's post-independence conflicts can be classified into six categories, including direct and indirect inter-state wars and armed conflicts; cross-border inter-communal conflicts; civil wars and civil conflicts; conflicts among rebel groups mostly over differences of political programmes and power struggle; intra-state inter-communal conflicts; and one-sided violence perpetrated upon civilians by the state or other armed political groups.[3] The distinction between wars and other types of armed conflicts follows, whenever possible, the differentiation drawn by the Uppsala Conflict Data Programme (UCDP).[4] Lack of reliable data on casualty figures, however, does not always allow adherence to this differentiation.

Inter-State Wars

Every country in the region has been involved in some type of armed conflict with its neighbours. Among the key factors for the conflicts are: (1) territorial and boundary disputes; (2) interference in internal affairs of neighbouring countries by supporting rebel groups either because of ethnic ties or in order to destabilize unfriendly regimes; and (3) containment of unwanted ideological and religious doctrines and movements, such as Islamic fundamentalism, often with support from actors outside the region.

Among the region's direct inter-state wars and armed conflicts are the three wars fought between Ethiopia and Somalia. The first one, which was fought over Somalia's claims of the Somali-inhabited Ogaden region of Ethiopia, started in 1961, escalated in 1964, and lingered until 1967 as a low-intensity conflict. The second Ethiopia–Somalia war, which was again fought over the Ogaden problem, broke out in 1977 when the Somali National Army, along with the Western Somali Liberation Front (WSLF),[5] invaded the Somali-inhabited Ogaden region of Ethiopia in an effort to free it from

Ethiopia. Initial success by the Somali army provoked direct external intervention by Cuba and the USSR, which provided arms, technical advisors and soldiers in support of the Marxist-leaning military regime in Ethiopia (see chapter 6 for more details). The initial success of the Somali army was reversed rather quickly and, despite some US assistance, Somalia suffered a staggering defeat, which triggered the rise of various rebel groups against the weakened regime of Siad Barre. The regime, along with the Somali state, finally collapsed in 1991.

The third war between the two countries occurred between 2006 and 2009. After over a dozen unsuccessful attempts to establish a national government, in May 2006 Somalia was largely brought under the control of the Union of Islamic Courts (UIC) and the Somali state with a national government was *de facto* re-established. The UIC, an essentially bottom-up grass-roots organization, defeated the warlords, who in the aftermath of the collapse of the state had torn the country up into fiefs. Unfortunately, Ethiopia viewed the UIC's Islamist rhetoric as a threat to its territorial integrity and stability and intervened pre-emptively to dislodge the UIC from power. Ethiopia supported the Transitional Federal Government (TFG), which was constituted in 2004 in Nairobi as Somalia's government, largely through external mandate, and had remained ineffective and unable to extend its authority beyond the town of Baidoa until Ethiopia's intervention.

Ethiopia's invasion of Somalia obtained the backing of the USA, which in the wake of the September 11, 2001 terrorist attacks, was engaged in the war on terror and viewed some of the UIC's leaders as having connections with al-Qaeda. The chairman of the UIC, Hassan Dahir Aweys, for example, was included in the list of 189 individuals and organizations designated terrorist under Executive Order 13224.

Ethiopian troops succeeded rather quickly in dislodging the UIC from power but could not pacify the country. The TFG, which was essentially composed of warlords, had little popular support and Ethiopian support made it even less legitimate. A more radical Islamist insurgency group, the al-Shebab, emerged as the main resistance to the TFG and external intervention and, along with other remnants of the

UIC, which assumed a new name, Alliance for the Re-Liberation of Somalia (ARLS), continued to fight the TFG and the Ethiopian invasion. By late 2008 al-Shebab and its allies managed to establish control over most of southern Somalia and it became apparent that Ethiopia had failed to pacify Somalia. As the TFG's position became increasingly untenable, the UN, along with Djibouti and other external actors, arranged negotiations between the TFG and a wing of the ARLS led by Sharif Sheikh Ahmed. An agreement was forged that entailed the withdrawal of Ethiopian troops from Somalia and the transfer of power to a new leadership of the TFG under the presidency of Sharif Sheikh Ahmed, the former chairman of the UIC and the leader of a wing of the ARLS which often is referred to as 'moderate'.[6] This new TFG assumed power in December 2009. However, like its predecessor, it came to be seen as foreign installed and was rejected by both the al-Shebab and the Sheikh Aweys-led wing of the ARLS (which came to be known as Hizbul Islam), and the country's civil war continued unabated, as discussed in greater detail in chapter 6.[7]

The Ethiopia–Eritrean border war of 1998–2000 is perhaps the largest inter-state war the region has seen in the post-colonial era, at least in terms of casualty figures. Following Eritrea's independence in 1993, the two countries formed an economic integration scheme with free mobility of goods and services, capital and labour. By 1997, however, policy differences placed relations between the two regimes and the economic integration scheme under severe strain. Under these conditions, a border dispute in the environs of a small border town, called Badme, in southwestern Eritrea escalated into a full-fledged war between the two countries in May 1998. In December 2000 the Treaty of Algiers was signed ending the war. The Treaty also established the Ethiopia–Eritrea Boundary Commission with the mandate to draw the entire boundary between the two countries on the basis of pertinent colonial treaties and applicable international law.[8] The Hague-based Commission rendered its decision in 2002. It delimited the entire border and placed Badme town, the flash point of the war, on the Eritrean side of the border. According to the Algiers Treaty, the Commission's decision was 'final and binding'. Ethiopia's reaction to the ruling has, however, varied from outright rejection to conditional acceptance. Its most recent position seems to be 'dialogue before demarcation'. Eritrea's reaction, by contrast, has been 'unconditional demarcation' to be followed by dialogue and normalization of relations. In any case, in the absence of any progress on the physical demarcation of the border, the Boundary Commission declared its task completed after undertaking a virtual demarcation of the border. The border problem, however, remains unsettled since Ethiopia has not accepted the virtual demarcation or allowed physical demarcation of the border. The regimes in the two countries have also used the border stalemate and continued tensions as mechanisms for diverting popular attention from various internal political challenges. The Ethiopian regime, on its part, blames Eritrea for practically every insurgency activity that takes place in the country. Along with the US government, it also accuses the Eritrean regime of supporting the Somali insurgency, especially since the leaders of the UIC had taken refuge in Eritrea after being dislodged from power by the Ethiopian invasion. The Eritrean regime vehemently denies supplying arms to the Somali insurgency and accuses the US, and the UN, of doing nothing to put pressure on Ethiopia to abide by the ruling of the Boundary Commission. It also views their meddling, along with Ethiopia's invasion to be the main obstacles to the re-establishment of the Somali state by Somalis themselves. The UN Security Council imposed sanctions on Eritrea and its leaders on 23 December 2009 for alleged support of al-Shebab. More sanctions were imposed on the country on 12 September 2011. The Eritrean regime has also used the border stalemate as a pretext in denying constitutional governance and democratization of the country's political life. The country's constitution, which was ratified in May 1997, has yet to be implemented.

Kenya and Somalia were involved in a border war (1963–7) which is estimated to have resulted in casualty figures ranging between 4,000 and 5,000 people. Uganda and Sudan also experienced armed conflicts and tense relations over accusations and counter-accusations of supporting each other's rebel groups. With the National Resistance Movement (NRM), which had close ties with the Sudan People's Liberation Movement (SPLM), coming to power in Kampala in 1986, Sudan resorted to supporting Uganda's Lord's Resistance Army (LRA) in retaliation to Uganda's alleged support of the SPLM. Border scrimmages between Eritrea and Djibouti in 1994 and in June 2008 are other of the region's inter-state conflicts. A Qatar-led mediation has de-escalated this conflict and Eritrean troops have allegedly withdrawn from the disputed areas, which are said to be monitored by Qatari observers.[9] However, the border dispute has yet to be resolved.

The most recent inter-state conflict in the region is the April 2012 conflict between Sudan and South Sudan over the disputed oil rich town of Heglig. Disagreements over the sharing of oil revenue or the payment by South Sudan for using the pipelines of the North are other factors. The two countries also engage in destabilizing each other by supporting each other's rebel groups.

Some of the countries of the Horn were also involved in conflicts against non-Horn neighbours. The Tanzania–Uganda war of 1978–9, where Tanzania invaded Uganda in support of the Ugandan National Liberation Army (UNLA), which was fighting to remove Idi Amin's repressive regime from power, is one such war. In addition, Uganda was engaged in an on and off conflict with the Democratic Republic of the Congo (DRC) between 1997 and 2007 over various issues. In August 2007 the conflict between the two countries was over ownership of Rukwanzi Island on Lake Albert as well as over the operations of Uganda's rebel groups, such as the Allied Democratic Forces (ADF) and the National Army for the Liberation of Uganda (NALU) from bases in the DRC. Uganda and the DRC, along with South Sudan, have, however, begun to cooperate in a joint offensive against the LRA. Sudan was also involved in a series of scrimmages against Chad between 2005 and 2008. Eritrea also fought a minor war against Yemen in December 1995 over the control of the Hanish Islands in the Red Sea. That conflict was settled in

1998 when Eritrea accepted the ruling of the Permanent Court of Arbitration, which determined that much of the archipelago belonged to Yemen.

In addition to the direct wars, the countries of the Horn have fought many proxy wars against each other and against non-Horn neighbours by supporting each other's insurgency movements. Some of these conflicts are clearly related to the manner in which the states in the region were formed and the partitioning of ethnic groups into several states, which has fostered irredentist movements. In other cases, proxy wars are fought for other political motives, including destabilizing enemy regimes or in retaliation against a hostile regime's support of internal enemies. Regardless, since the insurgencies in most cases are domestic forces, these conflicts are discussed under intra-state conflicts.

Intra-State Conflicts

The region's most frequent and devastating conflicts are the intra-state conflicts, which conceptually are of four types, although in reality they are often hard to distinguish from one another. By far the most devastating type of intra-state conflict the region has experienced consists of 'civil wars' and chronic strife between the state and organized political groups, which are mostly ethnic, religion or region-based.[10] The second type of domestic conflict is the inter-communal conflicts, which are fought among ethnic, clan and occupational groups (pastoralists vs sedentary farmers). These conflicts are generally over resources, such as land, water and livestock (cattle rustling) and they are often provoked by resource scarcity, resulting from a rapidly deteriorating environment and fast growing populations.[11] The third type consists of conflicts among armed opposition groups who also fight among each other while they fight against the state. The reasons for these conflicts are many and rivalry for power and differences in political programmes are among them. The fourth type of intra-state conflict is the one-sided conflicts which entail atrocities perpetrated by governments and rebel groups upon unarmed civilian populations for a variety of reasons.

Civil Wars

Every country in the region has faced at least one civil war during the post-independence era. In most cases they have fought multiple civil wars. A civil war is a violent conflict between the state or militia groups created by it and an armed group or groups, such as ethnic, regional, religious or other political organizations. Yet distinguishing civil wars from civil conflicts or one-sided atrocities is rather problematic. Much of the literature identifies civil war as (1) a conflict between the state or forces affiliated with it and an organized domestic force; (2) where the conflict inflicts at least 1,000 casualties; and (3) where the challengers of the state inflict at least 5 per cent of the casualties on the government's side (Cramer, 2006; Sambanis, 2002a)[12] – below this casualty threshold the conflict would be classified as a civil conflict. In addition to the controversies about the arbitrariness of the casualty threshold, absence of accurate data on casualty figures complicates the process of distinguishing civil wars from civil conflicts and one-sided conflicts.

As noted already, some of the civil wars in the Horn are closely linked with inter-state conflicts, as many of the sub-state actors which fight against the state either serve as proxies of other states or are at least supported by other states. The countries of the Greater Horn have engaged in what Cliffe and White (2002: 54) call 'mutual intervention' in each other's internal conflicts. Some regimes support insurgencies in a neighbouring country either because of ethnic ties with the rebelling groups or because such groups destabilize regimes they have poor relations with.[13] Insurgency movements in Ethiopia's Somali-inhabited Ogaden, such as the WSLF, for example, were supported by Somalia between the early 1960s to the time of the collapse of the Somali state in 1991.[14] The 'Shifta wars' in Kenya's Somali-inhabited North Eastern province, between 1963 and 1967, were also backed by Somalia, which aspired to unite all Somali-inhabited areas in the region under the Somali state. Somalia's invocation of self-determination of Somali people under one state received little sympathy from many other African states or from the Organization of African Unity (OAU), which adopted in 1964 a resolution that declared colonial boundaries to be sacrosanct. The OAU adopted such a doctrine due to concerns that tampering with the colonial boundaries would open a Pandora's Box and lead to wars all over the continent. Ethiopia and Kenya also responded to what they perceived as a Somali threat to their national integrity by establishing a mutual defence pact in 1964. Moreover, successive Ethiopian regimes countered Somalia's sponsorship of irredentist policy by supporting insurgency movements, such as the Somali National Movement (SNM), against the Somali state in order to weaken its ability to pursue its claims over the Ogaden.

Sudan supported Eritrea's liberation movements against both the imperial and the Mengistu regimes in Ethiopia. It also supported the Tigray People's Liberation Front (TPLF) against the Mengistu regime. Ethiopia for its part supported the Sudan People's Liberation Movement (SPLM) against successive Sudanese regimes. Eritrea currently hosts various Ethiopian rebel groups against the Ethiopian regime, while the Ethiopian regime reciprocates by supporting some Eritrean rebel groups. Sudan and South Sudan have also supported each other's insurgencies, as noted earlier.

The civil wars in the region are not simply products of proxy engagements by other states, however. Most of them are reflections of broad problems of nation-building, including real or perceived uneven development, even though they might get external support. Some others are reactions to repressive and overly centralized rule. The factors for civil wars are discussed in greater detail in chapter 5. The aim here is to point out that most of the countries of the region continue to face a plethora of civil wars and civil conflicts.

The collapse of the Somali state in 1991 is largely attributable to the country's civil wars, although the 1977–8 war with Ethiopia weakened the government and made it vulnerable and more repressive, triggering the rise of various insurgency groups. Since the collapse of the state in 1991, Somalia has fractured with Somaliland declaring its independence. Puntland has also become largely autonomous without declaring independence. Much of the rest of Somalia has remained a battleground of various contestants for state power with considerable external intervention.

Sudan has perhaps faced the most deadly civil wars given the casualty figures of the Southern Sudan and Darfur wars. Ethiopia also has encountered a large number of mostly ethnic-based civil wars. Uganda has also faced a number of these conflicts and has yet to overcome the challenge posed by the Lord's Resistance Army. Kenya, on the other hand, has faced a relatively smaller number of civil wars, although the country is deeply divided, as manifested by ethnic conflicts in 1963–7, 1991–3 and the deadly post-election violence in 2007. Djibouti, Eritrea and South Sudan have also not been immune to the factors that have engendered such conflicts. Djibouti has faced periodic rebellions from its Afar minority. The Afar-based Front for the Restoration of Unity and Democracy (FRUD) engaged the government in an active war between 1991 and 1994. Eritrea also faced some low-level conflicts against a Jihadist movement, Harakat al Jihad al Islami, in the early 1990s. Currently, there are some Ethiopia-supported groups, such as the Red Sea Afar Democratic Organization (RSADO) and the Democratic Movement for the Liberation of the Eritrean Kunama (DMLEK), who claim to wage armed struggle intended to topple the regime. Their impact so far has, however, remained negligible. Since its independence in 2011 South Sudan has also already faced civil wars. The South Sudan Democratic Movement/Army (SSDM/A), the South Sudan Liberation Army (SSLA) and the rebellion led by George Athor are the most significant. Table 2.5 provides a list of some of the most important civil wars of the region.

Conflicts among Rebel Groups

A type of violent conflict that is not given much attention in the literature is the conflict among rebel groups. While

Table 2.5. A selected list of civil wars and civil conflicts in the Horn of Africa

Country and main factors	Civil war
Djibouti Ethnic	The Afar Front for the Restoration of Unity and Democracy (FRUD), 1991–4 (1994–2001 low intensity)
Eritrea Religious	The Jihadist movement, Harakat al Jihad al Islami (1994–2003 low intensity)
Ethiopia Ethnic, religious and ideological	Eritrea's independence movements, the Eritrean Liberation Front (ELF) and Eritrean People's Liberation Front (EPLF) 1961–91; Ethiopian People's Revolutionary Party (EPRP), 1975–7; Tigray People's Liberation Front (TPLF), 1975–91; Western Somali Liberation Front (WSLF), 1974–8; the Somali Abo Liberation Front, 1975–8; Afar Liberation Front (ALF), 1975–97; the Afar Revolutionary Democratic Union/Front (ARDUF), 1996; Gambela People's Liberation Front, 1985–91; Oromo Liberation Front (OLF), 1975–present; the Ogaden National Liberation Front (ONLF), 1996, 1998–present; the Ethiopian People's Patriotic Liberation Front (EPPLF), 2006–present
Kenya Ethnic and irridentism	Shifta wars (1963–7); post-election violence, 2007–8
Somalia Regime change, state formation and power struggle among armed rival (clan/religious) groups	Somali National Movement (SNM), 1990–1; Somali Patriotic Movement (SPM), 1990–1; United Somali Congress/Somali National Alliance (USC/SNA), 1991–6; civil war 1989–91; Puntland, 2004; Union of Islamic Courts (UIC), 2005–6; al-Shebab and Hizbul Islam, 2008–present
Sudan Ethnic, religious and regional	North–South 1955–72; Sudan People's Liberation Movement/Army (SPLM/A), North–South 1983–2005; Darfur conflict, Justice and Equality Movement (JEM) and Sudan Liberation Movement (SLM), 2003–present; Beja Congress and Rashaida Free Lions, 2005–6; Nuba Mountains, 1987–2002; South Kordofan and Blue Nile, 2011–present
South Sudan Ethnic and inter-elite power struggle	The South Sudan Democratic Movement/Army (SSDM/A); the South Sudan Liberation Army (SSLA); and the rebellion led by George Athor, 2011–present
Uganda Ethnic, regional and religious	Ugandan National Rescue Front (UNRF), Ugandan National Liberation Army (UNLA) 1980–5; Ugandan National Rescue Front (UNRF II), 1997; National Resistance Army, 1982–6; Uganda People's Democratic Army (UPDA), 1986–8; Lord's Resistance Army (LRA), 1987–present; West Nile Bank Front (WNBF), 1996; Allied Democratic Forces (ADF), 1996–2002, 2007

Source: Uppsala Conflict Data Programme, http://www.pcr.uu.se/research/UCDP

challenging the state, these groups often war against each other for a variety of reasons. A good example of such wars is the wars fought between Eritrea's independence movements, the Eritrean Liberation Front (ELF) and the Eritrean People's Liberation Front (EPLF). These two nationalist movements fought sporadic battles against each other in the late 1970s and early 1980s. Both movements were fighting to drive the Ethiopian government out of Eritrea while they also engaged in a deadly power struggle against each other. Another example is the wars fought by the Tigray People's Liberation Front (TPLF) against a rival movement, the Tigray Liberation Front (TLF) and against the Ethiopian People's Revolutionary Party (EPRP) in the late 1979s. The Sudan People's Liberation Movement (SPLM) also fought against various splinter groups throughout its history. Somalia's rebel movements that brought about the fall of the regime of Siad Barre also fought against each other and brought the collapse of the state.

Inter-Communal Conflicts

The Horn countries have also faced a large number of inter-communal violent conflicts. As already noted, these are conflicts fought between ethnic and clan groups often over resources, such as land, water and livestock.[15] These conflicts tend to affect pastoral communities in drier areas disproportionately, although they are not limited to pastoralists. Often governments aggravate such conflicts by interfering on one side or another. If certain identity groups engage in rebellion or resist certain policy measures, governments tend to intervene by supporting rival identity groups, as in Darfur. In other cases, inter-communal competition over resources may intensify into deadly conflicts due to the inability of governments to address such conflicts on a timely basis. In some cases, governments even worsen the land and water shortages by appropriating communal land. Regardless of the specific factors, a growing number of inter-communal conflicts, whose magnitude has intensified with environmental degradation and availability of small arms, have contributed to the instability and economic disruptions of the region. These conflicts are generally sporadic and of much lower intensity compared to the inter-state or the civil wars. Yet because of their large numbers they are highly destructive. South Sudan's inter-communal conflicts in the Jonglei area are, for example, estimated to have resulted in over 2500 deaths and the displacement of some 350,000 people in 2009 alone (BBC News online, 22 January 2010). Table 2.6 attempts to identify the most notable of such conflicts. Inter-communal conflicts also have considerable impacts on the economy as they lead to destruction of property and disruption of production.

Cross-Border Community Conflicts

Another type of conflict the region has experienced is the destructive cross-border communal conflicts. These are essentially conflicts among pastoral communities of neighbouring countries and they are mostly over access to resources, such as water and pastures. Often they are also over cattle rustling. These conflicts are of significant magnitude. Frequent droughts, limited control over border areas and the inflow of small arms have contributed to the growing frequency and intensity of such conflicts. IGAD established the Conflict Early Warning and Response Mechanism (CEWARN) in 2000 to monitor and mitigate such conflicts through early warning mechanisms and timely intervention. CEWARN's effectiveness in controlling such conflicts is unclear, however.

One-Sided Violence against Civilians

In addition to the five types of conflicts identified, civilian populations in the region have also been subjected to violence by either their own governments or by various armed rebel groups (see table 2.7). When confronted with protests, governments in the region often resort to violence and when they

Table 2.6. A selected list of inter-communal armed conflicts in the Horn of Africa

Country and main factors	Inter-communal conflicts
Ethiopia Main factors include land, water and cattle rustling	Afar – Issa tribe (2002); Afar – Kereyou (2002–3); Amaro – Guji (2006); Anuak – Guji (2006); Anuak – Dinka (2002); Anuak – Nuer (2002–3); Bi'idyahan – Ismail (2003); Borona – Guji (2006); Borona – Gabra (1992); Borona – Konso (2008); Burji – Guji (2006); Dawa – Gura (2003); Derashe – Konso (2008); Dizi – Surma (2002); Gabra – Guji (2005); Gumuz – Oromo (2008); Majeerteen – Ogaden (2004); Marehan – Majeerteen (2006); Merille – Turkana (2005); Murle – Nuer (2006); Nyangatom, Toposa – Turkana (2006); Ogaden – Sharif Sheikh Ahmed (2002); Oromo – Somali (2003, 2005)
Kenya Main factors include cattle rustling, land and water	Borona – Gabra (2005); Dassanetch vs Turkana (2006); Dongiro – Turkana (2006); Garre – Murle (2005, 2008); Kalenjin – Kikuyu (1998, 2008); Kalenjin – Kisii (2008); Luo – Kikuyu (2008); Nyangatom – Turkana (1993, 2006, 2008; Pokot – Turkana (2006, 2008); Toposa – Turkana (2008)
Somalia Main factors include water and land	Afi sub-clan – Abtisame sub-clan; Agon-Yar sub-clan – Warsangeli sub-clan; Ali-Gaf sub-clan – Mahadade sub-clan; Dabare sub-clan – Luway sub-clan; Da'ud sub-clan – Warsangeli sub-clan; Dir clan – Marehan sub-clan; Dir clan – Sa'ad sub-clan; Duduble sub-clan – Suleiman sub-clan; Galje'el clan – Jejele sub-clan; Garre sub-clan – Marehan sub-clan; Huber sub-clan – Yantar sub-clan; Habar Jaalo – Habar Yunis; Jareer sub-clan – Jiddo sub-clan ; Marahan – Majeerteen; Marehan sub-clan – Fiqi Mohamed sub-clan; Mohamed Muse sub-clan – Warsangeli sub-clan; Ogaden – Sharif Sheikh Ahmed; Sa'ad sub-clan – Suleiman sub-clan
Sudan Main factors include cattle rustling, land and water	Aqar (Dinka) – Aqok (Dinka) (2006); Dinka – Nuer (2010); Ereigat Abbala Arabs – Zaghawa (2002); Habaniya – Falata (2007); Habaniya – Rizeigat Baggara (2006, 2009); Hotiya Baggara – Newiba, Mahariba and Mahamid (2005); Jikany Nuer – Luo Nuer (1993); Masalit – Rizeigat Abbala (1998–9); Misseriya – Rizeigat Baggara (2008); Murle – Bor Dinka (2007); Murle – Nuer Lou (2006); Nuer Lou – Hol Dinka (2008); Rizeigat Baggara – Ma'aliyah (2002, 2004); Terjam – Rizeigat Abbala (2007); Toposa – Didinga (2007); Terjam – Rizeigat Abbala (2007); Zaghawa – Ma'aliyah (2008)
Uganda Main factors include cattle rustling, land and water	Bokora Karimojong – Jie Karimojong (2000, 2003, 2007); Bokora Karimojong – Pian Karimojong (2003); Bokora Karimojong – Matheniko Karimojong (1999); Dodoth – Jik Karimojong (2000, 2005); Karimojong – Pokot (1998, 2000); Pian Karimojong – Pokot (2003); Pokot – Sabiny (2003)

Source: Uppsala Conflict Data Programme, http://www.pcr.uu.se/research/UCDP

Table 2.7. A selected list of one-sided violence against civilians in the Horn of Africa

Ethiopia	Government of Ethiopia – civilians (1989–2007); the Derg government (1974–91); the government massacred people in Sheib and surrounding villages in Semhar district, where between 600 and 1000 civilians were massacred; the Red Terror (1976–8); the Ethiopian People's Revolutionary Democratic Front (EPRDF) (1991–present); the ONLF – civilians (2007)
Kenya	The government of Kenya police-army vs civilians in 2008 with casualty figures ranging from 64 to 205; the Sabaot Land Defence Force said to have killed some 600 people and caused the displacement of over 66,000 others; the Mungiki sect is another armed entity that commits violent acts upon civilians
Somalia	Government of Somalia – civilians; Rahanwein Resistance Army (RRA) – civilians; SPM/SNA-OJ – civilians; United Somali Congress (USC) – civilians
Sudan	Government of Sudan – civilians (1989–present); Janjaweed – civilians (2001–present); JEM – civilians (2003); Sudan Liberation Army-Minni Minawi (SLA-MM) – civilians (2006); SLM/A – civilians (2005); SPLM/A – civilians (1989–2004); Somali Salvation Democratic Front (SSDF) – civilians (1991–3)
Uganda	Government of Uganda – civilians (1990–1); Allied Democratic Forces (ADF) – civilians (1997–2000); LRA – civilians (1989–2008); Ugandan National Rescue Front (UNRF) II – civilians (1997); Uganda People's Army (UPA) – civilians (1990)

Source: Uppsala Conflict Data Programme, http://www.pcr.uu.se/research/UCDP

face insurgencies they tend to adopt 'scorched earth' measures and commit massacres upon their civilian populations, especially when the civilian population is suspected of lending any kind of support to rebel groups or even sympathizing with them. The 12 May 1988 massacre in the village of Sheib in Eritrea and the 1976–8 Red Terror unleashed in many parts of Ethiopia are cases of state violence against civilians committed by the regime of Mengistu Hailemariam. The former was committed against villagers for their alleged sympathy and cooperation with the Eritrean liberation movements. The latter was mostly committed against students and members of the intelligentsia for alleged cooperation with or sympathy for the Ethiopian People's Revolutionary Party, a leftist political organization. According to Henry (1991) during Mengistu's regime (1974–91) roughly 150,000 were killed in campaigns of persecution; another 100,000 died in forced resettlement; and roughly 1,000,000 died in ensuing famines.

Uganda's Idi Amin, who is often referred to as the 'Butcher of Uganda', is said to have killed between 200,000 and 800,000 people (Fulford, 2003). Kaufman (2003) estimated the number of people killed under Idi Amin at 300,000. Amin was also strongly anti-intellectuals and he wiped out a large number of that country's educated people. Milton Obote's regime was also responsible for the massacre of some 2000 Buganda people at Mengo in 1966. From the regime's point of view it was a battle to crash Buganda's secessionist aspirations. Some observers, however, view the incident as one-sided violence since the Buganda were hardly armed (Mutibwa, 2008).

The region's governments have also used militia groups as counter-insurgency force. The government of President Nimieri of Sudan (1969–85) armed the Muraheleen militia from Southern Darfur and Southern Kordofan against the rebellion in Southern Sudan led by the Sudan People's Liberation Movement (SPLM). Likewise, despite its claims to the contrary, the Omar al Bashir regime has used the Janjaweed militia against rebel groups in Darfur, the Sudan Liberation Army (SLA) and the Justice and Equality Movement (JEM).

The campaign of terror and atrocities committed by the Jan-jaweed against civilians belonging to the Fur, Zaghawa and Massleit farming ethnic groups and the alarming size of the killings and displacements have led UN officials to describe the situation as 'ethnic cleansing' (UNHCHR, 2004). The indictments by the International Criminal Court (ICC) of President Omar al Bashir for crimes against humanity and genocide are highly controversial. Nevertheless, there are well-founded claims that the atrocities have been committed upon the civilian populations by militia groups, with the tacit approval of the government. The Janjaweed is, for example, said to be closely tied to the Sudanese armed forces (Salih, 2005).

Siad Barre's regime in Somalia is also accused of killing large numbers of people in different parts of the country during his last few years in power. Although the estimates vary widely, his regime is said to have massacred some 50,000 people in Somaliland alone between 1988 and 1990. The Museveni government of Uganda has also engaged in violence against civilians in its war against the LRA as well as in its attempts to disarm the Karamoja pastoralists.

Elections and alleged rigging of results have also triggered repression of opposition groups and violent suppression of protests in some of the countries of the region. The violent conflicts which ensued the 2005 election in Ethiopia and the 2007 election in Kenya are good examples. The post-election violence in Ethiopia claimed some 200 lives while that of Kenya claimed about 1,300 lives.

Rebel groups also often commit atrocities against civilian populations for a variety of reasons. In some cases they commit violence in order to expose the weakness of governments and to send a message about their cause and operations. They also attack civilians for alleged cooperation with the government and in order to undermine economic projects of governments. The Ogaden National Liberation Front (ONLF), for example, attacked an oil drilling project by a Chinese contractor, Zhonguyuan Petroleum Exploration Bureau, on 24 April 2007 and killed seventy-four workers in order to prevent oil exploration in the region until there is a political solution to the Ogaden problem. The ONLF also accuses oil companies of destroying the livelihoods of the pastoral local population by clearing large tracts of vegetation in their search for oil. In other cases, rebel groups may represent the interests of certain identity groups and attack identity groups that have rival interests. Attacks by the Janjaweed, who have close ties with the Baggara herders, on the farming communities of the Fur, Zaghawa and Massleit identities is a good example. The Baggara herders have land-based conflicts with the farming communities.

In some cases it is hard to find a rational and consistent objective for the violence committed upon civilians by rebel groups. The Lord's Resistance Army, which initially appeared to fight against the marginalization of the Ocholi people of northern Uganda, has engaged in brutalizing the civilian population not only in Uganda but also in neighbouring countries, including South Sudan, the DRC and Central African Republic by killing, torturing and maiming, raping and abducting civilians. The group has become notorious for abducting children to serve as child soldiers and sex slaves. Its violence is said to have caused the displacement of over 500,000 people in the Gulu and Kitgum districts in Uganda.

Human and Material Costs of the Wars

The region's various wars have produced exorbitant political, human and economic repercussions. One of the most harrowing effects at the political level is the collapse of the Somali state, which was brought about by a combination of inter-state and civil wars and inter-rebel group conflicts. Another effect that has changed the region's political landscape is the break-up of three of the region's countries. These include that of Ethiopia, with Eritrea's independence, Sudan, with the secession of South Sudan, and Somalia, with Somaliland's declaration of independence.

The human costs have also been enormous. Data on the region's casualty figures from the post-independence era wars and armed conflicts often do not exist and when they do, they are highly unreliable. From the anecdotal estimates that are available, however, the total fatalities (combatants and civilians) are frighteningly high. The first (1965–72) and second (1983–2005) North–South civil wars of Sudan are said to have produced over 2 million total deaths, 420,000 refugees and over 4 million displaced (Elnur, 2008; Jok, 2007). According to various estimates, the casualty figures of the Darfur conflict also range between 200,000 and 400,000 deaths and 2 million displaced (Qugnivet, 2006).[16] Eritrea is said to have lost over 50,000 combatants during its war of independence (1961–91), while the combatant casualty figures on the Ethiopian side from that war are said to be about 200,000. The casualty figures of Ethiopia's various civil wars between 1962 and 1992 are estimated at about 1,400,000 (Twentieth Century Atlas, n.d.). The Ethio–Eritrean border war of 1998–2000 is estimated to have claimed between 70,000 and 120,000 battle deaths and resulted in the displacement of hundreds of thousands. The figures for the Ogaden war between Ethiopia and Somalia (1997–8) are estimated to exceed 31,000, while the estimates for the Somali civil war (1991–present), range between 300,000 and 400,000. The ongoing Somali civil war is believed to have brought about the deaths of over 18,000 people and the displacement of over 1.4 million people between the start of 2007 and the end of 2009. Ethiopia's invasion of Somalia in 2006 is said to have resulted in over 8,500 deaths on the Somali side alone. The casualty figures of Uganda's civil war (1982–6) are unknown but it is estimated that some 750,000 people were displaced by that war. Kenya's post-election violence is also estimated to have led to the death of roughly 1,300 people. No doubt, the various other civil wars and numerous communal conflicts also continue to add to the casualty figures (table 2.8 provides rough estimates of casualty figures).

The conflicts, along with environmental degradation, have also made the region distinguish itself as one of the largest sources of refugees in the world (see table 2.9 for estimates of refugees from the region). Many of the refugees have encountered enormous hardships. Unknown numbers have died crossing the Red Sea, the Mediterranean Sea, as well as

Table 2.8. Estimates of casualty figures in conflicts in Horn of Africa

	Civil wars	Inter-communal conflicts	Violence against civilians	Inter-state wars/conflicts
Ethiopia	1,400,000	1,926–2,302	600–1,000 (1989)	126,058–176,058
	(d)* N.A.	(d) 40,000	(d) N.A.	(d) N.A.
Kenya	14,518	699–964	189–373	
	(d) 300,000	(d) N.A.	(d) N.A.	
Somalia	300,553–400,789	1,817–2,458	890–5,436	40,320
	(d) N.A.	(d) N.A.	(d) N.A.	(d) N.A.
Sudan	2,201,254;	1,891	16,810–70,909 ;	542
	(d) 6 million	(d) N.A.	(d) 1,000s	(d) N.A.
Uganda	No data	327	6,350–7,401	201
	(d) 790,000	(d) N.A.	(d) N.A.	(d) N.A.

* (d) represents people displaced due to conflict.
Source: Estimates taken from the Uppsala Conflict Data Programme, http://www.pcr.uu.se/research/UCDP/

Table 2.9. Refugees from the Greater Horn

	Djibouti	Eritrea	Ethiopia	Kenya	Somalia	Sudan	Uganda
Refugees by country of origin, 2012	602	251,954	70,610	8,745	1,077,048	500,014[*]	5,680
Internally displaced, 2012	0	0	0	300,000	1,356,845	2,422,520[*]	29,776

[*] These figures may include some people from South Sudan.
Source: UNHCR country operations profiles, 2012, http://www.unhcr.org/cgibin/texis/vtx/page?page= 49e483836&submit=GO

the Sahara desert. There are also accounts that some are subjected to gross human rights violations, including enslavement, rape and organ extraction, especially in the Sinai (Pleitgen and Fahmy, 2011).

In addition to the large numbers of casualties, refugees and internally displaced, the region's conflicts have also led to gross human rights abuses, especially on women and children; massive destruction of property; and profound socioeconomic disruptions. Most of the region's governments are often accused by various human rights organizations of violations of human rights, which include disappearances, torture and incarceration of political opponents and journalists without due process of the law. The region's governments are also accused of impeding fair elections by harassing candidates of opposition parties and their supporters and by the rigging of election outcomes. The 2005 and 2010 elections in Ethiopia, Kenya's 2007 elections and Sudan's 2010 elections were all characterized to have been marred by various types of irregularities and rigging. Uganda's February 2006 elections were also said to have been compromised by bribing, intimidation, counting and tallying irregularities, problems of multiple voting and ballot box stuffing in some areas. By contrast, the much delayed presidential election in Somaliland took place on 26 June 2010 and is generally viewed as fair and peaceful. Kenya's 4 August 2010 Constitutional Referendum as well as the 2013 election were also conducted peacefully.

The economic costs of the various wars and conflicts are also likely to be huge in the context of the economic needs of the region. The border war with Eritrea is, for example, said to have cost Ethiopia over $2.5 billion, while estimates of the costs for Eritrea range from $500 million to $1.5 billion. Uganda also estimates the costs of its conflict against the Lord's Resistance Army, over the 1986–2002 period to be around $1.33 billion, roughly 3 per cent of its GDP (APRM, 2009).

The full extent of the economic costs of the various wars is difficult to estimate, however. Military expenditures as a ratio of total public expenditures (see table 2.10) give us some indication. Yet, they only portray a part of the costs as they

Table 2.10. Expenditures on military as a ratio of total public expenditures

	Djibouti	Eritrea	Ethiopia	Kenya	Somalia	Sudan	Uganda
% of government expenditure allocated to health (1998–2007)	N.A.	N.A.	1	7	1	1	2
% of government expenditure allocated to education (1998–2007)	N.A.	N.A.	5	26	2	8	15
% of government expenditure allocated to defence (1998–2007)	13.6* 1995–2005	34.88* 1995–2003	17	6	38	28	26

* *Source:* US State Department, World Military Expenditures and Arms Transfers, 1995–2005; UNICEF, Information by Country, March, 2010, http://www.unicef.org/infobycountry/

give little information on the actual costs of all six types of the conflicts, especially on the economic costs to civilian populations. It is safe to assume that the costs of the various conflicts are bound to be large enough to make a notable difference to the region's development. According to some analysts, the conflicts in the region constitute the single largest factor in the region's economic crisis (Mwaura et al., 2002). If this assessment is indeed correct, it would also mean that ending the conflicts would render huge benefits to the region's development process.

3 | The Legacy of Empires

Introduction

Many of the chronic conflicts that have ravaged the countries of the Greater Horn region since the era of decolonization have roots that can be traced to major developments that occurred in the region roughly between the early 1800s and the late 1950s. One of the developments was the process of state formation and empire-building in parts of the region during the first three-quarters of the nineteenth century. The second development was colonization of much of the region during the period between the 1880s and the early 1960s. These two developments brought about considerable turmoil, conflicts and changes in socioeconomic and institutional systems, as well as in inter-identity relations in the region, as they did in much of the rest of the continent. Some studies (Besley and Reynal-Querol, 2012) have shown significant correlations between the conflicts that occurred in the pre-colonial and colonial epochs and those that have taken place in the post-independence era. The principal aim of this chapter is to examine, without delving into details of historical account, how the socioeconomic contexts, including inter-state and inter-identity relations, partition of ethnic groups and dichotomy of economic and institutional systems, which were established during the pre-colonial and colonial eras, have continued to engender conflicts in the region in the post-decolonization era. The chapter is organized into two parts. The first part explores how the processes of state formation and empire-building during the pre-colonial era left behind socioeconomic arrangements and inter-identity relations that still continue to foster conflicts. The second part examines how the political, economic and institutional systems established by the colonial state altered inter-identity relations and left behind socioeconomic contexts that continue to engender intra-state and inter-state conflicts in the post-decolonization era.

Legacies of Pre-Colonial Empires and Kingdoms

The region had rather diverse political systems and governance arrangements before colonialism. Large parts of the region, which are often referred to as stateless and acephalous, were characterized by decentralized village or elder-based systems of governance. Others were centralized kingdoms or proto-states, which attempted to expand and build empires. At the time the region was subjected to colonization by European powers there were also at least two empires of notable sizes, the Abyssinian empire in present-day Ethiopia and the Mahdiya state in the present-day Sudan.

Stateless Societies

Our knowledge of the decentralized pre-colonial systems is rather patchy but it appears that many communities, such as the Kikuyu, Messai and Luhya of Kenya, never established states. In some cases stateless communities emerged after the collapse of kingdoms and empires that governed them. Present-day Somalia, for example, had witnessed the rise and fall of several kingdoms and empires between the thirteenth and the end of the nineteenth century. Among such kingdoms were Ifat, Adal, Ajuraan and the smaller Majeerteen sultanates of Boqor and Hobyo. At the time of colonization, however, the inhabitants of present-day Somalia were essentially stateless, although they were able to undertake an organized resistance to colonization by the dervish movement under the leadership of Mahammad Abdille Hasan, the Mad Mullah. The dervish movement conducted a war of resistance against the Abyssinian empire and British colonization between 1899 and 1920.

In some other cases the decentralized political systems were part of empires, which either collapsed completely or shrunk in size, leaving some areas to become stateless. There were also communities which were on the fringes of empires and largely governed themselves through their own institutions, although they were subjects of an empire. Communities such as the Borona in southeastern Ethiopia and the Nuer in the southwestern part of the empire were parts of the Abyssinian empire, since the last years of the nineteenth century and the beginning of the twentieth century. However, they were largely self-governing.

Communities in the decentralized political systems governed themselves through customary law and various village or elder-based institutions. Governance in stateless Somalia, for example, relied largely on elders and on two institutions, customary law (*xeer*) and the customary blood compensation system (*diya*). The leadership in these decentralized systems was often group based (council of elders), although the council of elders invariably had a senior leader (principal elder), who chairs the council's deliberations and announces its decisions. In some cases they had authorities who convened meetings of the council of elders and presided over meetings. The sultans in Somalia, for example, performed such tasks. Decentralized communities in much of present-day Eritrea also were governed by their customary law, which in some cases, such as the laws of *Logo Chewa* and *Adgine Tegeleba*, were written. Decisions in these systems were made in the village *baito* (assembly) on a consensual basis.

Many of the pre-colonial decentralized governance systems still exist, even though they may have undergone notable changes. Examples of present-day decentralized systems include the Njuri Ncheke (council of elders) of the Meru in central Kenya, the Kaya elders of the Mijikenda in coastal Kenya, the Pokot council of elders in west Kenya and the Azmach and Yejewoka (assembly) of the Gurage in Ethiopia, the village *baito* (assembly) in highland Eritrea and the Gada system of the Borona, to name a few.

The literature on traditional institutions of governance largely ignores the decentralized communities. Our understanding of the social systems and institutions of decentralized communities is, thus, rather limited. Nevertheless, the land ownership patterns among such communities were largely communal. In many cases, they suffered land-takings by the state, both colonial and post-colonial. In other cases, as in post-colonial Kenya and Uganda, they have seen land privatization through land registration. Although land ownership laws have evolved in some cases, customary owners are viewed as tenants on public land. In Ethiopia and Eritrea the state has assumed ownership of all land.

In the decentralized systems the elder-based political system did not constitute a political class which appropriated surplus production from members of the community. Inter-communal conflicts in decentralized governance systems often centred around livestock raids and land disputes, especially during periods of migrations of communities that tended to displace others (Larick, 1986). While these communities were by no means peaceful, conflicts were generally less organized and of a short-term nature. Internally, these communities applied various types of customary law to settle conflicts. If existing processes are any indication, the deliberation process of conflict resolution in these systems was participatory and was open to all male adult members of the community.

These decentralized communities of the pre-colonial era have hardly left behind socioeconomic structures that foster conflicts. They have, however, left behind the culture of cattle raiding, which is a major factor in communal conflicts in many parts of the Greater Horn. With the inflow of small arms to the region, these conflicts have now become more deadly, as evidenced by the size of casualty figures from the conflicts between the Luo Nuer and Murle communities in South Sudan.[17]

Pre-Colonial Kingdoms

As noted already, the nineteenth century was a period of state formation in the region. Kingdoms sprouted in different parts of the Greater Horn in the early nineteenth century. These kingdoms were often characterized by concentration of authority and hereditary leadership of varying levels of autocracy. Often these kingdoms warred against each other over control of resources, slaves and trade routes.

Empires were also built by kingdoms that were successful in expanding by absorbing other kingdoms or stateless societies. The processes of kingdom formation and empire-building involved widespread conflicts and subjugation of some identities by others. In what is present-day Ethiopia, for example, a number of kingdoms in the northern parts of the country (Abyssinia proper) were engaged in endless wars against each other during the period of the country's history known as the 'Era of Princes' (roughly 1769–1885). Among such kingdoms were those of Tigray, Gonder, Gojjam and Shewa. These kingdoms emerged with the fragmentation of the Abyssinian empire, which was formed in the late thirteenth century around 1270 AD, although historians often link the Abyssinian empire to empires that existed in the region before it. Among the older empires were the Zagwe dynasty, centred in Lalibela, and the Axumite empire centred in Axum.

In the southern parts of present-day Ethiopia a number of kingdoms also emerged in the nineteenth century. Among them were Jimma, Limmu, Guuma, Gomma, Geera, Sidama and several others. These kingdoms also often warred against each other over control of trade and in an attempt to expand and build empires (Mohammed Hassen Ali, 1990).

Among the most notable kingdoms in what is present-day Sudan in the nineteenth century were: Taqali, Darfur, Dar al-Maslit, Dar Qimir, Funj Sultanate of Sinner and Kordofan. In present-day South Sudan the kingdom of Shilluk was the most notable one. Among the nineteenth-century kingdoms in present-day Uganda were those of Buganda, Bunyoro, Toro, Busonga and Ankole. These kingdoms also fought against each other in an attempt to absorb each other (Ofcansky, 1996).

Pre-Colonial Empires

The most successful empires in the region in the nineteenth century were the Abyssinian empire and the Mahdiya state of Sudan. The modern Ethiopian state (the second Abyssinian empire) was formed between the beginning of the second half of the nineteenth century and the early years of the twentieth century by unifying the different kingdoms in Abyssinia proper and by conquering the various kingdoms to its south, southwest and southeast. By the second decade of the twentieth century, when the country's territorial composition took its present form, eight of the country's thirteen provinces were incorporated into the empire by conquest between 1850 and the end of the first decade of the twentieth century.

Unlike the Abyssinian empire, which was re-established by conquering other kingdoms, the Mahdiya state (1881–98) was formed by defeating an oppressive foreign rule, the Turkish–Egyptian rule. Present-day Sudan came under the Ottoman rule in 1820, when the Ottoman empire's viceroy in Egypt, Muhammad Ali, expanded the empire southwards. Mohammad Ali's troops defeated the various kingdoms in the Sudan and extended the empire into Central Africa. The Mahdiya state was established through a revolt against the Turkiya empire, which placed upon its subjects an oppressive tax system. The Mahdiya state, however, lasted less than two decades, as it fell prey to an Anglo-Egyptian colonial expedition in 1898. By contrast, the Abyssinian empire was able to maintain its independence by defeating an Italian colonization effort in 1895 in the well-known battle of Adwa.

Unlike the decentralized political systems, the kingdoms and empires have left behind socioeconomic contexts that still foster inter-state and intra-state conflicts. The various wars and conquests of kingdom formation and empire-building as well as the political, economic and cultural relations that were left by the empires have left behind notable socioeconomic contexts that still have some lingering effect on nation-building. Among the specific contexts they left behind are the scars from the violence, looting and most importantly, slave raids, enslavement and slave trade. Both the Abyssinian empire and the Mahdiya state engaged in slave trade and the destructive raids involved. As Reid (2011) notes, these empires encountered endless wars of resistance from marginalized identities' frontier regions, which often were subjected to looting and plunder. Many of the kingdoms in the region also utilized slave labour and were involved in slave trade. The Oromo kingdoms in the southern parts of Ethiopia, such as Jimma, were slave traders. Kings and nobles in Jimma and other kingdoms in the Gibe and Didessa valleys possessed estates worked by thousands of peasants and large numbers of bonded labourers. In Jima, for example, the monarch, Abba Jifar II, is said to have possessed as many as 10,000 slaves and wealthy men commonly owned more than 1,000 slaves (Fernyhough, 2010: 75). There were also some 80,000 slaves in the kingdom of Keffa in 1897 (Fernyhough, 2010).

Along with the slave trade, the empires and kingdoms of the era also established hierarchical societies with first class and second class subjects and citizens. The Mahdiya state, which professed Arab and Muslim identity, denigrated non-Arab and non-Muslim identities and subjected them to slave raids, especially those in its southern frontiers. It thus left behind complex scars in inter-identity relations, particularly between northern and southern identity groups, hindering nation-building and fostering conflicts for years to come (Deng, 2010). Similarly, denial of cultural rights to non-Christians and to speakers of non-Abyssinian languages was common in pre-1974 Ethiopia. As a result of its Amharization policy, Ethiopia's empire state is also said to have banned the use of the Oromo language in public settings (Mekuria, 1994).

Pre-colonial empires and kingdoms also established foundations for uneven economic opportunities among different identities within their populations. The Abyssinian empire was perhaps the most noted in this regard. As the empire expanded southwards, the land of the conquered subjects was often confiscated and given to the conquering troops and administrators in lieu of salaries. The new subjects were then reduced to a class of landless tenants who worked the land of the new landlords on share-cropping terms (Pankhurst, 1968).[18] Some of the legacies of the empire, like the landlessness created by land appropriation, have largely been reversed by the 1975 land reform. The cultural inequalities have also been mitigated with the institution of a federal system by the country's 1994 constitution. However, disparities in access to political and economic power remain important sources of conflict, as evident from the activities of liberation movements, such as the Oromo Liberation Front and the Ogaden National Liberation Front. The pre-colonial kingdoms and empires established a lasting socioeconomic order, where the state was largely an expression of the cultural values of the identities that spearheaded its formation. For the subjugated identities, on the other hand, the state represented an apparatus of their political, economic and cultural subordination.

The conquests and political, economic and cultural subjugation of the vanquished are not unique to the kingdoms and empires of the region. State formation often is accomplished through conquest, which involves the subordination of the conquered by the conquerors. The violent process of state formation is, however, often followed by a process of nation-building, which involves socialization of the population by the state that it represents their collective interests while it also attempts to extend citizenship rights to all segments of society. This process of nation-building was not undertaken by the states of the region. Major factors may be colonization and threat of colonization of the countries of the region by European powers not long after their formation. In any case, long after the creation of the empires, nation-building strategies in Sudan and Ethiopia were 'unity in conformity' in Sudan and assimilation of the different cultures to the dominant culture in Ethiopia. Of course, these strategies proved serious impediments to peaceful nation-building in both countries.

Legacy of Colonialism

All of the countries of the Greater Horn except Ethiopia fell under colonial rule during the 1880s and remained colonies for roughly sixty or so years (see table 3.1). Within that time frame the colonial state transformed the structures of the economy, fragmented the institutions of governance and altered inter-identity relations in the colonies. The post-colonial state, in many respects, still operates within the socioeconomic context established by the colonial state. It is beyond the scope of this chapter to identify the various changes brought about by the colonial state and to analyse their implications. The concerns of this chapter are limited to the structural changes that left behind a conflict-fostering socioeconomic context in the region. Ethiopia avoided colonization, although it was occupied by Fascist Italy for a brief period of time (1936–41). Despite its ability to repel colonization, however, Ethiopia did not escape many of the conflict-engendering impacts of the region's colonization. The undeveloped nature of its economy also did not allow the country to occupy a different position in the global division of labour than its colonized neighbours.

Table 3.1. Colonial rule in the Greater Horn region

Country	Date of colonization	Date of decolonization
Djibouti	1884–5	27 June 1977
Eritrea	1885–1941 (Italian)	1–5 July 1991
	1941–52 (British as UN Trustee)	
	1952–62 federation with Ethiopia	
	1962 (annexation by Ethiopia)	
Ethiopia	1936 (Italian occupation)	1941
Kenya	1895	12 December 1963
Somalia	Northern Somalia 1886 (British)	1 July 1960
	Southern Somalia 1885 (Italian)	
Sudan	1898 (Anglo-Egyptian)	1956

The colonial state brought to an end the various nine-teenth-century conflicts which were triggered by the processes of state-formation and empire-building. Ending those wars did not, however, bring peace to the region. Colonization itself triggered wars of resistance as well as wars of liberation. Among the most notable wars against colonization were those waged by the Abyssinian empire in the 1890s. The 1895 battle of Adwa, where a large Abyssinian army defeated an Italian army, was perhaps the most notable. The 1936 con-quest of Abyssinia by Italy was another war of colonization. The colonial war that destroyed the Mahdiya state in Sudan and the wars against the dervishes in Somalia were other notable wars. Colonialism also triggered various rebellions and liberation struggles in the region. Beyond the wars, colo-nialism left behind many conflict-fostering legacies that still subject the region to various conflicts.

One critical conflict-engendering legacy is the problem of inter-state boundaries, which often are neither demarcated nor clearly delineated. The vagueness of boundaries, which Ethiopia also did not escape because its boundaries were also defined by the colonial boundaries of its neighbours, has caused a number of border disputes. The Eritrea–Ethiopia border war (1998–2000) is the biggest of such wars, but border disputes are rather rampant among all the countries of the region. Although British colonialism kept South Sudan largely separate from the North, the boundar-ies between the two remained unclear and are presently causing serious problems between the two countries. While border conflicts are mostly inter-state conflicts, they also have serious implications on state-identity and inter-identity relations as they entail various types of hardships on border communities, especially when their loyalty to the state is questioned. The Misseriya and Dinka Ngok identities, for example, have conflicting positions in the wrangling between Sudan and South Sudan about ownership of Abeyei and other border places.

In addition, colonial powers often engaged in transferring ownership of territory from one colony to another, as in the case of the Ogaden, which at different times was held by different powers (see chapter 6). The British and Italian governments also attempted to dismantle Eritrea by giving the southern and eastern portions to Ethiopia and the western portions to Sudan, during the UN deliberations about the disposal of the former Italian colonies following Italy's defeat in the Second World War. Only emphatic local opposition prevented the implementation of the plan, known as the Bevin–Sforza plan (Bereket Habte Selassie, 1989). The British also entertained plans to separate Southern Sudan from the rest of Sudan and join it with their East African empire. Such attempts at territorial rearrangements also contributed to post-independence conflicts. As discussed in more detail in chapter 6, South Sudan, Ogaden and Eritrea have seen major conflicts related to colonial territorial arrangements.

A second legacy, which is related to the arbitrariness of inter-state boundaries, is the splitting of various ethnic groups into different countries. State boundaries are generally arbitrary, since states are often formed through wars. Avoiding partitioning of identity groups is hardly a consideration in state formation. Thus, the problem of partitioned identity groups is not a problem that is unique to the Horn of Africa or to the continent of Africa. The degree of arbitrariness of boundaries and the number of partitioned ethnic groups, however, seem to be disproportionately high in Africa, where the states are mostly colonial creations. The fact that these countries are relatively young and still in the process of nation-building may also magnify the magnitude of the problem. Table 2.2 in the previous chapter provides a list of some of the ethnic groups that are split into several states in the Greater Horn region. Ethiopia, despite successfully rebuffing colonization, has not been immune to this problem. A combination of its own expansion and European colonization of the areas adjacent to its frontiers ensured that it too shared with its neighbours the problem of partitioned identities.

Partitioned ethnic groups face a number of socioeconomic problems that make them prone to conflicts. A major problem relates to the disruption of their social and cultural ties as well as their economic process, especially when the partitioned communities are pastoralists and inter-state relations are poor and border crossings are impeded. Often partitioned identities are also grieved about their national identity. The Afar in Ethiopia, Eritrea and Djibouti, for instance, aspire to a single Afar political entity to replace their partition into three countries (Berhe and Adaye Afar, 2007). While the partition of the Somali identity group, which led to three major wars between Ethiopia and Somalia, is the most conspicuous problem, many of the fragmented ethnic groups in the region have rather poor relations with their home states. Often they also face political and economic marginalization and repression when they react to their marginalization. Given such problems, partitioned identity groups tend to engage in various forms of resistance against the state. In some cases they also form armed movements, which demand self-determination. Roughly 34.5 per cent of the partitioned ethnic identities listed in table 2.2 have seen some armed rebellion against the state. When they rebel against the state, partitioned identities tend to obtain cross-border support from members of their identity, which tends to create inter-state tensions and conflicts. The Ogaden Somalis, the Afar in Djibouti and Ethiopia and the Beja of eastern Sudan are examples of armed struggle by partitioned identities.

A third conflict-fostering legacy of colonialism is the fragmentation of the economies of the colonies. The colonial state transplanted to the colonies a small capitalist economic sector that operated like an island in the sea of the traditional subsistence sector. The new sector produced mostly primary commodities geared to the markets of the colonial powers. However, it also became the priority of policy and the focus of investment resources. By contrast, the large traditional subsistence sector, which was largely driven by local consumption, was marginalized from access to resources. The two sectors represented two different modes of production and operated parallel to each other with limited interdependence between them. Instead of developing symbiotic relations and shared dynamics for mutual growth, the two sectors were characterized by conflict. Often the capitalist sector's expansion in important industries takes place at the expense of the traditional sector in part because the property rights of the traditional sector are either not recognized or not respected. Expansion of extractive industries and commercial farming, for example, resulted in land-taking from the traditional sector and evictions of peasants and pastoralists.

Although actual figures are hard to compile, there is little doubt that the colonial state appropriated large parcels of communal land from the traditional sector, especially the pastoral segment. The aim of the land-takings was to promote the growth of the capitalist sector and to keep land reserves for its future growth. Land appropriation triggered rebellions at different periods and in different locations. One of the early rebellions took place in Eritrea when a local leader, named Bahta Hagos, led a rebellion in 1894. The rebellion was, however, quickly crushed. A much better known rebellion is that of the Mau Mau in Kenya, which started in 1952. Despite popular protests in various parts of the region, the colonial state continued the process of land-taking and in some cases it simply declared all land as state property without denying use-rights to customary holders of land in order to facilitate land-taking, as needed. The fragmentation of the economic system and deprivation of the traditional sector created conditions for the stagnation of the traditional sector and for the impoverishment of the population operating in that sector. The post-colonial state has largely adopted much of the colonial land policy, as discussed in greater detail in chapter 7. Land-takings, along with population growth, have fostered land scarcity and various land-based intercommunal conflicts, as well as rebellions against the state.

Institutional Fragmentation

The dichotomy of modes of production is associated with a dichotomy of institutions of governance. The laws and norms that govern one economic system do not work well in another. Institutions of a non-capitalist subsistence economy could not govern a capitalist economy. But the reverse is also true. The capitalist sector, for example, requires a market-based private land tenure system for it to function unencumbered. The traditional non-capitalist pastoral and mixed farming systems, by contrast, cannot operate unhindered under a private land tenure system, which tends to restrict the mobility of livestock from place to place for grazing.

In establishing a capitalist economic sector, the colonial state also introduced a new set of corresponding institutions of governance. However, as it did not eradicate the traditional subsistence economic system, it also did not eliminate the traditional institutions of governance, which correspond with that economic system. One of the major legacies of the colonial experience in the countries of the Greater Horn, as in the rest of Africa is, thus, a dichotomous system of institutions of governance. Long after colonialism, the segment of the population in the traditional subsistence sector still adheres to the traditional system's customary property rights laws; its resource allocation mechanisms, and its conflict resolution and dispute adjudication practices.

The parallel institutional systems do not exist in isolation of each other. As discussed in greater detail in the next chapter, the dichotomous systems have complex interrelationships. They are incompatible in many respects and complement each other in others. With respect to the judicial system, for instance, the two systems complement each other in dealing with major crimes, such as murder, rape and theft. Such crimes are adjudicated by the formal courts and the offenders are given their sentences. However, in the traditional system criminal offences are generally the responsibility of the offender's extended family (or clan) and not only of the individual offender. Under such circumstances, the families have to be reconciled through various forms of compensatory arrangements for the conflict to end. Punishment of the offender by the state is generally not sufficient to bring an end to the conflict. There are also economic linkages of various types between the two systems. Moreover, new technologies in communication, such as radios and cell phones, have increased the connections between the two socioeconomic spaces. Despite such linkages, however, the traditional economic and institutional system remains entrenched and the dichotomy of institutions remains a norm in much of the region, as well as the rest of Africa.

The socioeconomic implications of the presence of parallel institutional systems have not received much attention in the literature. However, there is little doubt that it has been a source of various problems. Institutional fragmentation, along with the dichotomy of economic systems, creates separate socioeconomic spaces, which make governance and policy-making very challenging. Under parallel socioeconomic spaces, it becomes likely that policy would favour one system or the other unless there is a leadership that vigorously pursues policies of reconciling the parallel systems. In the absence of such leadership the state in a global capitalist system generally utilizes the market system in much of the resource allocation process in line with the capitalist order. The traditional subsistence sector, which operates on the fringes of the market system, finds itself on the fringes in terms of access to resources.

The population under the traditional socioeconomic space also faces marginalization in terms of access to judicial service. The formal judicial system is generally inaccessible and often unsuited to the traditional sector. The formal system often involves costs for legal representation and for the filing of cases. It also often entails long distance travel to the courts. In many cases illiteracy and language barriers also contribute to its inaccessibility. The laws that the formal courts apply are often incompatible with the realities in the traditional sector. The rulings of the formal courts, especially in criminal cases, are also essentially retributive rather than restorative and do not bring an end to disputes in rural settings.

Given such constraints, the population in the traditional socioeconomic space largely relies on its own traditional judicial system to settle disputes. Unlike in the formal courts, the rulings of the traditional courts are restorative, intended to bring an end to disputes through a system of compensation and reconciliation. The deliberation process in the traditional courts is conducted in local languages and it is participatory and open to all adult males in the community.[19] The rulings in most cases are rendered by elders in an open assembly and, thus, provide much better safeguards against corruption. Perhaps the most fundamental reason why the traditional judicial system has remained resilient is that the formal courts operate in socioeconomic and cultural settings that do not reflect the realities in rural areas. The two judicial systems, thus, operate side by side catering to the two socioeconomic spaces.

Due to its limited influence on policy, the traditional institutional space is also marginalized with respect to access to public service facilities, such as schools and hospitals. It is also marginalized politically, since it is unable to influence policy, mainly due to lack of education and access to information and the means of expressing input on policy. The socioeconomic space, under which the overwhelming majority of the population operates, thus, endures general marginalization.

The marginalization of rural inhabitants, along with the institutional detachment of the state from this large segment of the population, has in many cases adversely affected the legitimacy of the state and state–society relations. Often the marginalization of rural inhabitants affects some identity groups more than others. Geography seems to play some role in this regard. The further an ethnic group's location is from urban centres, the more it relies on traditional institutions and the more limited its access to public services becomes. In any case, inequalities often lead to problems of diversity management and ethnic conflicts, which often exacerbate the inequalities and undermine the process of nation-building.

The dichotomy of institutional systems has caused violent conflicts, especially when the state engages in land-takings. Conflicts in the Nuba Mountains in Sudan, in Gambela in Ethiopia and the violent inter-communal conflicts in the Tana River area of Kenya are some examples. Moreover, under fragmented socioeconomic spaces with marginalization of the overwhelming majority of the population, economic development, stable governance, state-building and democratization are all likely to be adversely impacted. It is unlikely that countries that leave behind the overwhelming majority of their citizens would have dynamic economies and stable democratic governance. It is also difficult to envisage effective governance under conflicting parallel economic, institutional and judicial systems, since governments would find it hard to cater appropriate policy to the two socioeconomic spaces simultaneously.

Uneven Development among Regions

Another legacy of colonialism is uneven development among regions and ethnic groups within the countries of the region. One of the primary goals of colonialism was to exploit resources from colonies. Accordingly, the colonial state concentrated its infrastructure development in the colonies in areas it viewed to be profitable. Similarly, private firms operating in colonial Africa invested in those same areas. Regions that were deemed to be unprofitable and populations living in those areas were largely left marginalized. The Buganda areas of southern Uganda were privileged relative to the rest of the country (Mutibwa, 2008). In Kenya the British identified central Kenya and the Rift Valley as profitable areas, while the western and northeastern regions, which were viewed as unprofitable and troublesome, were marginalized (APRM, 2006; Mwaura et al., 2002). Southern Sudan and northern Uganda were among other areas within the region that were relatively marginalized by the colonial state. The problems of marginalization and uneven development have proven to be intractable. All the areas that were marginalized by the colonial state have remained centres of conflict (APRM, 2006, 2009).[20]

Religious Conflicts

Another conflict-fostering legacy of colonialism was in the area of religious policy. Religious diversity and religious conflicts in the region predate colonialism. A long-term view of the region reveals that, despite its religious diversity, it has faced relatively few religion-based wars. Yet, there were important episodes in which economic and political rivalries, along with religious differences, led to serious wars and conflicts. Wars between the Abyssinian empire and various Somali Sultanates date back to the fourteenth century. These wars had religious motives, although they were also rivalries about control of trade routes to the Red Sea and the Gulf of Aden. Similarly, the wars between Ottoman Egypt and the Mahdiya state against Emperor Yohannes IV of Abyssinia had religious overtones, although they were wars that revolved around expansion of empires. However, colonialism also contributed in spreading religious conflicts through its policy of religious discrimination. In many parts of the Greater Horn colonialism was accompanied by missionaries of different Christian denominations. In rare cases, there were even conflicts between the different missionaries. The 1892 civil war between Catholics and Protestants in Buganda was one example of religious conflict. Favouring the spread of Christianity, colonialism was not characterized by religious freedom or equal treatment of all religions. The British colonial administration, for example, did not allow the preaching of Islam or the influence of northern culture in South Sudan. Colonial rule also left education largely under the control of missionaries, who often discriminated against non-Christians.

Perhaps the most important conflict that can be, at least in part, attributable to colonial religious policy is the conflict between North and South Sudan. Needless to say, that conflict was not merely due to religious differences but religion was certainly a major factor. In any case, the impacts of the colonial policy on religion, along with the rise of Islamic fundamentalism and the war on terror, have increased religious strife throughout the Greater Horn region.

4	The State as a
	Source of Conflict

Introduction

The nature of the post-colonial state has been a major source of various socioeconomic problems in the Horn of Africa, as in much of the rest of the African continent. The state has especially been a critical factor in the region's crisis of state-building as well as in many of the region's chronic conflicts. This chapter aims to examine the direct and indirect mechanisms by which the nature of the state in the region engenders conflicts. More specifically, the chapter has two principal objectives. One is to examine the nature (characteristics) of the post-colonial state in the Horn of Africa, including its institutional systems, its governance structures and its leadership qualities. The second is to analyse how the nature of the state has impacted state–society relations and fostered conditions that promote both inter-state and domestic conflicts, which, in turn, undermine the process of state-building, democratization and stimulate further conflicts. A systematic analysis of the nature of the state in the region or how its characteristics foster general socioeconomic problems and conflicts requires that we first conceptualize the state. It also requires that we briefly sketch what the structures of a properly functioning and democracy-fostering state entail so that we have a point of reference against which to compare the nature of the existing state in the Horn of Africa.

What is the State?

The state is the chief organizer of socioeconomic life in every country in the world. Yet, there is hardly any agreement on how to define it. Although the terms state, country and government are often used interchangeably, the state is not the same thing as the country nor is it the same as the government. Somalia for almost two decades since 1991 has been essentially without a state and a functioning government but it has not ceased to exist as a country and this tells us that the terms state and country do not exactly refer to the same thing, despite their close association with each other. What stateless Somalia lacks is the overarching set of organizations that organize socioeconomic life in the country and a government that administers the interlocking set of organizations.

At the time of writing this chapter Egypt is facing mass demonstrations and the Mubarak-led government has collapsed. The demise of the government did not result in the collapse of the Egyptian state, however. The other organizations of the state, such as the country's military and the judiciary, for example, appear to continue to operate, protecting life and property in the country. The state is, thus, something more than the government, although, where the state is not well developed, the distinctions between the state and the government or even between the state and the governing regime may not exist or may not be apparent.

In some cases the state is said to encompass a population, fixed sovereign territory, which is recognized by other states, and a government with leaders and a legitimate monopoly of the power of coercion (Samatar and Samatar, 2002). This definition, however, does not differentiate the state from a country that is independent, since the said components of the state are not different from those of the country. It would be hard to explain the role of the state or the characterization of the state as 'developmentalist', 'predatory', etc., on the basis of this definition. Of course, there is no state without a country and a population. The state, however, is more specific than the broad requisites for its existence.

The state is also defined as an organization that extracts resources through taxation and attempts to extend coercive control and political authority over a particular territory and the people residing within it (Skocpol and Amenta, 1986). This definition is also problematic because it attempts to define the state by what it does but the identified tasks, which essentially exclude the positive roles that the state may play, can be performed by organizations other than the state. Even thuggish rebel groups can extract resources and exercise coercive control, at least temporarily.

Max Weber's (1958) definition that the state is a human community that establishes a monopoly of the legitimate use of physical force within a given territory is also an incomplete definition because it does not distinguish the state from the government. The idea of legitimate use of physical power may also be problematic since legitimacy of coercive power depends on the legitimacy of the state. When the legitimacy of the state is lost or questioned, by citizens as well as by other states, its monopoly of coercive powers also ceases to be legitimate, as demonstrated by the civil wars in Libya and Syria, two countries where the state is not clearly demarcated from the regimes. From the point of view of the rebel group (the Transitional National Council), Muammar Gaddafi's regime did not command any legitimacy, although such a claim would be contested by the supporters of the Gaddafi regime. Similarly, the Assad regime in Syria commands little legitimacy, at least from the point of view of the opposition forces. Legitimacy of the coercive powers of the state is thus contingent on the legitimacy of the state and often the state may not be viewed to be legitimate by the population or may be viewed legitimate by only a segment of the population.

Part of the challenge in defining the state may be attributable to the changing nature of the state and its changing relations with society over time. Another explanation may be due to differences in the characteristics of the state in different countries, which may be at different levels of socioeconomic development and at different levels in the development of the state. In any case, a satisfactory definition of the state needs to identify all the essential characteristics of the state, while separating it from other closely related entities. A working definition for our purposes is that the state is an overarching set of interlocking organizations that collectively organize socioeconomic relations of the population of a given country (Wallis and North, 2010). Although they may differ slightly from one political system to another, the interlocking set of organizations consists of the constitutional courts, the military, the bureaucracy, the central bank, the electoral commission and the government, with its legislative, judiciary, and executive branches, which administers the whole set-up but does not supplant the different organizations (see figure 4.1). A properly functioning state has a monopoly of coercive power and the power to extract resources from society in a given territory and is expected by the population in that country to provide security and to facilitate the attainment of a range of other public services that would enhance their well-being. Societies are, however, often diverse and different identity groups have competing interests. States face difficult challenges in managing diversity and often tend to advance the interests and vision of powerful groups, who are able to exert influence or even to determine the political lives of state

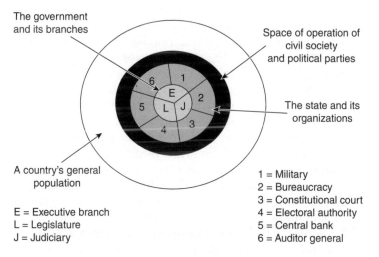

Figure 4.1. Conceptualization of the State

functionaries. In general, however, the state may serve different interests at different times. It can advance general public interests, private interests, or manage different interests by arbitrating or forging compromises between competing interests, depending on the balance of power among social groups within society and the governance structure in place. Thus, as Sekyi-Otu (1996) notes, the state, at its best, is a necessary source of collective empowerment and well-being. At its, worst, however, it can be a debilitating burden.

Genesis and Nature of the State

Theories on the genesis of the state provide some useful insights on the nature of the state, including what roles it plays and whose interests it represents, even though how the state is formed does not necessarily determine its nature in perpetuity. A brief discussion of some of these theories follows.

The Consent Theory of the State

This theory contends that the state is a spontaneous institution that naturally evolves from a community when members of that community require protection both from external and internal threats. According to this theory, the state, as an overriding institution, is said to naturally evolve to establish the laws by which society is governed and to act as a policeman and final arbiter of disputes. From this perspective the state is organically linked with society and it essentially acts as a protector of society and broadly as a promoter of its interests. Locke's social contract theory complements the consent theory of the state, since the social contract is voluntary and each person who lives within a community and accepts its benefits is said to tacitly agree to the rules by which that community is governed. Rousseau's *general will* theory is also similar to the consent theory since a state that advances the general will is likely to be rooted in the general consent of citizens.

Real cases approximating the consent theory of the state may exist at two different levels. At one level we have the pre-colonial African traditional institutions of governance, especially those elder-based decentralized systems. Communities in such systems organized themselves in a manner that the laws governing them were established in an assembly of a council of elders, laws were also enforced by all members of the community and all able-bodied men were organized, often along age groups, to provide security as needed without forming a professional army. In some cases, the communities evolved to form hierarchical systems and to incorporate other communities. Such metamorphosis of these decentralized community organizations (proto-states) was, however, halted by colonialism. In other cases they were disrupted by the expansion of pre-colonial empires, such as the Abyssinian empire in the case of Ethiopia.[21] Nevertheless, these traditional institutions show us that states can be formed along the lines of the consent theory, although they may not remain consent-based in perpetuity. In the post-colonial era, these traditional institutions of governance still operate at the local level, albeit in a much changed form and circumstances. The Aba Gada system of the Borona in southeastern Ethiopia, the Njuri Ncheke of the Meru people in central Kenya, the Kaya elders of the Mijikenda in the east coast of Kenya, the Pokot elders in western Kenya, the Nuer chiefs in southwest Ethiopia and the Gurage elders in central Ethiopia are among such traditional institutions that still operate in a system where the community is involved in law-making (living customary law) and in the implementation (enforcement) of the laws (rules) with little differentiation between the community's organization (proto-state) and the members of the community (society). In other words, unlike the modern state, these proto-states operated with little separation of powers and with limited differentiation of the organs of the state. Instead, they relied on a system of direct participation of the population (except women and youth in most cases).

At another level, the more advanced a democratic system of governance becomes, the more the state would resemble a consent-based system, even though it may not have been initially formed through the consent of society. In other words, regardless of how the state was formed initially, democratic transformation, which generally results from popular struggle, leads to the establishment of consent-based state–society relations. In a mature democratic system the state operates on the basis of legal systems and policies that would be controlled by the population, through its representatives at the national and regional levels and through direct participation at the local level.

The State as a Creation of a Dominant Class

A second theory of state formation is Marxian theory, which views the state as a creation of dominant classes for the purposes of protecting their property and advancing their interests at the expense of those of the rest of society. Such states may emerge as constructs of specific classes or other identities and may be highly partial in the political, economic and cultural interests they advance. However, states that advance the interests of dominant class or ethnic groups do not have to be constructs of dominant groups originally. Even states formed through consent can evolve into states that represent dominant classes or other identities if the balance of power in society shifts in a manner that certain groups establish a dominant position. According to this theory, the state, which is designed to protect the privileges and advances the interests of a dominant class, cannot grant equal citizenship rights to all citizens. Hence the state is characterized by perpetual class conflicts.

The Conquest Theory of the State

A third theory claims that the state emerges from external conflicts. According to this theory, communities form states in order to either conquer other groups or to defend themselves against attacks by others. Charles Tilly's (1990) contention that war made states and that in wars states were gradually able to monopolize organized violence by eliminating private armies and other contenders, corroborates this theory. It is debatable if wars precede the formation of the state. It is plausible that groups who want to attack others may first form a state-like organization. It is also reasonable for identities that perceive a threat to establish an organization to help them defend themselves. Such organizations may not embody all the characteristics of the modern state, however. In any case, from the perspective of the conquest theory of the state, down to its foundation, the state was never meant to preserve justice, property rights or the peace. Rather it is an instrument associated with aggression.

Colonial Conquest

We can also add colonial conquest as another mechanism of state formation. It is, by far, the most common form of state formation in the Horn of Africa, as in the rest of the African continent, although, as noted in chapter 3, it is by no means the origin of statehood in the region. The region's existing countries are either curved out or shaped by European colonization. The Abyssinian empire was the only one in the region to escape direct colonization after thwarting Italy's attempts by defeating it in the battle of Adwa in 1895. Nevertheless, the map of present-day Ethiopia also is shaped by a combination of the empire's expansion and by colonial conquests of territories surrounding it by European colonizers. Despite Ethiopia's ability to maintain its independence, the nature of its state and its socioeconomic structures was heavily influenced by external influences.

Characteristics of a Democracy-Fostering State

From the identified theories of the genesis of the state, views on the nature of the state vary in a spectrum between two extremes. On one extreme is the view that the state is an ideal expression of society, as depicted in Plato's Republic. In this case the state is an agency for advancing the well-being of society at large. On the other extreme is the view that the state is an instrument of domination and exploitation, as expressed by the conquest theory. A variant of this latter view is the libertarian perspective that the state is a vicious parasite riding on the back of society (Rothbard, 2002). In reality the state at different times and in different countries lies at different locations in a continuum between the two extremes. Many factors, including changing relations and balance of power among social classes as well as changes in broad socioeconomic development of society can lead to changes in the nature of the state and in how it relates with society. In other words, the state, as an organizer of socioeconomic life, shapes society but societal relations and balance of power among socioeconomic classes and levels of socioeconomic development also shape the nature of the state.

Ideally, the state, like a club where all citizens are members, would serve as an agency for advancing the well-being of all its members. The democratization effort, which attempts to create mechanisms by which all citizens are represented in policy-making and other decisions, is intended to ensure that the state serves as an agent for advancing the well-being of all citizens. However, given the competing interests of diverse groups of citizens, the state tends to serve the interests of certain groups, such as a dominant class and/or the elites of dominant ethnic groups. In other cases it may serve the interests of dominant social groups, such as the military, or it may simply advance the interests of its functionaries, conforming to what Caporaso (1982) refers to as the 'state for itself' conception of the state.

Samatar (2002) identifies five conceptions of the state ranging from the ideal or the *integral* state, which advances the common good effectively, to the *cadaverous* state, where civic life has ceased and the state is practically dead. In between these two extremes are three types of states. One is the *developmentalist* state, which actively promotes national accumulation and improvement of human capital. Another is the *prebendalist* state, which is largely preoccupied with the protection and reproduction of the immediate interests of the regime and its associates. Another type is the *predatory* state, where the functionaries of the state are essentially engaged in scavenging for dwindling public resources, oblivious to the collective good.

The nature of states, thus, ranges from those that are enabling to those that are debilitating. An essential characteristic of an enabling state is that it has mechanisms that safeguard broad social interests and hinder the state's tendency to degenerate into a debilitating entity. Among such mechanisms is a coherent system of institutions of governance that foster equitable access to political, economic and cultural resources to all citizens. In the absence of such institutional systems a state would likely be either self-serving or partisan and the more the state becomes self-serving or an agent for the advancement of particular interests, the more likely that it faces problems of diversity management, including resistance by disadvantaged groups and social conflicts. Among the critical attributes of a properly functioning and enabling state is, thus, that its institutions are suitable for dispensing citizenship rights equitably among all citizens.

Another critical aspect of an enabling state is that the governance structures are built in a manner that they empower citizens to hold the state accountable. Among the requirements of such governance structures is establishing structures that ensure a level of independence of the different interlocking organizations of the state from each other and from the executive branch of government, so that there is horizontal accountability among them. The judiciary, the central bank and the electoral commission, for example, cannot operate credibly without independence from the executive. It is also critical that such independence creates a political space where civil society, opposition parties and individuals engage freely in the political process with full protection of the law from possible transgressions and restrictions by the government. Such a political space would allow non-state actors to organize and hold the state accountable. Moreover, it is essential that the government itself has a built-in system of checks and balances with separation of powers.[22] Independence of the legislature and judiciary from the executive body is, for example, crucial for safeguarding accountability of the executive branch of government and for ensuring the rule of law. The legislative body would hardly serve as a meaningful representation of citizens if it is used as a rubber stamp of the executive body, as often is the case in many African countries.

A third criterion is that the state has an effective electoral system to ensure that a leadership which fails to develop the structures and institutions of the state that empower citizens to advance their security and broad socioeconomic well-being is removed from office and replaced by a leadership that the population places its trust in. While the identified criteria give us characteristics of a properly functioning and mature state, it is important to recognize that the development of the state, like that of the society it represents, is work in progress. It also does not necessarily progress in a linear manner.

The Nature of the State in the Greater Horn of Africa

Rising from the ashes of the colonial state through nationalist struggle, the post-colonial state in Africa was expected by the general population to serve as an agent of liberation of the victims of colonialism.[23] Unfortunately, the state, in most cases, has not been a liberator. To the contrary, the African state is described by many observers as a 'state without citizens' (Ayoade, 1998), 'vampire state' (Ayittey, 1993, 1998), 'predatory' (Samatar, 2002), 'juridical' and not empirical (Jackson and Rosberg, 1982), 'quasi-state' (Jackson, 1990), 'suspended state' (Hyden, 1983), 'collapsed states' (Zartman, 1995), 'lame Leviathans' (Callaghy, 1987), 'bifurcated' states (Mamdani, 1996), 'disconnected' states (Dia, 1996) and 'imported states' (Englebert, 1997). As a result, there has been widespread advocacy for the reconstitution of the African state to bring it under the control of citizens, and thereby to reconcile its institutions with those of the African masses and to coordinate its policy with broad societal interests.

The state in the Greater Horn shares most of the characteristics of the state in the rest of the African continent. It has, thus, been far from enabling. The above identified three attributes of an enabling state can be used to appraise the nature of the state in the Horn. Of course, these three criteria are not the only characteristics of a good state, but they represent core requirements and provide essential benchmarks for examining the nature of the state in the region and why the state has become a major factor in the region's conflicts both directly and indirectly.

Institutional Fragmentation

As noted, the post-colonial state is largely a product of popular nationalist struggle but it is also erected upon institutional systems established by the colonial state. It thus shares with the colonial state some institutional characteristics. The colonial state introduced a capitalist socioeconomic system while largely precluding capital accumulation by the native subjects. It also imposed European institutional systems of governance upon its colonies without eliminating the African institutions of governance that existed at the time of colonization, although it often modified them to serve its purposes. The colonial state, thus, organized the colonies in a manner that pre-colonial indigenous institutions of governance and traditional (non-capitalist) modes of production, consisting of subsistence peasant and pastoral economies, existed side by side with the European institutions of governance and an embryonic capitalist economic system. In Ethiopia, which escaped direct colonialism, the development of an institutional system followed a somewhat different trajectory. The Abyssinian empire imposed its own institutional system on its newly acquired southern provinces, which were incorporated by conquest in the late nineteenth century. At the same time, the empire itself fostered economic and institutional duality by allowing the expansion of the foreign-dominated commercial sector and by copying institutions of the western world in the name of modernization. Some nationalist modernizers in the country, referred as 'Japanizers' by Addis Hiwet (1975), expressed concerns that the expansion of the commercial sector with new technology would be harmful to the country if it were not properly designed to bring about economic transformation of the citizens.

The capitalist economic sector has expanded modestly since decolonization. Yet, the countries of the Horn of Africa, like most other African countries, are still characterized by a duality of modes of production and institutions of governance. The parallel systems of production are evident from the nature of the economies, which range from a small sector of a fairly developed capitalist system, symbolized by modern banking systems and stock markets, to a rather large sector of subsistence peasantry and pastoral systems. The parallel modes of production have also sustained parallel institutional systems of political, economic and social governance. As pointed out in chapter 2, the state, along with the capitalist sector of the economy, is run on the basis of the state-sponsored (formal) institutions, which were partly inherited from the colonial state and partly imported during the post-colonial era. The large traditional sector, on the other hand, is largely run on the basis of institutions that originate in pre-colonial systems of governance.[24] The 'traditional' systems, which were formal institutions in the pre-colonial era, varied from place to place in line with the governance systems that existed at the time.[25]

Some of these traditional systems of governance have written laws. In Eritrea, for instance, different regions have their own written traditional laws, such as those of *Logo Chewa* and the *Adgine Tegeleba* of Akle-Guzai and several others. In most cases, the traditional laws are not coded. A list of examples of such institutions in the Horn include the Gada of the Oromo, the Kicha of the Gurage, the Kaya of the Mijikenda on the coast of Kenya, as well as the Njuri Ncheke of Meru in central Kenya. Irrespective of whether their laws are coded or not, the traditional institutions continue to play a significant role in the governance of African societies, especially in rural areas. A recent survey, for example, shows that, despite variations from community to community, survey respondents believe that over 56 per cent of disputes in Kenya's Mijikenda, Meru and West Pokot are settled by the traditional judicial system while in the Gurage, Borona and Nuer communities in Ethiopia the figure is over 78 per cent (Kidane Mengisteab et al., 2011).

Institutions, which represent an enduring collection of formal laws and informal rules, customs, codes of conduct and organized practices, shape human behaviour and interaction. As institutional scholars inform us, when formal and informal institutions are in discord they tend to lead to social instability, as they promote competing property rights laws and send conflicting signals about expected appropriate social behaviour (Eisenstadt, 1968: 409; Olsen, 2007).

The parallel institutional systems, of course, do not exist in complete isolation from each other as communities and individuals have to negotiate the two systems in their daily lives. In many respects the two systems even complement each other. However, neither one of the systems is fully compatible with the economic and cultural systems of the other.

The implications of fragmented modes of production and institutional systems for governance and general socioeconomic transformation are understudied. Yet, it is clear that parallel modes of production and institutional systems represent separate socioeconomic spaces and they create a number of socioeconomic problems related to management of diversity, nation-building and democratization. Among the most important are the following:

- Conflicting property rights laws, along with differences in the rationale that governs allocation of resources, often hinder the making of coherent economic policies that coordinate resources with the interests of the communities in both socioeconomic spaces. Land-takings by the state, for example, are often for purposes of giving land concessions to investors in large-scale commercial farming, to firms in the extractive industries and to developers in urban areas. The policy may seem reasonable from the point of view of development imperatives. However, it often is done with little regard for the interests of peasants and pastoralists, who often face evictions and impoverishment. The policy, thus, produces growth in one sector and violation of property rights and misery in the other.

- The communities that live under the traditional modes of production and institutional systems face marginalization in access to resources, such as public services, as they remain largely delinked from the primary agents of resource allocation, the state's institutions and the market mechanism.[26] These communities lack the political clout to influence the state's resource allocation policy in their favour and they are largely unable to attract resources through the market for a number of reasons. Among them is that their production and resource allocation systems are dominated by use value rather than exchange value. Their productivity is rather low as they employ rudimentary tools in their production process. These communities, thus, lack the purchasing power as well as transportation and communication facilities for active participation in the market system. This disjuncture of the rural communities from the state and the market implies that these two resource allocation mechanisms become rather ineffective in poverty alleviation and in transforming the subsistence sector of the economy.

- The communities in the traditional socioeconomic space operate under customary law and traditional judicial practices. The formal judicial system is often inaccessible to them for a variety of reasons. Regardless of the merits of the traditional judicial system, these communities are marginalized in access to the benefits of the formal judicial system, since the judicial system under which they operate is rarely recognized by the state and, thus, does not render state accountability.

- The existence of parallel institutional systems delinks the state institutionally from the majority of the population. Consequently, they weaken the legitimacy of the state and undermine the process of state-building. Englebert (1997) describes the African state as predatory, neo-patrimonial, rent-seeking and urban biased and he attributes these characteristics to its legitimacy deficit. Basil Davidson (1992) also attributes the ineffectiveness of the African state in bringing about sustained socioeconomic development to its neglect of traditional institutions and its failure to restore Africa's own history.

• By failing to reconcile the parallel institutional systems, the state has also failed to create conditions for nation-building and democratization. It is difficult to envisage a working democratic system emerging under conditions of parallel institutional systems that marginalize the overwhelming majority of the population.

Fragmented institutional systems may not be the direct cause of large-scale violent conflicts in the region. However, the above identified problems indicate that they foster conditions that engender conflicts. The political, economic and judicial inequalities they promote are major sources of conflicts and undermine peaceful processes of nation-building, as discussed in the next chapter. They hinder equitable access to citizenship rights among various identities and they impede the process of democratization by excluding large segments of the population from political and economic influence.

Structures of Governance

Another debilitating characteristic of the state in the Horn, as in the rest of Africa, is the absence or near absence of relative independence of the various organizations of the state from the executive branch of the government. Separation of powers and checks and balances within the various organizations of the state, as well as within the branches of government, constitute critical requisites for state accountability. It is also indispensable for creating space where non-state actors can participate in the political process. It is, for example, unlikely to have credible elections if the electoral commission is not independent from the government. It is also hard to safeguard the rights of citizens from possible transgressions by the executive without an independent constitutional court and judiciary. In all the countries of the region the executive branch of government dominates the other organizations of the state leaving little room for their independence. Despite some differences among them, the region's countries also have little separation of powers within the organs of the government for checks and balances and accountability. The executive branch in most cases dominates the other branches of government, the judiciary and the legislature. Moreover, the executive branch itself is often dominated by individual leaders in all the countries of the region, except perhaps in Kenya. Under such circumstances, the creation of political space for civil society and opposition political parties to operate in depends entirely on the whims of leaders, who invariably tend to restrict it severely. The different organs of the government, including the judiciary, which is supposed to protect the existence of such a space, are often subverted by the executive branch and more specifically the 'strongmen' leaders, who face few constraints in restricting political participation by opponents. There is also a glaring absence of mechanisms for representation of the different segments of the population in governance, since the legislature, to which representatives are elected, does not have much autonomy from the executive branch. Real decentralization of governance that would allow local participation is also hardly feasible under such conditions even when nominal arrangements of decentralization exist.

No doubt, there are notable differences among the governments of the region. Somalia, which is without a functioning state, Eritrea, which does not have a constitutional government, and Sudan, which has been engulfed by various intractable civil wars, are not in the same category as Kenya. Yet no country in the region has put in place the necessary level of separation of powers within the government or the necessary level of independence of the different organizations of the state. There are a number of indicators for the glaring absence of autonomy of state organizations from the government and the absence of governance structures that enable citizens to influence policy and to hold the governments accountable. Among the most conspicuous are the level of influence of civil society on government, autonomy from the government of electoral authorities (commissions), credibility of elections, judicial independence from the executive and ability of the legislature to hold the executive accountable. Direct empirical evidence on these indicators is rather sparse. However, expert opinion surveys for the African Governance Report by the United Nations Economic Commission for Africa (UNECA, 2009) show that the countries of the region score very poorly on all the identified indicators (see table 4.1).

Without the checks and balances that are made possible by separation of powers and independence of the

Table 4.1. Selected indicators of autonomy of state organizations from governments in the Horn countries[*]

	Djibouti	Ethiopia	Kenya	Uganda
Civil society has strong or fairly strong influence on government	–	23%	26%	25%
Civil society effectively or moderately able to promote gov't accountability	38%	23%	48%	22%
Electoral authority always or largely impartial	40%	26%	51%	25%
Electoral system acceptable or largely acceptable to all political parties	52%	27%	75%	33%
Legislative always or usually holds the executive accountable	40%	24%	26%	25%
Judiciary always or largely independent	35%	28%	28%	48%
Gov't fully or mostly respects rule of law	50%	–	–	25%

[*] Eritrea and Sudan are not included in the survey.
Source: UNECA, *African Governance Report II*, 2009.

organizations of the state, it is highly unlikely to have governance that is accountable and respects the rule of law. In other words, it is hard to prevent the rise of authoritarian rule without a system of checks and balances. As we will see in chapter 5, without separation of powers, it is also hard to envision proper diversity management, which requires genuine decentralization and credible representation of all segments of the population to ensure equitable disposal of citizenship rights and other opportunities and privileges among all identity groups.[27]

Leadership Quality

Selfless, committed and far-sighted leaders can become state builders by developing the structures of the state that promote accountability. They can also spearhead transformation of the fragmented economic and institutional systems. Leaders in the Horn countries, like their counterparts in the rest of the continent, face the daunting challenge of measuring up to these responsibilities. Those who commit themselves to state-building would have to do so at the expense of their own self-interest, which includes monopolizing power and extending their tenure in power. Building the structures of the state, which foster accountability, is antithetical to monopolizing power and perpetuating one's tenure in power. State builders, thus, would have to deny their own selfish interests and commit class suicide, as Cabral (1969) expected of African leaders. The Horn of Africa has not produced such leaders. Instead it is known for its infamous dictators, including Idi Amin, Mengistu Hailemariam and Siad Barre. Most of the region's current leaders are not far behind the identified notorious despots, in terms of their monopoly of power and subversion of institution-building in order to perpetuate their own control of power. In Eritrea the leadership has been in power since 1991 without implementing a constitution, without allowing the formation of opposition parties and without a free press. Needless to say, there is very little separation of powers among the component organizations of the state in the country. Under such conditions the country does not have any legal mechanisms of changing leadership.

Sudan does not have a term limit provision in its constitution, even though it allows a multiparty system and conducts elections. However, in the absence of the structures of checks and balances and accountability, elections are easy to manipulate. Depriving opposition parties the ability to compete on a level playing field through various means, seems to have enabled the Bashir leadership to monopolize power since 1989.

The leaders of Djibouti and Uganda also have been able to successfully amend constitutional term limits and to extend their tenure. President Museveni of Uganda, who came to power in 1986, ruled for ten years under a system known as the 'non-party system', which prevented political parties from fielding candidates for presidency. A multiparty system with a two-term limit on the tenure of the president was introduced and the first elections took place in May 1996. After serving two terms by winning the 1996 and 2001 elections, however, Museveni managed to repel the term limit provision in 2005. Again he won for a third term in the 2006 election and a fourth term in 2011. All in all President Museveni has been in power for twenty-seven years at the time of writing.

Ethiopia with its 1994 constitution instituted a parliamentary system with no term limit on the post of prime minister. However, the Ethiopian regime has successfully established a dominant party that faces little risk of losing an election, although a coalition of opposition parties claimed that it won the 2005 election and that the election was stolen by the ruling party through rigging and manipulation of vote counting. Regardless of the veracity of the claim, the late Prime Minister Meles, who died in office in July 2012, stayed in office for twenty-one years from 1991. Post-Moi Kenya is, perhaps, the only exception in adhering to the provision of a two-term limit for the president, although the 2007 election was alleged to have been marred by fraud and rigging, which led to post-election violence.

The length of stay in power among the region's current leaders is a good indication that these leaders are not building institutions and state structures that foster accountability.

The widespread violations of human rights and restrictions on press freedoms and freedom for opposition parties are other indicators of the prevalence of self-serving characteristics of leaders (see table 4.2). The length of stay in power, along with the failure to establish the mechanisms of accountability have also politicized ethnicity and fostered the widespread perception that the states in the region represent the ethnic identities of the leaders.

The absence of commitment to state-building is not limited to leaders who are in power. Opposition parties have also rarely articulated political platforms that would promote state-building by establishing structures of accountability and by addressing the problems of fragmentation of economic and institutional systems. Perhaps it is too unrealistic to expect, as Cabral did, the emergence of visionary leaders who would suppress their own interests in order to transform the state. Wishful theory aside, state transformation in reality may come not as a *gratis* from leaders but as a result of broad social struggle. Lack of state transformation has, thus, to be explained not only by the deficit of quality leadership but also by the weakness of organizations of popular struggle, including the lack of awareness among opposition parties and civil society groups about what it entails to transform the state. The demands of such groups, which include respect for human and civil rights, free press, freedom of opposition parties and fair elections, are, no doubt, essential. However, there has been little indication that opposition parties and civil society groups have a well-articulated agenda about how to address the fragmented modes of production and institutional systems. Opposition parties have also rarely established platforms that restructure the state to promote accountability.

Another problem with the leadership is that it is often aid-dependent and extroverted. During the Cold War self-declarations of being anti-communist or anti-imperialist were used as a scheme for obtaining aid and other support from external powers. In the post-Cold War era being an ally in the war on terror has become a new strategy within the region for extracting foreign aid and securing leniency on their

Table 4.2. Selected characteristics of leaders in the countries of the Horn of Africa

	Djibouti	Eritrea	Ethiopia	Kenya	Sudan	Uganda
Length of stay in power (yrs) of current leaders (to 2012)	13	21	21	10	23	26
Gov't service* fully or modestly addresses needs of the poor	22%	–	25%	18%	–	10%
Watchdog* organizations fully or largely effective	35%	–	12%	26%	–	15%
Gov't* always or usually respects human rights	50%	–	26%	26%	–	26%
Executive largely or completely corrupt	35%	–	33%	49%	–	65%

* Expert opinion from UNECA, *African Governance Report II*, 2009.

human rights violations, especially given the Somalia crisis. This issue is discussed in greater detail in chapter 6. For now it suffices to note that excessive reliance on foreign powers has led to loss of independence in policy-making. Aid-dependence and extroversion have also afflicted opposition parties and even civil society organizations. Opposition parties often compete with the leaders in government for external support, which usually comes with conditions that do not necessarily facilitate the transformation of the state in the region.

Given the gaping deficit in leadership and the weaknesses of civil and political organizations, fundamental change, which goes beyond the replacement of leaders, is not likely to come quickly in the region. Perhaps it is prudent to put in perspective this pessimistic view of the nature of the state in the Horn. The region, like the rest of the continent, has a state where the coercive powers are more developed than the aspects that empower citizens. This is perhaps partly due to the colonial heritage of the state and partly a reflection of the low levels of general socioeconomic development of society. Like other socioeconomic conditions of the region, the state represents work in progress. In its present form it has championed neither its own transformation nor the transformation of society. Instead it has been a major factor in the region's many conflicts.

The State as a Factor in Conflicts

The identified characteristics of the Horn region, including (1) the absence of strong mechanisms of checks and balances in the governance structures, (2) the fragmentation of modes of production and the dichotomy of institutions and (3) the self-serving proclivity of the leadership, create conditions that foster a number of conflicts. Fragmented modes of production and dichotomous institutions, for example, promote or perpetuate uneven development among various geographic regions, identity groups and economic systems. Sustained inequalities in economic opportunities, political power and cultural resources, in turn, foster various diversity-related conflicts. As we will see in the next chapter, many of the civil wars in the Horn of Africa are rebellions against the state by identity groups which are marginalized or perceive themselves to be marginalized. Conflicts in various parts of Sudan, including Darfur, the Nuba Mountains, South Kordofan, the Blue Nile and the Red Sea region are, for example, grievance-driven. The long civil war in the south, which culminated in the secession of South Sudan, also revolved around chronic political, economic and cultural marginalization of the south. Similarly, conflicts in the Ogaden in Ethiopia, western Uganda and western, eastern and coastal Kenya are largely driven by grievances over marginalization.

While direct rural–urban conflicts do not exist in the region, fragmented modes of production and institutional dichotomies have also led to conspicuous marginalization of rural areas. They have also impeded ways of addressing the appalling poverty in many rural areas. Consequently, rural areas have increasingly become breeding grounds for conflicts both through the growing rural to urban migrations, which swell the urban destitute, as well as by supplying foot soldiers to rebel groups. The institutional dichotomies, which allow the state to engage in acquisition of land under the customary ownership of communities, have often aggravated the marginalization of rural communities, creating tense conditions in some areas, including Gambela in Ethiopia and the Nuba Mountains in Sudan.

5   Failures of Governance and Nation-Building

Introduction

A major factor in the Greater Horn's chronic conflicts, especially the state–identity civil wars, is the problem of nation-building. The nation-building problem, in turn, is to a large extent related to the failure of diversity management by the states of the region. As noted in previous chapters, the countries of the Greater Horn are characterized by diverse populations with differential access to political, economic, social and cultural rights and opportunities. Such differences in empowerment have made management of diversity and peaceful nation-building highly challenging. This chapter has two principal aims. One is to investigate the main factors that have hindered a peaceful process of nation-building and why the post-colonial states of the region have not been able to overcome the obstacles to nation-building since the era of decolonization, over half a century ago.[28] The second goal is to examine some of the key implications of the persistence of the problems of nation-building.

The chapter is organized into three parts. The first briefly conceptualizes the key terminologies, such as nation-building, state-building and identity groups and diversity management. The second explores the key factors that engender crisis of nation-building and conflicts and why the post-colonial state has not been effective in addressing such factors. The third part analyses briefly the most important implications of the crisis of nation-building, including the effects on the processes of state-building and democratization.

Conceptualizing Nation-Building

Nation-building entails integration of the diverse identity groups within the population of a country to form a community of citizens sharing a system of institutions of governance. Success in the process of nation-building requires that the state, which organizes the socioeconomic life of a given society, (1) provides to all identity groups equitable citizenship rights that ensure equitable access to participation in the political, economic and cultural affairs of their country; (2) forges, through the representation of all identity groups, an institutional system of governance that accommodates the interests and aspirations of all groups and advances the well-being of all citizens; and (3) ensures that the rule of law is respected so that the conflicts are resolved through peaceful means and that the institutional arrangements are safeguarded. Failure of nation-building, on the other hand, is manifested in the absence of shared loyalty to existing institutions of governance resulting in state–identity conflicts, which may spill over to inter-identity and inter-state conflicts.

In situations where state-building and nation-building are both in a formative stage, as in the Horn of Africa, these processes become mutual requisites for each other because state institutions cannot be developed when different identity groups do not accept them. Successful nation-building also depends on successful state-building because poorly conceived and developed state institutions are unlikely to ensure equitable access to citizenship to all identities and to safeguard the rule of law. As a result, the two processes, which are intricately interrelated, need to be cultivated concurrently. This, no doubt, is a daunting task, in part because the state, which is a critical agent in nation-building, is itself underdeveloped in the sense that its different organizations do not have the structural independence to keep each other accountable and to allow citizen participation in the political process. The state institutions are also too weak to be able to provide the different services states normally provide citizens, including security and various other public services. A committed and knowledgeable leadership can be instrumental in overcoming this conundrum. In the absence of such leadership, however, the state tends to concentrate on building up its coercive powers over its organizing capacity.

Conceptualizing the State

As noted in the previous chapter, the state is an overarching set of interlocking organizations that collectively organize socioeconomic relations of the population of a given country. The interlocking set of organizations varies from country to country depending on the governance systems countries establish. In most cases, however, they consist of the constitutional courts and the judiciary, the military, the bureaucracy, the central bank, the electoral commission and the government with its legislative and executive branches that administer the whole state system. In a properly functioning (democratic) state the different organizations of the state command relative independence from each other and especially from the executive branch of government. Such relative independence of the different organizations of the state fosters accountability, reduces concentration of power in the hands of one organization, and creates more space for citizen participation in the political process. Such checks and balances within the state also reduce the likelihood that the state is an expression of a dominant identity group and enhance the neutrality of the state with respect to the ongoing competition among various identity groups.

As noted in the chapter 4, independence of the different organizations of the state hardly exists in most of the countries of the Horn. Concentration of power in the hands of the executive branch of government and individual 'strongmen' is rather the norm. Such concentration of power undermines the process of nation-building by hindering participation of citizens in establishing the institutional arrangements by which they are governed. Concentration of power in the hands of strongmen with long tenure in power also creates the tendency for the population to identify the state with the ethnicity of the autocratic leaders.

Conceptualizing Diversity Management

Diversity of identities and its management are critical for a successful process of nation-building as well as for state-building. For this reason a rather detailed conceptualization of identity is provided here. Diversity refers to the plurality of identity groups that inhabit individual countries (Deng, 2008). Identity also refers to real or imagined (often socially constructed) markers that social groups attribute to themselves or to others in order to set themselves apart from others and to distinguish others from one another. The distinguishing markers of identity groups are often moving targets and difficult to pin down. Nevertheless, they can be classified into primordial and social categories. While primordial (ascribed) markers constitute the network into which every child at birth finds itself to be a member, social identity markers, which are attained, can be formed across primordial markers.[29]

Primordial identity markers can be categorized into two levels. At one level are the exclusive identity markers, such as race, ethnicity, religion, language, kinship, clan and region. Primordial identity markers, however, are not limited to the exclusive markers. Nationality or citizenship of a country, for instance, is an identity marker, which distinguishes the citizens of a given country from those of others, while binding together, as a community of citizens, the diverse identities within that country. While the exclusive markers can lead to sub-nationalist narratives, which accentuate citizenship of an identity group, the inclusive markers lead to narratives of national unity and national citizenship, transforming citizenship of identities to national citizenship.

Different identity groups develop disparate cultures, which are forms of expression of a given identity. While culture is challenging to define, it is essentially an identity signifier and encompasses a worldview, a system of values, norms, attitudes, beliefs, orientations and underlying assumptions of an identity group. Like other identity markers, culture also has national (inclusive) and sub-national (exclusive) dimensions, which may be inversely related to each other, depending on the level of nation-building and the political environment that exist in a country.

Many of the primordial markers of a given identity group overlap with those of other groups, as linguistic and religious communities often extend far beyond the kinship or ethnic entity. Race, ethnic, kinship and clan identities also do not necessarily constitute homogeneous groups, since such groups may practise different religions, operate under different modes of production with different institutional systems and belong to different social classes. Race, ethnic and clan identities also are not confined to the jurisdiction of a given state. As indicated in chapter 2, the Luo live in Kenya, Uganda, Sudan, Ethiopia and Tanzania, while the Somalis are partitioned into four of the Greater Horn countries. (For a partial list of partitioned ethnic identities in the Greater Horn region, see table 2.2 in chapter 2.) Some of the primordial markers are also not rigid over time. Identity groups may change their mode of production, economic and political systems, institutions, religion, and over time, they may change even their clan and ethnicities. Some ethnic and clan groups split into different groups. Others are absorbed by or assimilated into other groups over time.

Other identity markers which have important impacts on nation-building are modes of production and institutional systems of governance. As noted in chapter 4, the modes of production that prevail in the Horn of Africa and the rest of the continent range from fairly advanced capitalism, symbolized by modern banking systems and stock markets, to subsistence peasantry and pastoral systems. Pastoral communities in rural areas and business communities in urban areas, no doubt, represent different identities with different institutional systems and cultural values even when they belong to the same ethnic or religious groups. Such fragmentation of modes of production creates different economic, political and cultural spaces within countries as well as within ethnic and religious identities. The diversity of modes of production also perpetuates diverse corresponding institutional systems. The parallel existence of different modes of production and institutional systems does not facilitate nation-building, which entails shared institutional systems. The incoherence between the traditional and formal institutional systems with respect to land ownership has contributed significantly to state–identity and inter-identity conflicts and to the problems of peaceful governance. Conflicting property rights laws with respect to land ownership have been a major source of conflicts and tension in many of the regions' countries, including Ethiopia, Kenya and Uganda (see APRM, 2006, 2009, 2011). The two Sudans have also faced widespread tensions and communal conflicts over conflicting land rights laws.

Different ethnic groups may also be represented by different political parties, as in Ethiopia and Kenya. Under such circumstances, power struggle among groups is likely to be intense and elections may be ensued by violent conflicts, as witnessed in 2005 in Ethiopia and in 2007 in Kenya.

African societies, like other societies, also embody other identity markers, such as those based on gender, age, sexual orientation and origin (indigenous and migrant). The conflicts that arise from lack of proper management of such identity markers are likely to be limited in scope compared to those that arise from the exclusive markers, such as ethnicity, clan and religion, although immigrants and refugees have been victims of exclusion, denial of rights, violence and abuse in many countries. Ethiopia and Eritrea as well as Sudan and South Sudan have also engaged in denial of citizenship rights to people originating from each other following their breakups. Splitting of families where the spouses were of different ethnic identities was common during the expulsion of people of Eritrean origin from Ethiopia, following the 1998–2000 border conflict between the two countries. Given their huge numbers, refugees in the Greater Horn countries are also at times susceptible to insecurity in their host countries.

Gender, class, sexual orientation and age are also important identity markers in the countries of the Horn. Denial of rights and equitable access to opportunities to such identity groups can lead to serious violations of human rights, which may have broader destabilizing effects even if they don't lead to large-scale violent conflicts. The youth, who often encounter a host of problems, especially unemployment, for example, have contributed to broad social instability. One important challenge the youth face is the failure of the educational systems to prepare them for gainful employment. Lack of access to land and/or off-farm employment also exposes them to rural–urban migration and hardship. Exposure to foreign culture through various media outlets during their formative years alienates them from their own culture. Under such conditions the youth can easily become a source of social instability by leading or participating in anti-regime and anti-establishment protests, riots and revolutions, as in Ethiopia in the 1970s.

Repressive labour laws and gross social inequalities, especially when they coincide with ethnic and religious identities, are also potential sources of violent conflicts and instability. Conflicts in western and northeastern Kenya, in northern Uganda and in various parts of Sudan are largely triggered by social inequalities (see tables 5.3–5.6).

In much of the Greater Horn women also continue to face exclusion from access to resources, opportunities and decision-making (see table 5.1). At a young age girls are often faced with lower access to education compared to their male counterparts for a variety of reasons. As adults, they are often denied the right to participate in decision-making both at home and in the public sphere. Early marriage often contributes to their inability to participate in decision-making at home. Often they are also denied rights of inheritance and even the rights of child custody in cases of divorce. In many cases also, the practice of bride-wealth places women in bondage, where they cannot abandon abusive marriages unless their parents pay back the bride-wealth paid by their husbands.[30]

The second group of identity markers are often referred to as social identity markers (Martin, 1995). This type of

Table 5.1. Beliefs about women's participation in decision-making and rights*

Participation of women	Ethiopia		Kenya		Somaliland	
	Yes (%)	No (%)	Yes (%)	No (%)	Yes (%)	No (%)
As leaders	24.0	76.0	84.8	13.2	–	–
As elders	67.0	33.0	69.6	28.8	18.2	–
In meetings	92.5	7.5	97.2	1.2	51.5	7.1
In obtaining land	54.7	42.0	55.2	43.2	56.1	40.8
In inheriting property from parents	34.0	62.0	59.0	40.5	87.8	10.2
In inheriting property from husbands	71.3	21.3	94.0	6.0	90.8	7.1
In obtaining equal share of property if divorced	51.3	44.8	28.0	70.8	5.1	90.1

* No significant differences were found between the responses of men and women.
Source: Data taken from a survey in Kidane Mengisteab et al., 2011.

marker is expansive in the sense that they can be formed across the primordial identities as well as across national citizenships. These markers are often based upon purposive choices, tactical necessity and common interest or incurred moral obligation (Geertz, 1963; Rex, 1995). Among such markers are: occupational associations, political affiliation, media groups, business organizations, labour unions, academic associations, human rights and various other civil society groups. It seems that the more the social identity markers develop, the more likely interdependence and networks of interaction across primordial identity groups are promoted. The expansive social identity markers can facilitate nation-building by building bridges across primordial identity groups. However, such markers are more developed in countries where state-building, economic diversification and interdependence, educational facilities, communication networks and social capital (civic institutions that lie above the family and below the state) are more advanced. Unfortunately, social identity markers are rather weak in the countries of the Horn, as in much of the rest of Africa, in part due to limited diversity of the economy and failure of governments to allow the establishment of the political space that facilitates the development of civil society organizations. One problem stemming from the underdevelopment of social identity markers is that many political parties are organized along the lines of primordial identity markers, such as ethnicity, religion or region. Competition for power among such parties tends to lead to problems of relations among primordial identities.

Diversity of identities in itself does not hinder the process of nation-building nor does it foster conflicts. However, as actors in the socioeconomic arena, identities compete against or cooperate with each other in order to enhance their access to political and cultural power and economic resources. Such interaction with other identities, no doubt, creates conflicts of interests and vision. Managed properly, such inter-identity interactions do not hinder the creation of a community of citizens (nation-building). When mismanaged by the state and citizenship rights are inequitable among identity groups, however, diversity of identities, especially those of ethnic and religious groups, can foster violent state–identity and inter-identity conflicts. The risk of such violent conflicts is particularly high in countries where there is a historical memory of conflicts, subjugation and marginalization. In any case, identity relations are largely determined by the nature of the socioeconomic arrangements that govern societies. We now examine the factors that undermine nation-building by poisoning state–identity and inter-identity relations in the Greater Horn.

Manifestations of Problems of Nation-Building

Establishing a community of citizens, who share common institutions, involves policy measures that depoliticize the exclusive primordial identity markers and narratives and promote the inclusive primordial and social identity markers and narratives. Such a transformation in state–identity and inter-identity relations, in turn, requires a participatory process of creating socioeconomic institutions that accommodate the political and economic interests and cultural values of the various identities within the citizenry, especially those historically marginalized. Populations that have socioeconomic arrangements that do not accommodate their general values and aspirations are subjects rather than free citizens and they are likely to aspire to change their predicament when a suitable time arises. As shown in chapter 4, the structures of the state in the Greater Horn hardly allow the participation of citizens, in general and identity groups with grievances in particular, to participate in crafting political arrangements that address their concerns. In most cases, from pre-independence Eritrea and the Ogaden in Ethiopia and South Sudan and Darfur in Sudan, the executive branch of government with little input from the concerned groups simply imposes arrangements and attempts to suppress any resistance by violent means. When ethnic or regional identities are not represented in the making of the political arrangements that incorporate them into a given country and when they perceive that the arrangements do not accommodate their interests, different types of reactions can be expected to ensue. Some of the reactions can be violent and lasting.

Violent Manifestation

The most violent type of reaction to the state-imposed socioeconomic arrangements by affected identity groups (mostly but not exclusively ethnic groups) is waging a civil war, usually after a period of less violent measures, such as protests, riots and rebellions. As we saw in chapter 2 (see table 2.5), every country in the Greater Horn region has faced many forms of violent resistance and civil wars. Among the most significant civil wars Ethiopia has experienced since the 1960s were: the wars against the Eritrean liberation movements (1961–91); the Western Somali Liberation Front (WSLF), 1974–8; the Ogaden National Liberation Front (ONLF) (1984–present); the Ethiopian People's Revolutionary Party (EPRP), 1975–7; the Tigray People's Liberation Front (TPLF), 1975–91; the Afar Liberation Front (ALF), 1975–97; and the Oromo Liberation Front (1975–present). The first three were secessionist struggles while the others were largely demands for political, economic and cultural rights, although the agendas of the different groups often changed periodically.

Among Sudan's most important civil wars are included: the first North–South war of 1955–72; the second North–South war of 1983–2005; the Darfur Conflict, 2003–present; the ongoing conflicts in the eastern part of the country led by the Beja Congress and the Rashaida Free Lions; the rebellion in the Nuba Mountains; and more recently the Blue Nile and South Kordofan civil wars.

Somalia has been in a series of civil wars at least since its 1977–8 war against Ethiopia over the Ogaden. With Somalia's defeat in that war, the regime of Siad Barre faced wars by a number of rebel groups including the Somali National Movement (SNM), the United Somali Congress (USC), the Somali Salvation Front (SSF), which evolved into the Somali Salvation Democratic Font (SSDF), and the Somali Patriotic Movement (SPM). The civil wars, which aimed to dislodge Siad Barre from power and bring about political and economic changes, succeeded in removing the Barre regime from power in 1991. However, they also brought about the collapse of the Somali state and ignited a new cycle of civil wars, mainly revolving around power struggle. With atrocities committed by the Barre regime during the civil war and the continued power struggle and turmoil engulfing the country, especially the former Italian colony (Somalia), Somaliland, the former British colony, declared its independence. Somalia has since 1991 remained in a perpetual civil war among constantly changing actors. The country's most significant ongoing civil war is between the UN and African Unity-supported Transitional Federal Government (TFG) and the al-Shebab rebel outfit.

Djibouti has also seen a civil war as well as tensions between the government, which is often dominated by the Issa Somalis, and rebels from the country's minority Afar population. The Afar-based Front for the Restoration of Unity and Democracy (FRUD) waged an active war against the government in 1991 and 1994. Since then the situation has remained generally calm with occasional flare-ups.

Uganda has also seen coups and civil wars. The most notable include: Idi Amin's coup in January 1971; the war waged by the Ugandan National Rescue Front (UNRF) against the regime of President Obote, 1980–5; the war by the National Resistance Army (NRA), 1982–6; the war of the NRA government against the Uganda People's Democratic Army (UPDA), a rebel group which operated in northern Uganda between 1986 and 1988; the war waged by Allied Democratic Forces (ADF), which operated in western Uganda; and the conflicts against the Lord's Resistance Army (LRA), 1987–present.

Kenya has seen less civil war compared to the other countries of the region, although in the early 1960s it faced a low intensity irredentist civil war against its Somali inhabitants in the North Eastern Province. Moreover, the country has faced a number of ethnic riots and post-election violence including the post-2007 election violence, which dangerously spilled over into inter-ethnic violence. The demand for independence of the coastal parts of the country by a separatist group, the Mombasa Republican Council (MRC), is also a potential risk, although the group has not waged a notable armed struggle yet. Eritrea has also seen some violent activities by the Eritrean Islamic Jihad Movement (EIJM), the Ethiopia-based Eritrean Salvation Front (ESF) and the Red Sea Afar Democratic Organization (RSADO). The region's newest state, South Sudan, which only gained its independence in July 2011, also has already faced violent rebellions as well as various inter-identity conflicts. Some of the rebellions against the new state are over allocation of positions of power among representatives of various identity groups and alleged horizontal inequality in access to power and other resources among various identity groups (Richardson, 2011).

Non-Violent Resistance

Civil wars are not the only manifestations of the crisis of nation-building in the Greater Horn. The presence of small minority groups, which are marginalized but are powerless to resist, is, for example, not likely to be manifested in violent conflicts, although it might be displayed by protests and riots. More importantly, the presence of large marginalized segments of the population, who live under traditional institutions of governance largely outside the state's institutional system, is also an indicator of the problem of nation-building. These segments of the population, mostly pastoralists and subsistence farmers, are economically, politically, socially and culturally marginalized. Higher rural poverty rates and lower rates of access to public services, such as educational and health services, among these segments of the population show their marginalization. The fact that they live under a different institutional system is another indicator of their marginalization. The presence of dichotomous institutional systems also reveals that a community of citizens governed by a shared institutional system remains elusive. The peasants and pastoralists often engage in sporadic and localized uprisings. However, they often provide the foot soldiers when rebellions are organized by other groups, as manifested by the various liberation movements in the region.

Theories of Civil Wars and Their Relevance to the Greater Horn

A large number of theories of violent conflicts, such as civil wars, are available in the literature (see Wulf and Debiel, 2009 for a list of some of the models). The relevance of three of the more widely known theories to the civil wars in the Greater Horn is briefly discussed here. Perhaps the most dominant is the relative deprivation (or 'grievance and justice seeking') theory. According to this theory, collective violence is driven by relative deprivation, which is defined as the gap between what a social group believes it deserves and what it gets (Gurr, 1970). In other words, conflict occurs when there is real or perceived uneven access to political, economic, social and cultural resources by different identity groups and when the institutions of distribution of resources are viewed to be unfair by some groups. Aggrieved groups generally protest against their condition and when the state responds with repression, the protests are transformed into armed rebellion. Civil war, according to this theory, is largely between social forces or identity groups who want to either change their disadvantageous socioeconomic position or to preserve their privileged position, and the state, which is the main dispenser of access and privilege. A number of studies (Auvinen and Nafziger, 1999; Nafziger and Auvinen, 2002; Stewart, 2000, 2001) contend that there is a strong positive empirical relationship between income inequality and occurrence of civil wars. Stewart (2000: 248), for example, draws a very bold contention that 'if there is group conflict, we should expect sharp economic differences between conflicting groups associated (or believed to be associated) with differences in political control'.

A rival explanation contends that measures of socioeconomic or political grievances, such as income inequality and oppression, do not systematically affect the risk of conflict, and that the measures of grievance, to the extent that they factor at all, amount to little more than a rebel discourse used to mask and to justify their predatory activities among those whose support they seek (Collier and Hoeffler, 2002). This theory, which is generally referred to as the 'greed/opportunity' ('greed and loot-seeking' or 'acquisitive desire') theory, is largely based on the 'rational actor' perspective of economics literature, which views rebellion as an economic activity with payoffs (Collier and Hoeffler, 2002). This theory contends that greed or economic motivation and prospects of success, in part due to the weakness of the state (opportunities/constraints), rather than socioeconomic or political grievances explain the onset and perpetuation of conflict (Collier and Hoeffler, 2002).[31] Accordingly, poor countries that have abundant resources are more likely to face civil wars because the resources raise the payoffs, which proponents of the theory view as the main driver of conflicts. The theory also contends that financial support from diaspora populations and neighbouring countries are other opportunities that motivate civil wars by weakening the constraints.

In resource-rich countries, such as Sierra Leone, the DRC and Angola, the deprivation and greed theories seem to merge since inequality amidst resource wealth is likely to increase the intensity of relative deprivation among marginalized groups while also raising the payoffs. In such countries, therefore, explanations of conflicts which are triggered by nation-building crises have to incorporate the grievance-engendering socioeconomic arrangements and institutional systems with the opportunity-enhancing (constraint-reducing) resources and the weaknesses of the state.

The greed/opportunity theory, however, hardly reflects the main factors of the conflicts in the Greater Horn of Africa. Most of the rebellions in the region, such as South Sudan and Darfur in Sudan, Afar, Oromo and Ogaden in Ethiopia, Somalis in Kenya and Ancholi and Karimojong in Uganda, are by politically, economically and culturally marginalized identities. Hardly any of these identities have notable resources or even opportunities that could serve as drivers to the conflicts. Of all these rebellions only South Sudan has succeeded after roughly half a century of conflicts.

Eritrea's war of independence also could not have been motivated by greed and resources, since Eritrea during its armed struggle hardly had any known resources, which the country's liberation fronts might have wanted to control. If anything, the prevailing view by observers was that the country would not be economically viable even if it secured its independence. Similarly, the TPLF war was about the marginalization of Tigray and there were no known resources that the front wanted to control. The Ogaden wars in Ethiopia also could not be explained by greed. There are claims that the Ogaden has oil and gas deposits of unknown quantities. However, there is little indication that these resources were factors when the wars started in the early 1960s. Moreover the constraints of these wars could not have been low since the Ogaden war is still going on. The Eritrean war also lasted three decades while the TPLF war was over a decade and half long.

The civil wars in Somalia led by various groups including the Somali Salvation Democratic Front (SSDF), the Somali National Movement (SNM) and the United Somali Congress (USC) were hardly motivated by greed and resources either. Rather, they were fought to overthrow the regime of Siad Barre, which the various opponents considered to be repressive and also favouring some clans over others in order to extend its tenure in power. It is also difficult to attribute Somaliland's declaration of independence from the rest of Somalia to any known resource wealth. There are also no known resources that could have motivated the insurgency of the Shifta wars of the 1960s in Kenya's North Eastern Province. Similarly, there is hardly any resource base that sustained or motivated the Afar–Issa conflicts in Djibouti.

Financial support from diaspora populations and neighbouring countries would be substitutes to resource wealth, according to the greed theory. Financial inflow from diaspora groups to the Greater Horn countries is substantial, as shown in table 5.2. Yet the argument that such financial inflow motivates the onset of the identified conflicts is simply unconvincing. The size of the diaspora population at the time most of these wars started was minimal. Most of the civil wars predate the formation of sizeable diaspora populations. The size of the diaspora grew in large part due to the wars. It is, however, reasonable to argue that financial support from diaspora groups would help sustain ongoing wars or wars that start after the diaspora population is formed. Similarly, foreign support is generally cultivated after the wars start, unless foreign intervention is involved in the onset of the war.

Perhaps the only case in the Horn where the greed theory may have some relevance is in explaining the South Sudan conflicts. The onset of the pre-independence South Sudan's civil war predates the discovery of oil by over two decades. It is, however, likely that oil wealth played a role in motivating the Sudan People's Liberation Movement (SPLM) to change its long-held opposition to independence after the death of its leader John Garang de Mabior. South Sudan's post-independence conflicts may also be, at least in part,

Table 5.2. Remittances compared to foreign direct investment and ODA (official development assistance) inflows (averages for 1995, 2005 and 2010)

	Djibouti	Eritrea	Ethiopia	Kenya	Somalia	Sudan	Uganda
Remittances as % of GDP	–	26.5*	0.75	4.4	–	3.0	4.4**
Amount ($US m)	30.5	226.3†	280.6	1718.4***	–	2031.6	655.8
FDI inflows average 2005–10 ($US m)	113.5	9.2	257.7	195.2	94.7	2524.7	701.5
Net ODA inflows average 2005–10 ($US m)	123.8	180.2	2866.2	1301.0	492.8	2161.2	1611.8

* Average for 1995–2002.
** Average for 2005 and 2010.
† Annual average for the 1993–2002 period.
*** Average for 2006–8. The average amount for the 2005–12 period, according to Kenya's Central Bank, is $1,119,469,375.

Source: African Development Bank, *African Economic Outlook*, 2012; World Bank, *World Development Report*, 2013; Tekie Fessehatzion (2005).

motivated by payoffs as some of the conflicts are over government positions that provide access to resources.

The New War Theory

Since the early 1990s a new theory of war ('New War') has
emerged in the literature. This theory contends that with the
erosion of autonomy of the nation-state (or even 'implosion'
of the state) under the impact of globalization a new type of
war has emerged (Enzensberger, 1994; Kaldor, 1999). Among
the features of the 'new war' are that the violence is mainly
directed against civilians, the aim is to control territory
through political rather than military success, political control
is maintained through terror, atrocities are deliberate rather
than side effects, the war is financed through loot, plunder
and illegal trading and the actors depend on continued violence for political and economic reasons (Kaldor, 2000). The
relevance of the theory of new wars, i.e. if it adds anything
substantive to our understanding of wars or even if new wars
exist as a genre, is questioned by many analysts (Cramer,
2006; Kalyvas, 2001). With respect to the modes of warfare
and financing, wars have always been changing in these
respects. The variation is largely explained by technological
and organizational advances. In this respect, thus, it is rather
unclear if new wars are distinguishable from old wars, as
Cramer (2006) points out.

Kaldor (2009), in further clarification of the characteristics
of new war, notes that it is a mixture between war (violent
conflicts for political cause), crime (violence for private
motives) and human rights violations (aggression against
individuals). From this angle, perhaps the LRA of Uganda
and the warlords of Somalia might fit the new war characteristics, although it is hard to attribute the emergence of
these groups to globalization, which the theory contends is
the key driver of new wars. Moreover, in the case of the
Greater Horn one would be hard pressed to show any quali-
tative differences between the region's civil wars between the
early 1960s and the early 1990s and the wars over the last

decade and half. What the experience of the region seems to suggest is that a civil war (war against the state) can be transformed into a war between armed groups if the state collapses without a successor state being formed, as in Somalia. A related experience of the region is that, given that the state is not well differentiated from regimes that control it, when the regime collapses there is a serious risk the state will collapse along with it. Under such circumstances the civil war is transformed into an inter-group war, which shares some of the characteristics of what is referred to as a 'new war'.

The civil wars in the Horn of Africa, as those in the rest of Africa, differ from the civil wars that occur in parts of the world where state-building has matured. In the African case civil wars generally occur under conditions where the state is in a developmental stage or even contested, and nation-building is in a formative stage. Under such conditions inter-state and intra-state wars are not clearly demarcated. But these characteristics seem to be beyond the concerns of the theory of 'new wars'.

In the case of the Horn of Africa, thus, the relative deprivation (the 'grievance and justice seeking') theory, which incorporates political, economic and cultural marginalization as factors of explanation, is more applicable, even though it too has some limitations. As noted, many of the conflict areas in the region are disadvantaged. Data on inequalities of access to resources are hard to find in the desired form, nevertheless, the snapshots in tables 5.3–5.6, give some indication. It also needs to be pointed out that conflict and instability produce marginalization by disrupting economic activity. In many cases, therefore, the problem becomes a vicious circle. In other words, deprivation is a major factor for the onset of civil wars but civil wars also intensify and perpetuate the deprivation.

Despite its usefulness, the grievance and justice seeking theory, which is mostly based on uneven access to economic, political, social and cultural resources, does not explain all the civil wars in the Greater Horn of Africa. The theory does not deal well with political problems that are not only or primarily about uneven access or repression. The Ogaden

Table 5.3. Some indicators of the distribution of public services in Sudan, 2008

State	Population as % of total, 2008	Urban population % of state total	No. of hospitals		No. of secondary schools	
Sudan	100	29.51	377	100%	3478	100%
Northern states	**78.9**	**41.95**	**335**	**88.85**	**3387**	**97**
Northern	1.8	16.94	26	6.89	88	2.5
River Nile	2.9	29.60	30	7.95	160	4.6
Red Sea	3.6	31.55	14	3.71	69	1.98
Kassala	4.6	26.29	11	2.91	80	2.3
El Gadarif	3.4	28.45	22	5.83	90	2.6
Khartoum	13.5	81.01	28	7.4	1072	30.8
El Gezira	9.1	19.10	58	15.4	773	22.2
Sinnar	3.3	21.66	24	6.4	157	4.5
White Nile	4.4	33.59	26	6.9	263	7.6
Blue Nile	2.1	24.31	15	3.98	40	1.2
N. Kordofan	7.5	19.91	27	7.2	167	4.8
S. Kordofan	3.6	23.52	16	4.2	108	3.1
N. Darfur	5.4	17.31	16	4.2	111	3.2
W. Darfur	3.3	17.31	6	1.6	59	1.7
S. Darfur	10.5	21.55	16	4.2	150	4.3
Southern states	**21.1**	**17.01**	**42**	**11.14**	**91**	**2.6**
Upper Nile	2.5	25.31	9	2.4	*	
Jonglei	3.5	9.53	4	1.1	*	
Unity	1.5	20.65	4	1.1	*	
Warrab	2.5	8.72	3	0.8	*	
N. Bahr el Ghazal	1.8	7.68	1	0.3	*	
W. Bahr el Ghazal	0.9	42.86	2	0.5	*	
Lakes	1.8	9.35	3	0.8	*	
W. Equatoria	1.6	16.16	7	1.9	*	
Central Equatoria	2.8	34.65	4	1.1	*	
E. Equatoria	2.3	8.88	5	1.3	*	

*Upper Nile states = 33; Equatoria states = 33; and Bahr el Ghazal states = 25.
Source: Sudan Statistical Abstracts, 2005–8.

conflict is, for example, not only about marginalization and repression but also a case of an identity group, which has been partitioned into several states by colonialism, wanting political rearrangement that would unify the different parts of the group under one state. The Greater Horn, as noted in chapter 2, has many identity groups that are partitioned into several countries. Many of the partitioned identities find

Table 5.4. Some indicators of regional inequalities in Ethiopia

State/region	Urbanization % of population, 2004	No. of people/ medical doctor, 2004	Primary & secondary school enrolments % of population, 2004
Tigray	18.1	44,706	16.8
Afar	8.8	95,000	2.8
Amhara	11.1	124,267	12.5
Oromia	12.8	120,663	15.2
Somalia (Ogaden)	16.3	97,833	3.1
Benishangul/Gumuz**	9.4	34.941	21.2
Southern Nations	8.3	114,512	15.2
Gambela**	18.4	19,500	20.9
Harari*	61.6	3,700	17.6
Addis Ababa*	100	12,808	16.9
Dire Dawa*	73.5	11,935	12.7
Ethiopia	15.8	59,971	13.8

* These are urban areas and have higher access to public services.
** These are small states with a small population and have seen marked improvement in access to public health and education over the last two decades.
Source: Ethiopia, Statistical Abstracts, 2004.

Table 5.5. Some indicators of the distribution of poverty and access to some public services by region in Kenya

Region	Income poverty, 2000, % of total population of provinces	% households with access to electricity	% gross primary school enrolment, 2000
Nairobi	–	71.4	52
Central	35.3	19.2	106.0
Coast	69.9	19.3	71.0
Eastern	65.9	6.9	96.9
North Eastern	73.1	3.2	17.8
Nyaza	70.9	5.1	94.0
Rift Valley	56.4	10.5	88.3
Western	66.1	1.6	93.3

Sources: APRM, *Country Review Report of the Republic of Kenya,* 2006; Society for International Development, *Pulling Apart: Facts and Figures on Inequality in Kenya,* 2004.

Table 5.6. Poverty distribution by region in Uganda

Rural/urban & by region	Poverty estimate, % of total population by region	
	2005/6	2009/10
Rural	34.2	27.2
Urban	13.7	9.1
Central	16.4	10.7
Eastern	35.9	24.3
Northern	60.7	46.2
Western	20.5	21.8
Uganda	31.1	25.5

Source: Uganda Bureau of Statistics, Uganda National Household Survey, 2009/10, 2010.

themselves to be minorities in their respective countries and also face the problem of uneven development, which often triggers civil wars and strife. No doubt, inequitable access to citizenship rights and economic resources contributes to conflicts involving such groups. However, it is unclear if the partition of groups itself is not a factor in the conflicts in some cases. If it is, as claimed by some studies (Michalopoulos and Papaioannou, 2011), relative deprivation may not be a sufficient explanation of the conflict and mitigating the deprivation may not be a sufficient solution either. In other words, it is unlikely that absence of marginalization would have negated the irredentist conflicts involving the Somali populations in Ethiopia and Kenya.

Another conflict case that does not fit the relative deprivation theory very well is the Eritrean war of independence. When this war broke out in 1961, Eritrea was not marginalized in terms of access to resources relative to other parts of Ethiopia. Rather the problem was loss of political autonomy and self-determination. Eritrea was created as a separate political entity by colonialism and it was annexed by Ethiopia following a decade of a UN instituted federal arrangement between the two countries. The war was against the annexation, which is not explainable by the relative deprivation theory.

As noted already, another major factor for the crisis of nation-building in the Greater Horn, as in other parts of Africa, is the presence of dichotomous modes of production and parallel institutional systems. This dichotomy is not always a direct cause of war, as we don't see peasants and pastoralists marching against the state because of the dichotomy of modes of production and institutional systems. However, the state is institutionally delinked from these social classes and its legitimacy among these groups is rather weak. They are also economically, politically and culturally marginalized as a result of dichotomies in modes of production and institutional systems. When there are rebellions against the state, these two social classes generally provide the bulk of the foot soldiers, as was the case with the Eritrean and Tigrayan liberation fronts.

The grievance/justice seeking (relative deprivation) theory does not deal with the problems caused by the presence of parallel modes of production and fragmented institutional systems, which are fundamentally different than mere relative deprivation. A more comprehensive explanation of the conflicts related to problems of nation-building in the Greater Horn of Africa, therefore, needs to incorporate three inter-related conditions. These are the problems of (1) uneven access to resources and mismanagement of diversity, (2) failure to develop political arrangements that accommodate partitioned identities and political entities and (3) failure to transform (reconcile) fragmented modes of production and parallel institutional systems. We now examine why the post-colonial state in the Greater Horn of Africa has failed to overcome these three conditions and promote nation-building over the last fifty or so years.

Why Has the Post-Colonial State Failed in Nation-Building?

Despite their adverse impacts on nation-building, the post-colonial state in the Greater Horn region, like its counterparts in the rest of the continent, has failed to transform many of the conflict-fostering legacies of pre-colonial and colonial empires. A number of factors account for this historic failure. Perhaps the most important factor is the nature of the state itself. As noted in chapter 4, the structures of the state, which concentrate power in the executive branch and strongmen, has made the state incapable of effective nation-building. The strongmen have diverted the state into an instrument of preservation of power instead of an agent of change and empowerment of citizens. Change that addresses grievances and empowers citizens by democratizing the process of nation-building is simply incompatible with concentration of power fostered by the structures of the state.

A related factor is the nature of the political elite both those in power as well as the counter-elite, whose primary preoccupation is to trade places with those in power. The prevalence of strongmen, who dominate the executive branch of government with little accountability, tends to make such leaders become ethnocratic. Often such self-serving leaders poison inter-ethnic/clan relations when they find inter-identity animosities to be instrumental in extending their tenure in power. Somalia's Siad Barre is one of the leaders who resorted to clan politics, as the legitimacy of his government waned following his defeat in the 1977–8 war against Ethiopia. During the waning years of his rule, as the EPLF and TPLF forces were winning the war, Mengistu Hailemariam of Ethiopia also attempted to portray the insurgencies in Eritrea and Tigray as a drive to capture power by the Tigrigna-speaking (Tigray/Tigrigni) ethnic group in an effort to mobilize ethnic support for his regime from other parts of the country. The post-election conflicts in Kenya also exposed the ethno-cratic characteristics of that country's leadership. Even when the leaders do not directly fuel inter-identity conflicts, the fact that they dominate power for long periods of time tends to associate the state with the ethnicity of such leaders. The Ethiopian state, for instance, is often identified with the Amhara or Tigray ethnic groups.

Lack of understanding of the implications of fragmented modes of production and parallel institutional systems to the process of nation-building on the part of policy-makers is another serious factor in the failure of the state in transforming the pre-colonial and colonial legacies. As noted earlier, parallel institutional systems are incompatible with the process of creating a community of citizens under shared institutional systems. The governments of the region have also shown little indication that they have fully grasped the constraints on governance imposed by the fragmentation of the socioeconomic spaces. They continue to largely ignore the property rights laws, resource allocation mechanisms and conflict resolution systems in the traditional system when, in most cases, the overwhelming majority of their populations is governed by the traditional institutions.[32] They have invested little effort in reconciling the parallel institutional systems and transforming the traditional modes of production.

Implications of Failure in Nation-Building

Regardless of the reasons for the failure of the post-colonial state, the continued crisis of nation-building and the associated civil wars and conflicts have had and are likely to continue to have serious detrimental effects on the whole region. The most serious implications include:

- *Crisis of state-building:* The crisis of nation-building is closely intertwined with the crisis of state-building. Continued crisis of nation-building undermines the process of state-building, which, in turn, hinders nation-building, creating a vicious cycle. It is difficult to envisage success in building effective state institutions when the governance arrangements, which allow the establishment of a community of citizens, are not in place. In other words, where various identity groups have grievances against the state, state–society relations are poor and the legitimacy of the state is low. Under such conditions, both nation-building and state-building are simultaneously undermined. Almost all the countries of the region are ruled by despotic regimes, which are often perceived to represent the domination of the state by one ethnic group or another. Such a conspicuous failure in nation-building renders the states in the region highly unstable even when they appear stable in the short run. Given the nature of the regimes these countries are particularly susceptible to major instability or even the collapse of the state during periods of regime change.

- *Regional conflicts:* Continued crisis in nation-building and the ensuing conflicts also create risks of spilling over to neighbouring countries and bring about inter-state conflicts and instability. The crisis and civil war in Somalia is a good example. Neighbouring countries Ethiopia, Kenya and Djibouti have sent troops to support the Transitional Federal Government (TFG) against insurgency groups, such as the al-Shebab. The conflict has also created friction within the Intergovernmental Authority for Development (IGAD), which accuses Eritrea of allegedly supporting the insurgency in Somalia. The countries of the region have also seen various mutual interventions in each other's conflicts by supporting and hosting each other's insurgency groups. The crisis of nation-building is, thus, a major source of regional conflicts and instability.
- *Inter-communal conflicts:* Conflicts arising from nation-building problems also have the potential to spill over into inter-communal conflicts, which can lead to risks of massacres, ethnic cleansing and possibly even genocides. When under siege from insurgency activities, self-serving dictators tend to mobilize supportive ethnic identities. Often communities do not heed such mobilizations. However, the Darfur case and the 2007 post-election violence in Kenya are scary reminders of the dangers of inciting the ethnic card by the political elite. The risk of spilling into inter-communal conflicts is also great because identities with grievances tend to see the state as an expression of certain identity groups.
- *External intervention:* As is discussed in chapter 6, the Horn of Africa has been a strategic region in the global geopolitical rivalries. Various powers have competed to put the region under their sphere of influence. Internal

state–identity conflicts have given foreign powers a good opportunity to interfere in support of one side or another with the aim of advancing their strategic as well as economic interests. The Somali civil war and the problem of piracy have, for instance, become a pretext for transforming Djibouti into a hub of foreign military concentration.

*   *Continued economic crisis and poverty:* The continued crisis of nation-building and conflicts also hinder the region's economic development. As noted already, the Horn of Africa is one of the poorest regions of the world. It is also a region of chronic food shortages and frequent, devastating famines. The region is also engulfed by an alarming rate of environmental degradation. The enduring crisis of nation-building and the conflicts associated with it undermine the region's efforts to overcome the difficult economic challenges it faces.

*   *Impedes democratization:* It was already noted that transforming the state–identity conflicts requires establishing accommodating political arrangements through dialogue between the state and the various identity groups. Such a democratic approach to nation-building is unlikely to be possible under conditions of violent conflicts. The countries of the region, thus, seem to be caught in a vicious cycle. They need a democratic system to overcome the nation-building crisis and the conflicts associated with it. Unfortunately, the conflicts make democratization difficult to attain. Such a cycle could perhaps be broken by far-sighted leaders, which the region sadly lacks.

6 | Regional Instability and _____ External Intervention

Introduction

The Greater Horn of Africa has experienced considerable external intervention in the post-Second World War era and much of that intervention has had notable impacts on the region and its conflicts. External intervention is a complex phenomenon, which comes with diverse intentions, takes a variety of forms and leaves behind disparate outcomes. Some interventions might be altruistic, intended to help the recipients, for instance, in times of natural catastrophes and human-made disasters, or to mediate destructive conflicts and to keep peace. Some are intended to help in promoting development, although their approach and policy tools might at times be misguided. Often, however, interventions are imperialistic with purely self-serving intentions to advance the strategic, ideological, political and economic interests of those intervening, even though the real motives might be disguised. Such interventions generally have detrimental effects on the hosts. In some cases, the effects are significant enough to change the course of history and cause lasting damage in the affected areas.

Some self-serving interventions are carried out by states or intergovernmental organizations while others are carried out by non-state political organizations. Some of the interventions are by regional and continental actors while the most significant are by states and intergovernmental organizations from outside the continent, although such global actors may often use regional actors as agents.

The Horn of Africa, which has experienced frequent natural and human-made disasters, has been a notable recipient of the altruistic types of intervention. Various governmental and non-governmental actors have stepped in to rescue thousands of people from starvation during periods of natural and human-made catastrophes. Many governments across the world have hosted thousands of the region's refugees, who are victims of gross human rights violations by their own governments. This chapter does not intend to cover these humanitarian interventions, however. Its aim is rather limited to the self-serving interventions by states, intergovernmental organizations and non-state political organizations, mostly but not exclusively from outside the African continent. The scope is limited to those interventions of the post-Second World War era, which have had notable destabilizing effects on the whole or parts of the Greater Horn region. The reason for this focus is in order to concentrate on the types of intervention that contribute in significant ways to the region's instability and conflicts, which constitute the principal concerns of this book.

Self-serving interventions often entail rewarding friendly regimes and political organizations with political and diplomatic backing as well as with military and economic support of various kinds. These rewards or incentives are paid to client regimes or political groups for carrying out policies that advance the interests of the intervening powers, including destabilizing regimes or political organizations which may be viewed as hostile to the interests of the intervening power or powers. Intervention against adversaries in some cases includes direct military attack. In other cases, it involves a variety of sanctions to deny such regimes or political organizations access to military equipment, technology and markets in an effort to cripple them militarily, diplomatically and economically.

Among the main objectives of this chapter are (1) to examine the factors that have made the region a major theatre of external intervention and to identify some key interventions; (2) to explore the most important adverse impacts of the most significant interventions; and (3) to explain why the region has not been able to ward off external intervention. The chapter is organized into three parts. The first part examines the key global factors for intervention and identifies some of the major interventions. The second part examines some regional and domestic developments that motivated external intervention. The third part examines the most important impacts of the interventions on the region's stability and why the region has not been able to shelter itself from the numerous interventions, despite their many adverse impacts.

Global Factors for External Intervention

The Greater Horn region borders the Red Sea and the Gulf of Aden, through which over 20,000 ships sail every year. This strategic significance of its location is an obvious context for the high level of external intervention the region has endured. More recently, competition for access to and control of the region's resources has also become an increasingly notable factor in external intervention in the region. Given these contexts, a combination of global and regional and domestic factors has fostered much of the external intervention in the Horn of Africa. The global category of factors relates to the rivalries and conflicts among global powers that stem from the configuration of power in the global system.

The global factors of intervention can be categorized into three time periods: (1) the period between the end of the Second World War and the era of decolonization, roughly between 1945 and the early 1960s; (2) the era between decolonization and the end of the Cold War (mid-1960s–1991); and (3) the post-Cold War era, 1991 to the present. Much of the external intervention in the period between the end of the Second World War and the region's decolonization revolved around attempts to restore and maintain colonial rule and to rearrange boundaries of the countries of the region. One critical issue for intervention during this period was related to the disposal of the former Italian colonies in the region, especially Eritrea but also Somalia. Another issue was related to the territorial composition of the countries of the region in general and Somalia in particular. Whether the Somali-inhabited Ogaden and the Northern Frontier District of the British colony of Kenya were to become parts of Ethiopia and Kenya respectively or parts of Somalia was particularly controversial. Whether Southern Sudan was to remain a part of Sudan or was to be joined with the British East African empire was another issue of contention.

Following the fall of the Italian empire in East Africa in 1941, the British military, which defeated the Italian forces in the region, came to administer both Eritrea and Somalia. The British also liberated Ethiopia from Italian occupation and restored the Ethiopian monarchy. However, they kept the Somali-inhabited Ogaden region and the border regions with French Somaliland under their control (Anglo-Ethiopian Agreement of 1944). When the war ended, Britain continued to administer the former Italian Somalia until 1949 and Eritrea until 1952.

The disposal of Italian Somalia was relatively less contentious than the disposal of Eritrea. The UN resolved that Somalia attain its independence after ten years of administration by a caretaker Trustee and the trusteeship was given to Italy in 1949. The disposal of Eritrea and the geographic composition of Somalia, however, became highly controversial, due to competing interests of various powers. Four sets of interests were pertinent for decisions on these two issues. The most dominant interest was that of the competing superpowers and their allied camps at a time when the Cold War was unfolding. Another set of interests was that of the region's colonial powers, which aspired to maintain their colonial dominions. A third interest was that of the states of the region. At that time, however, only Ethiopia was independent and able to represent its own interests. A fourth set of interests was that of local communities, although their capability to express let alone to defend their interests was rather limited. The question of the disposal of the former Italian colonies and the geographic composition of the states of the region are examined within the context of the above identified competing interests.

Ethiopia claimed the Ogaden on the basis of a 1897 Anglo-Ethiopian treaty, which it saw as affirmation of its claim of the Ogaden following the conquest of the territory by the expanding Abyssinian empire in the 1890s. Ethiopia also claimed Eritrea, on the grounds that it needed an outlet to the sea and also alleging that Eritrea was part of the Abyssinian empire before Italian colonization severed it from the empire. Britain, on the other hand, sought to unify all the Somali-inhabited territories to form Greater Somalia and rule it along with British Somaliland.[33] On the issue of Eritrea, Britain proposed to dismember Eritrea, joining the northern and western lowlands with Anglo-Egyptian Sudan and ceding the rest of Eritrea to Ethiopia. The British expected that acquisition of eastern and southern Eritrea would win Ethiopia's agreement to cede the Ogaden to Somalia under Britain. On the Sudan side, the British sought to break up Sudan by joining South Sudan with their East African empire of Uganda and Kenya. Another broader interest on the part of Britain, which was shared by other western powers, was to ensure that the Soviet Union did not get a foothold in this strategic region.

The British position with respect to Eritrea did not materialize due to vocal outcry by Eritrean leaders at the UN in New York against the dismemberment of the country. However, some powers, led by the US, opposed Eritrean independence and supported Ethiopia's plea for a sea outlet. The fact that Ethiopia emerged from a brutal aggression by Fascist Italy may also have won it some sympathy. More importantly, the US sided with Ethiopia because of its interest in maintaining the strategic naval radio station, Radio Marina, which was left behind by Italian rule in Asmara, Eritrea's capital city. The station was handed over to the US by the British Military Administration of Eritrea in 1943. Located on nearly the same longitude as the Soviet deep space command centre in the Crimea, the station, which was renamed Kagnew, was a Cold War listening station later furnished with large dishes used to monitor telemetry from a variety of Soviet spacecraft. The base eventually became a joint project of the North American Aerospace Defense Command, the Army Security Agency, the Central Intelligence Agency, the Army Security Agency, the US Strategic Communications Command and the Navy Communications and signal research unit.

Given its interest in the Kagnew base, the US objected to Eritrea's independence out of concern that an independent Eritrea might terminate the US's access to the base, which was considered at the time 'one of the most valuable U.S. telecommunications centers in Africa, Asia, and the Middle East' (Schraeder, 1992: 590). It is unclear why the US believed that it could not maintain the Kagnew base under independent Eritrea. The country was, however, regarded to be a Muslim country, due to its large Muslim population, and it was feared that it might ally itself with the Arab world and turn the Red Sea into an 'Arab Lake' and threaten American as well as Israeli interests in the region (Okbazghi Yohannes, 1991). Ethiopia, on the other hand, was viewed to be a country with a strong Christian heritage that would be inclined to be favourable to western interests. Despite such a perception/misperception, however, the ratio of Muslim to Christian populations in the two countries is not very different. The Ethiopian monarch, Haile Selassie, was also viewed as a staunch anti-communist. On the basis of religious prejudice (Islamophobia) similar to that of the US, Israel also adhered to a policy that strongly opposed Eritrean independence. Like their American counterparts, Israeli policy-makers believed that an independent Eritrea would be an 'Arab-oriented' (and anti-Israel) state that would turn the Red Sea into an 'Arab Lake' (Schraeder, 1992: 579–80).

The UN finally devised a compromise solution of federating Eritrea with Ethiopia. The Ethio–Eritrean federation, which was established in 1952, however, lasted only ten years, as Ethiopia unilaterally annexed Eritrea in 1962. The annexation of Eritrea was of little surprise to those who opposed the federal arrangement on the grounds that such an arrangement between two unequal countries would not work. This group, which was led by the Soviet Union and included many Arab countries, had warned that the federal arrangement gave Ethiopia a blank cheque to annex Eritrea. In reality, the UN settlement of the Eritrean case was essentially an accommodation of the geostrategic interests of major global powers at the expense of the rights of the Eritrean people to self-determination. This was made plainly clear even by the leader of the US delegation to the UN, John Foster Dulles, who served as Secretary of State between 1953 and 1959. Secretary Dulles stated that 'From the point of view of justice, the opinions of the Eritrean people must receive consideration. Nevertheless, the strategic interests of the United States in the Red Sea Basin and considerations of security and world peace make it necessary that the country [Eritrea] has to be linked with our ally, Ethiopia' (Bereket Habte Selassie, 1989: 37). For Eritrea the arrangement charted its postwar history, the toll of which included a thirty-one-year-long war of independence (1960–91) at a sacrifice of roughly 50,000 fighters, unknown numbers of civilian casualties and economic ruin. Even the country's post-independence border war with Ethiopia can be attributed to that fateful UN arrangement.

The US operated the Kagnew base for thirty-four years, from 1943 until 29 April 1977, by which time advances in communication technology had reduced the significance of the base and Ethiopia had also undergone major changes in its political system and ideological orientation. The monarchy was overthrown in 1974 by a self-proclaimed Marxist military junta, the Derg, led by Mengistu Hailemariam, and the country shifted its alliance to the Soviet Union. Throughout the period between the early 1950s and 1977, however, Ethiopia enjoyed US military and economic support.

On the Somali side, Britain also under US influence handed over the Ogaden to Ethiopia in 1948. The Somali aspiration of Greater Somalia under one state was, thus, dashed. With independence in 1960, Italian Somalia and British Somaliland were united to form the Republic of Somalia. The new state continued to pursue the goal of unifying all Somalis, including those in the Ogaden, which is known as Western Somalia for Somalis, and those in Kenya's North Eastern Province, as well as those in French Somaliland (Djibouti). Local movements in support of unification with Somalia, along with the Somali state's pursuit of the policy of 'Greater Somalia', however, led the country to wars, known as the 'Shifta wars', against Kenya in the early 1960s and three major wars against Ethiopia, as was noted in chapter 2.

By the time Sudan became independent, Britain also did not partition South Sudan from the rest of Sudan after keeping the region mostly isolated from the rest of Sudan throughout its colonial rule and also after creating expectations among the Southern Sudanese that Southern Sudan would be separated from the rest of the country. In Uganda also, the British colonial administration had established a special status for the Buganda kingdom, due to the kingdom's role in facilitating the colonization of the rest of Uganda. To the dismay of the leaders of Buganda, however, the British left no provisions for the special status of the kingdom within Uganda. On a number of fronts, therefore, the arrangements external powers designed for the region in the aftermath of the Second World War became direct sources of many of the region's lengthy inter-state and intra-state wars. As noted, the Ethio-Eritrean war was fought for thirty years, 1961–91. The Ogaden saw three major wars between Ethiopia and the Republic of Somalia and it still remains a major conflict zone within Ethiopia. Somalia and Kenya also fought the Shifta wars in the early 1960s, while Southern Sudan fought a civil war between 1956, when Sudan gained its independence, and 2011, when South Sudan became an independent state. During that entire period there was only a ten-year window of peace (1974–83), when the south was granted self-rule under the Addis Ababa Agreement.

Cold War Era Interventions

The territorial and political arrangements which were crafted for the countries of the region mostly by external actors in the aftermath of the Second World War became critical sources of the region's most intractable conflicts. They have fostered violent conflicts between those who strived to change these arrangements and those who wanted to sustain them. Eritrean nationalists waged their war of independence to undo Ethiopia's annexation of their country and achieved that goal in 1991. Somali inhabitants of the Ogaden and Kenya's Northern Frontier District also waged wars of secession against Ethiopia and Kenya respectively. These insurgencies have remained active, although those of Kenya are mostly of low intensity. The Somali Republic also pursued its quest of establishing a Greater Somalia that encompasses all Somali-inhabited territories in the region. To this end it supported the secessionist movements in both Ethiopia and Kenya and engaged in both proxy and direct wars against those two countries. The wars against Ethiopia contributed considerably in bringing about the collapse of the Somali state. Yet, the insurgencies in the Somali-inhabited regions of Ethiopia and to a lesser extent those in Kenya still continue and the composition of Somalia still engenders conflicts, although these conflicts are mostly fought within Somalia since the collapse of the Somali state.

With the formation of the Anyanya I insurgency in Southern Sudan in 1955, the conflict between Sudan and South Sudan also broke out as soon as Sudan embarked on its independence. A successor to the Anyanya insurgency, the Sudan People's Liberation Movement (SPLM), finally brought about the independence of South Sudan in July 2011. At the time of writing relations between the two countries remain tense, mainly over boundary disputes and disagreements over the sharing of revenue from oil, which is extracted mostly from South Sudan but is pumped to Port Sudan through pipelines in Sudan.

The Ugandan state under Milton Obote also waged a brief war (the Mengo Crisis) in 1966 to crush what it considered Buganda's challenge (Mutibwa, 2008). Tensions still remain between the Ugandan state and the Buganda kingdom for a variety of reasons. Djibouti, which remained a French colony until June 1977, was the only country in the region that escaped violent conflicts until the Afar insurgency in 1991, led by the Front for the Restoration of Unity and Democracy (FRUD).

The parties to the various conflicts have competed to secure external patronage in order to obtain armaments, military training and other types of support. External actors also competed to secure local clients that would facilitate their ability to influence or even have access to bases and service facilities in this strategic part of Africa. This convergence of interests of the patron states and their client actors transformed the region into a locus of perpetual external intervention. The Cold War rivalry among the superpowers and their respective allies perhaps motivated the most consequential external interventions in the region. Among the most important cases of intervention during the Cold War are the following.

Ethiopia: US/Israel (1950–77)
Ethiopia was the main attraction of supportive external intervention in the region during the Cold War. This was perhaps in part because it is the largest country in the region and in part because of the challenges it faced in its efforts to keep Eritrea as well as the Ogaden as part of its territorial composition. Both superpowers and their allies intervened in support of Ethiopia's cause at different times during the Cold War. Israel also provided notable support to Ethiopia throughout the Cold War. As noted already, the US provided Ethiopia with very strong diplomatic support during the UN deliberations on the disposal of Eritrea and Somalia in the late 1940s. As a result, Ethiopia was successful in securing control over Eritrea through a federal arrangement, which in reality was a prelude to annexation of the latter. With US influence Ethiopia was also able to obtain the Ogaden from Britain in 1948. The interest on the part of the US in supporting Ethiopia was the continued access to the Kagnew base in Asmara. On the part of Ethiopia, it anticipated resistance both in Eritrea and in the Ogaden and needed help in strengthening its security apparatus and armed forces.

Given their mutual interests, the two countries signed a Mutual Defence Assistance Agreement in 1953 and the US secured a twenty-five-year lease of the Kagnew base. Following the emperor's ability to secure a $100 million low-interest credit from the Soviet Union in 1959, the US in 1960 concluded a secret military agreement with Ethiopia and agreed to provide support for a 40,000 member Ethiopian army. The US dispatched to Ethiopia a Military Assistance Advisory Group (MAAG), consisting of some 300 personnel to train Ethiopian military personnel. Some 23,000 Ethiopian service personnel received advanced training from American personnel while about 4,000 of them were trained at facilities in the US. Under the defence pact Ethiopia became the largest recipient of US military and economic assistance in Africa. US military aid to Sub-Saharan African countries between 1955 and 1976 was estimated to be about $750 million and roughly 80 per cent of it went to Ethiopia (Lefebvre, 1991).

Israel also joined the US in supporting Ethiopia, especially in terms of military training. Israel saw Ethiopia, where the Organization of African Unity (OAU) headquarters is located, as an entry point to the rest of Africa in terms of expanding its relations. It also saw independent Eritrea as 'another Arab-oriented (and anti-Israeli) state effectively turning the Red Sea into a hostile "Arab lake"' (Schraeder, 1992: 580). Israel, thus, consistently pursued a policy of preventing Eritrean independence (Schraeder, 1992). By contrast, Israel saw Ethiopia 'as the only non-Muslim riparian state and therefore a deterrent to Arab efforts to make the Red Sea either an Arab or an Islamic lake' (Bard, 1988/9: 4). The fact that Emperor Haile Selassie and his family spent part of their time in exile in Jerusalem following the Italian conquest of Ethiopia in 1936 was also a factor in creating warm relations between the two countries. Furthermore, the Israeli government, along with the US, helped save Haile Selassie's reign when he faced a coup in December 1960. Israel also deployed Mossad agents to train Ethiopian police. The Eritrean commando, which was established with the specific purpose of fighting the Eritrean liberation fronts, was also trained by Israeli agents (Bard, 1988/9).

Both the US and Israel, then, saw Eritrean independence as harmful to their respective strategic interests. The leftist orientation of the Eritrean nationalist movements and their reliance on Arab support, along with Haile Selassie's self-proclaimed anti-communist stand, reinforced the resolve of the US, Israel and other western powers in supporting Ethiopia not only in its war against Eritrean nationalists but also against Somalia as well as against various other rebellions within the country.

Ethiopia's close ties with the US and Israel continued even after Emperor Haile Selassie was deposed in 1974. Despite this continued support, however, the challenges Ethiopia faced from Eritrean nationalists continued to grow. Ethiopia's relations with the US finally broke down after the Ethiopian military regime, which overthrew the emperor, was able to secure a much larger military support from the USSR than what the US was providing. In 1976 a delegation of Ethiopia's military junta (the Derg), led by Mengistu Hailemariam, visited Moscow and secured an arms agreement with the Soviet Union valued at $385 million. This agreement essentially ended the Cold War era US–Ethiopia security relations, which were characterized by a near monopoly of the US on arms supplies to Ethiopia.

In April 1977 the Ethiopian government closed down all US military facilities in the country, ordered the MAAG personnel to leave the country and terminated the lease of the Kagnew base. Israeli relations with Ethiopia, however, continued even after Ethiopia shifted its ties from the US to the USSR in 1977, largely due to the two countries' mutual opposition to Eritrean independence. Israel continued to provide Ethiopia military trainers as well as arms, alongside the Soviet Union.

Somalia: USSR (1963–77)

Given its territorial ambitions, as well as US and Israeli support of Ethiopia, Somalia faced the imperative of building up its military. US acquisition of the Kagnew base in Asmara also motivated the USSR to seek a point of entry into the strategic Red Sea region. Somalia and the Soviet Union thus became a good match for establishing a patron–client relationship. In 1963 the Soviet Union offered Somalia some $30 million in military aid and agreed to assist in establishing the Somali air force and to train and equip the army which was to expand its size from 4,000 to 20,000 (Lefebvre, 1987). The Soviet Union established a base in the Somali port of Berbera and its military support to Somalia continued to grow with the size of the Somali army reaching about 35,000 by the time the Soviet Union left the country in 1977.

Ethiopia: USSR/Cuba 1977–90

With the Ethiopian military government proclaiming the country socialist and terminating its military ties with the US, a major shift in alliances took place in the region. The Soviet Union established ties with Ethiopia and started to supply Ethiopia with various armaments at the time when Somalia invaded the Ogaden in July 1977. Needless to say, the Somali government was angered by its ally, the USSR, supplying arms to its arch enemy and reacted by breaking diplomatic relations with the Soviet Union and closing the base at Berbera. The Ogaden war initially went rather well for Somalia and it occupied about two-thirds of the territory. However, the fortunes of the war changed, especially when the Soviet Union and Cuba intervened with massive military support for Ethiopia. The Soviet Union delivered about $1 billion worth of armaments to Ethiopia, along with over 1,000 military advisors, including a general, named, Vasilii Ivanovich Petrov, who led the Ethiopian counter-offensive (Gebru Tareke, 2000). Cuba also sent some 18,000 combat troops with their combat gear, including armoured cars and T-62 tanks (Gebru Tareke, 2000). In the words of Gebru Tareke (2000: 635), 'the dramatic and massive intervention by socialist countries enabled the Ethiopians to crush and repel the invading army, which never recovered fully from its stunning defeat'.

Somalia: US 1978–90

Egypt and Saudi Arabia supported Somalia during the 1977–8 Ogaden war against Ethiopia. Their support was no match to the massive Soviet and Cuban support of Ethiopia, however. By the end of March 1978 Somalia suffered a crushing defeat, which was followed by a civil war, as the Siad Barre regime faced a number of internal rebellions. At a critical stage when the Somali civil war was unfolding, the US Department of Defense on 28 June 1988, delivered $1.4 million in lethal aid to the Somali armed forces, including 1,200 M-16 rifles and 2.8 million rounds of ammunition (Schraeder, 1992). The US continued to aid the Siad Barre regime to the tune of about $800 million. Access to the former Soviet base at the port of Berbera was a factor for continued US support to the regime.

Sudan: US/Israel (1956–91)

Israel, along with Ethiopia, was a supporter of the Anyanya I insurgency in Southern Sudan. The US also had few relations with Sudan between the time of the country's independence in 1956 and 1976. US security assistance to Sudan during that period of time was a negligible amount of about $2 million out of roughly $750 million provided to Sub-Saharan Africa during the same period (Lefebvre, 1991). Sudan, for its part, was a strong adherent to a policy of non-alignment during these years.

Sudan, however, severed relations with the US following the 1967 Arab–Israeli war and between 1967 and 1976 the Soviet Union supplied Sudan some $65 million worth of armaments. However, following a communist inspired coup attempt in 1976, the Sudanese leader, Jaafar Nimieri, began to reassess his relations with the Soviet Union. The US, which had lost its security relations with Ethiopia to the Soviet Union in 1977, was also interested in exploring ties with Sudan. In addition to countering the Soviet presence in Ethiopia, the US was also drawn to Sudan by its motivation to control the regional designs of Libyan leader, Muammar Gaddafi (Lefebvre, 1991).

Sudan granted the US naval port call rights in Port Sudan and joined Egypt and Saudi Arabia in allying itself with the US. Between 1977 and 1985, US arms transfers to Sudan reached levels unprecedented for Africa (Lefebvre, 1991). The US provided Sudan with $135 million in military aid, $160 million in foreign military sales financing credits, $506 million in economic support and $581 million in foreign military sales cash arms transfers (Lefebvre, 1991).

US–Sudan relations begun to decline in the mid-1980s for a number of reasons. The Nimieri regime had instituted an Islamic rule by adopting *Sharia* laws. With the overthrow of Nimieri's regime the Transitional Military Council also repaired relations with Libya, in part to stop Libyan support to the rebellion in South Sudan. US military and economic aid to Sudan was finally cut off as soon as the National Islamic Front (NIF) took power through a coup in 1989. The fundamentalist character of the NIF was a concern for the US. With the end of the Cold War and the termination of Soviet security relations with Ethiopia's military government, the US also saw no pressing need for continued security relations with Sudan.

Post-Cold War External Intervention

The end of the Cold War marked a brief lull in external intervention and the region experienced some notable changes during the interlude. Despite some support from the US, the Siad Barre regime of Somalia was swept from power on 26 January 1991 by the combined efforts of several insurgency groups. Unfortunately, the Somali state also collapsed along with his regime. As Soviet support dried up, the military government of Ethiopia also crumbled and the head of the state, Mengistu Hailemariam, fled the country for Zimbabwe on 21 May 1991. Eritrea became a *de facto* independent state on 29 May 1991. The cessation of external intervention did not last long, however, as the Cold War was quickly followed by new developments that reignited another cycle of external intervention.

Geopolitical Interests and the China Factor
A major global development that has contributed in sparking a wave of intervention in the region in the post-Cold War era is the growing competition for access to and control of the region's oil and mineral resources between China and western

powers. Both powers have engaged in what Chau (2007) refers to as 'political warfare' in the region, as in the rest of Africa, to achieve their national objectives. The operations entail providing economic aid, development assistance training and arming military and security forces of African countries. China's economic engagement in Africa, as well as in the Greater Horn region, has expanded rapidly over the last decade. China's investments in Africa have, for example, expanded from roughly 3 per cent of China's total foreign investments in 2007 to roughly 14 per cent of its total foreign investments in 2010. In 2011 China invested about $16 billion in mining projects in Africa. In July 2012 Africa–China trade also reached $165 billion, tripling from what it was in 2006. Within the region, as shown in table 6.1, China has surpassed the US and has begun to challenge the European Union (EU) as the largest trading partner of the

Table 6.1. Comparison of the ratio of trade of the major countries of the Horn with China, the US and EU in 2010

Country	Ratio of imports	Ratio of exports	Ratio of total trade
Ethiopia	China 15.5% EU 11.7% US 9.7%	EU 32.1% China 14.0% US 6.8%	EU 15.3% China 15.2% US 9.2%
Kenya	EU 15.1% China 13.3% US 2.7%	EU 25.8% US 5.9% China 0.7%	EU 17.8% China 10.1% US 3.5%
Sudan	China 22.2% EU 14.7% US 1.3%	China 68.7% EU US 0.1%	China 44.3% EU 8.3% US 0.7%
Uganda	EU 18.6% China 8.5% US 3.1%	EU 26.4% US 3.2% China 1.4%	EU 21.3% China 6.0% US 3.1%

Source: *EU Bilateral Trade and Trade with the World*, Trade G.2. Total Merchandise Trade, 2008–2012, http://trade.ec.europa.eu/doclib/docs/2011/january/tradoc_147265.pdf (see by country).

larger economies of the Greater Horn region, including Sudan, Ethiopia and Kenya.

The rapid growth of China's economic engagement with Africa and its access to Africa's resources has raised concern among western powers, even though European corporations remain dominant in the region's resources, especially oil. According to US Secretary of State Clinton, for example, China's economic engagement in Africa displays 'traits of "new colonialism"'(Ighobor, 2013: 8). The Secretary notes that 'during colonial times, it is easy to come in, take out natural resources, pay off leaders and leave. And when you leave, you don't leave much behind for the people who are there. We don't want to see a new colonialism in Africa.'

In agreement with Secretary Clinton, Prime Minister David Cameron of the United Kingdom expressed condemnation of China's engagement in Africa during his visit to Nigeria. Cameron attested that 'the West is increasingly alarmed by Beijing's leading role in the new "scramble for Africa"'(Groves, 2011). Cameron added that he was keen to counter the 'Chinese invasion'. Why Chinese economic relations with Africa are any more imperialistic than western economic relations and if Africa needs western protection from 'colonization' by China are interesting questions. They are, however, outside the scope of this chapter. Regardless of its benefits for and risks to the region and the rest of the continent, China's growing economic engagement has provoked rivalry with western powers, which have dominated the continent's resources since the era of colonization, and has ignited another wave of external intervention in the region.

Beyond Secretary Clinton's rhetoric, the US has deployed a two-pronged strategy to counter China's growing engagement with Africa. One approach relates to establishing security ties with African governments. This approach revolves around the US Africa Command (AFRICOM), which was established in 2007 to serve as a key organization in the implementation of US foreign policy in the African continent. As Deputy Assistant Secretary of Defense for Africa, Theresa Whelan (2007) noted, Africa's growing importance in US national security objectives is the imperative behind the creation of AFRICOM. There is little doubt that Africa, primarily due to its resources, especially oil, has become important not only to the US but also to China and other major consumers of the continent's resources. Competition for access to the exploitation of the continent's resources has, thus, triggered more intervention to influence the policies of African governments.

In June 2012 the Pentagon established the Combined Joint Task Force – Horn of Africa (CJTF-HOA) with the stated goal 'to wage peace across the region, to deny the enemy a safe haven, to increase the capacity of host nations to provide services for their people and combat terrorism' (Chau, 2007: 12). The Pentagon then took over Camp Lemonnier (in Djibouti) in 2003, and stationed all four branches of the US military – Army, Air Force, Navy and Marine Corps – on the base. In 2006 the Pentagon expanded Camp Lemonnier by almost five times its original size, from 88 to 500 acres. It has since completed an airfield project in the country to provide parking spaces for C-130 Hercules and CV-22 Osprey aircraft and to support C-17 Globemaster III and C-5 Galaxy military transport planes. Although AFRICOM is headquartered at Kelley Barracks in Stuttgart, Germany, Djibouti, for all practical purposes, has emerged as the base for AFRICOM in Africa. Djibouti, which traditionally hosted a French military base, has also become the host of the UN-mandated mission Maritime Intercept Operation (MIO) in the war against Somali pirates. As part of the MIO mission, German, Dutch, Italian, Norwegian, Danish and many other navies are operating from the country, as we will see in the next section of this chapter.

Beyond Camp Lemonnier, the US has established military installations in much of the region. It has struck an agreement with Kenya that allows it access to the port of Mombasa and airfields at Embakasi and Nanyuki. It has also reached similar arrangements with Uganda. The US has constructed two K-Span steel buildings to house troops and equipment at Entebbe. The US has also sent a small contingent of troops to central Africa with the alleged objective of helping in the arrest of Joseph Kony, the leader of the brutal Lord's

Resistance Army. The EU has also joined in this effort by financing logistical facilities (Scimia, 2012). Moreover, the US has established a chain of drone micro bases in several countries in the region, including at Arba Minch, in Ethiopia, in Djibouti as well as in Seychelles (Whitlock and Miller, 2011).

This US-led militarization of the region is overtly for purposes of fighting piracy and terrorism. However, the activities of Somali pirates, al-Shebab, or the Lord's Resistance Army seem to hardly justify such a level of military build-up. Rather, the unstated objective appears to be designed to establish security ties with African governments in order to influence their policies and stamp the inroads China has made in accessing the continent's resources and markets.

A second approach the US has outlined to counteract the Chinese influence in the Greater Horn region as well as in the rest of the African continent is through greater economic penetration of the region. The 14 June 2012 announcement by President Obama of a new Africa strategy is part of this approach. The new strategy is short on details but it calls for increased US economic engagement with Africa in order to (1) promote an enabling environment for trade and investment; (2) improve economic governance; (3) promote regional integration; (4) expand African capacity to effectively access and benefit from global markets; and (5) encourage US companies to trade with and invest in Africa (Senate Foreign Relations Committee, 2012).

If managed properly by African governments, growing Chinese as well as US economic engagement through trade and investment can have positive impacts in the Greater Horn region as well as in the rest of the continent. Growing economic involvement by such major actors in the global economic system would enhance competition for African resources and markets while facilitating the opening of foreign markets for African products. Chinese involvement has, for example, largely liberated African economies from the bondage of structural adjustment programmes, which were imposed by the international financial institutions and western powers for the last quarter of a century. Enhanced competition for African products and investment opportunities can also improve the bargaining power of African governments as well as the private sector of African economies.

The security ties, which the US is forging with the governments in the Greater Horn, by contrast, are inconsistent with most of the objectives of the new Africa strategy the Obama administration has recently unveiled. The security ties are likely to have a number of adverse impacts. They are likely to be divisive within the region, as some governments are favoured over others, depending on their receptivity to American policy. They are also likely to change intra-region balance of power and trigger militarization and conflicts. In so doing, the security ties and external intervention are likely to hinder regional integration and cooperation in coordinating security policy.

As noted, military ties and external intervention during the Cold War contributed in intensifying, if not in initiating, conflicts in the region. There is little reason to believe that the new security ties the US is establishing in the Greater Horn would not have similar results. As they did during the Cold War, the new security ties are already supporting and strengthening undemocratic regimes against domestic opposition. In addition, they are likely to reduce competition among global economic actors in the markets of the region by favouring firms from the countries with security ties. Such developments are also likely to harm the region's economic interests and dampen its bargaining power.

Regional and Domestic Factors

Another category of factors for resurgence of external intervention in the region relates to regional and domestic developments, which posed challenges to the interests of global actors thereby motivating external intervention. Two such developments account for much of the external intervention in the region in the post-Cold War era. One is the penetration of the region by various militant Islamist movements and the war between these movements and the west led by the US. A second development that has motivated notable external intervention is the problem of piracy. We now briefly look at some key interventions that were motivated by these two regional and domestic developments.

War on Terror

The war on terror has been the most important factor as well as a pretext for external intervention in the region in the post-Cold War era. The Greater Horn has been greatly impacted by the rise of militant Islamist movements in the Muslim world since around the mid-1980s. With the 1989 coup that brought the National Islamic Front (NIF) to power, Sudan became an attractive destination of various Islamic movements from around the world. The founder of the NIF, Hasan al-Turabi, envisioned Sudan to become the centre of Islamic revival worldwide. To this end, al-Turabi founded a pan-Islamic organization, the Popular Arab and Islamic Congress (PAIC), which met annually in Khartoum and facilitated the congregation in the country of various Islamic movements from different countries. Osama Bin Laden and his al-Qaeda (the base) was one of the movements hosted by the NIF government. Bin Laden came to Sudan in 1991 at the invitation of the NIF and is said to have quickly established links with various Islamic movements, such as the Gamaa Islamiya of Egypt, the Islamic Salvation Front of Algeria, Hamas of Palestine, the Eritrean Islamic Jihad Movement (EIJM) and insurgents from Libya, Yemen and Somalia (Vidino, 2006). He also formed a coordinating council (*Shura*) composed of al-Qaeda's leadership and top members of Islamic movements from around the Muslim world and set up training camps in Northern Sudan.

From the point of view of the NIF leader, these organizations represented Islamic movements fighting for legitimate causes (Vidino, 2006). However, several of these movements are widely viewed as terrorist organizations by western governments as well as by some of the region's governments. Some of these movements are also said to have carried out a series of terrorist attacks both outside as well as within the region. Outside the Greater Horn, al-Qaeda and other Islamist movements with various levels of links with al-Qaeda were accused of the bombings of two hotels in Aden, Yemen, in 1992 and the bombing of the World Trade Center in New York in February 1993. Such groups were also linked to the June 1993 attempt to bomb the UN in New York and other landmark buildings in the United States. The suicide attack against the USS *Cole* in Yemen on 12 October 2000 and the 11 September 2001 attacks against the US were by far the most significant of the attacks.

Within the region, the government of Eritrea claimed that the EIJM conducted terrorist attacks in the country and the government accused the NIF government of Sudan of sponsoring a terrorist organization and subsequently severed diplomatic relations with Sudan in 1994. The 26 June 1995 failed assassination attempt of President Hosni Mubarek of Egypt, while he was on a state visit in Ethiopia, was also attributed to Sudan-based terrorist groups. The bombing of a Mombasa resort hotel and the failed missile attack on an Israeli passenger jet in 2002 are other attacks attributed to al-Qaeda in the region. Uganda also accused Sudan of supporting terrorism, although the terrorists in Uganda are not associated with any Islamic movements.[34] The US embassy bombings in Nairobi and Dar es Salaam on August 7 1998 were the largest attacks in the region attributed to al-Qaeda or its affiliates.

It is difficult to determine accurately the significance of the roles and numbers of foreign actors in the identified terrorist activities. Yet, it is safe to say that these attacks have incited external intervention by states and intergovernmental organizations often with the support of states and intergovernmental organizations from the region.[35] In the early 1990s the US provided some security assistance to Ethiopia, Eritrea and Uganda to counteract the terrorist threats from Sudan-based groups. Sudan was designated a 'state sponsor of terrorism' by the US in 1993 and in April 1996 the UN Security Council also imposed sanctions on Sudan. As Sudan faced mounting pressure from the US, the UN and neighbouring countries, Bin Laden left Sudan on 19 May 1996, concerned about his safety in the county. Sudan also expelled members of the Egyptian Islamic Jihad.

The US also destroyed the Al-Shifa pharmaceutical factory in Khartoum by a missile attack on 20 August 1998 claiming that the factory was producing chemical weapons. However, the evidence for the allegation was highly dubious (Barletta, 1998). Various accounts suggest that the factory was, in fact, producing malaria and tuberculosis drugs. The US Treasury unfroze the assets of the owner of the factory in response to his lawsuit against the US government and this might be viewed as an informal admission of a mistake (BBC News, 1999). The US never officially admitted that it had made a mistake, however.

With Sudan's growing isolation, al-Turabi as well as the NIF's internationalist and ideological wing lost influence. Al-Turabi himself was imprisoned in 1999 after falling out with President Bashir. Al-Turabi's vision of making Sudan the centre of Islamic revival, thus, came to an end. Despite Bin Laden's departure and the decline in the influence of the INF, the region has continued to be viewed as a hot spot for terrorism with stateless Somalia replacing Sudan as the centre of attention.

Somalia, Terrorism and Intervention

With the collapse of the state in 1991, stateless Somalia was widely expected to be an attractive location for international terrorism. Contrary to expectations, however, al-Qaeda in the early 1990s was unsuccessful in establishing itself in Somalia or in developing links with local Islamist movements, such as the Al-Itihad al-Islamiya (AIAI).[36] A number of factors are said to have hindered al-Qaeda's efforts at establishing roots in Somalia. One factor is said to be that *sufi* Islam, which is dominant in Somalia, is generally inhospitable to Taliban-style fundamentalism. Another reason is that the clan-based socioeconomic system is not easily penetrable by foreign identities, including 'Arab jihadi organizations' (Bruton, 2010; Cohn, 2010; US Military Academy, 2007). A third reason seems to be that the country's civil war made it difficult for foreign terrorist groups to attach themselves with any of the combatant groups without entangling themselves in inter-clan conflicts. Stateless Somalia, thus, offered transnational terrorist groups an easy passageway, due to its unguarded boundaries, but not an easy base for operation or success in the recruitment of followers, at least until the emergence of al-Shebab as the dominant insurgency after the defeat of the Union of Islamic Courts (UIC) by Ethiopian forces in December 2006.

Yet, well before the publication of the US Military Academy Report on Somalia in 2007 and the designation of al-Shebab as a terrorist organization by the US government on 29 February 2008, Somalia had already become a centre of external intervention as well as a theatre of the war on terror in the region. How this transformation of the country from one that was deemed inhospitable to terrorists to the centre of the war on terror in the region came about is rather challenging to explain. Was the analysis that interpreted Somali realities as inhospitable to transnational terrorism faulty? Did the realities in Somalia change so drastically to make it a safe haven for terrorists and if so, what factors account for the change? Or is there a problem of conflating Islamic movements with terrorist organizations? In other words, are the movements suspected of terrorism or designated as terrorist groups, essentially nationalist Islamist movements which have little interest in transnational terrorism? Or did external intervention play a critical role in transforming nationalist movements into transnational terrorist groups? These are difficult questions to answer, but there is little doubt that external intervention both from outside the region as well as from within the region have contributed in dragging the country into an abyss, where all forces, foreign and domestic, have grossly victimized innocent civilians.[37] It is also likely that the magnitude of external intervention has radicalized some elements within the Somali insurgency transforming the conditions in the country.[38] Bruton, for example, warned of the unintended consequences of external intervention by saying, 'unless there is a decisive change in U.S., UN, and regional policy, ineffective external meddling threatens to prolong and worsen the conflict, further radicalize the population, and increase the odds that al-Qaeda and other extremist groups will eventually find a safe haven in Somalia' (2010: 5).

Many state and non-state actors have intervened militarily and politically in Somalia. The stated reasons for the intervention range from combating terrorism and self-defence to helping to bring about peace to the war-torn country. Regardless of the stated goals, much of the intervention involved picking winners in the country's civil war. External actors have established one Somali government after another in the capital cities of neighbouring countries with little regard to how the Somali population would view such foreign-made and foreign-supported governments. The Sharif Sheikh Ahmed-led Transitional Federal Government (TFG) is no exception. The director of the Ansari Africa Center at the Atlantic Council in Washington, DC describes the transitional Somali government as follows: 'the idea of the Somali government, the so-called federal transitional government of Somalia, which is internationally backed, is a legal fiction that makes it convenient for us to pretend that there's some governing authority there' (PBS NewsHour, 2012).

The US and Ethiopia have waged the most significant interventions in Somalia. On 12 December 1992, the US launched a humanitarian intervention, Operation Restore Hope, to facilitate the distribution of food aid and alleviate starvation in the country. The US military, however, got entangled in the country's civil war when it attempted to apprehend General Mohamed Ali Farrah Aidid, chairman of the United Somali Congress (USC), who was accused of hindering the US and UN peace mission and of attacking UN forces. General Aidid, who was contending for power against Ali Mahdi Mohamed, another member of the USC, however, viewed the US/UN as exceeding their humanitarian mission and taking sides in the civil war. Regardless, the attempt to arrest Aidid entangled the US military with Somalia's clan and sub-clan conflicts as the two contenders for power belonged to two different sub-clans. Aidid, along with his clan, resisted the US attempt to arrest him and the conflict resulted in what has come to be known as the Black Hawk Down incident of 3 October 1993, where 18 US soldiers and between 1,000 and 1,500 Somalis died. President Clinton ordered the termination of operations by US forces soon after the incident.

The war on terror waged after the 9/11 attacks on the US by terrorists brought the US back into Somalia. In 2006 the CIA began to support the warlords, who organized themselves as the Alliance for the Restoration of Peace and Counter Terrorism (ARPCT) in order to receive US support. The aim of the CIA was to obtain the Alliance's support in tracking and capturing suspected terrorist elements in the country. Given the suffering the warlords had inflicted on the population for a number of years, the intervention to support them was extremely unpopular and it was opposed by the country's weak Transitional Federal Government. Even the Secretary-General of the UN at the time, Kofi Annan, strongly criticized the support given to the warlords.[39] It was also said to have galvanized the decentralized clan-based Islamic courts, which provided judicial and other services in different parts of the country. The Islamic courts were in the process of unifying to form the Union of Islamic Courts (UIC) and their militia, which was used to enforce rulings by the courts, defeated the ARPCT rather decisively in June 2006. The UIC then brought Mogadishu and most of the country under its control in June 2006 and *de facto* re-established the Somali state while the TFG remained cornered at Baidoa, a small town northwest of Mogadishu.

While the UIC was consolidating its control of the country, various external actors were also lining up to intervene; some to shelter the TFG and others to support UIC. In March 2005 the Intergovernmental Authority for Development (IGAD) proposed to form a peacekeeping force, IGASOM, to be deployed to back the TFG, even though the Islamic courts expressed strong opposition to the proposal. On 14 September 2006, the African Union, in support of IGAD, approved the formation of a peacekeeping force, which was to be called AMISOM (African Union Mission in Somalia) instead of IGASOM. In late November the US introduced a resolution in the UN Security Council to authorize an AU peacekeeping force to defend the TFG. Despite demonstrations in Mogadishu against the formation of such a force (Abdulle, 2006), the resolution was passed on 7 December 2006, giving AMISOM the blessing of the UN Security Council.

Within the region, Ethiopia was the backbone of the TFG, which was led by a long-time friend of Ethiopia, Abdulahi Yusuf. Uganda also sided with the TFG and later became one of the first countries to send troops to Somalia, as part of AMISOM. The UIC was also able to obtain some external support. The countries which are said to have provided some assistance include Egypt, Libya, Eritrea, Djibouti, Syria, Iran and Saudi Arabia. The types of support the UIC received ranged from uniforms, medicine to military training, arms and ammunition (United Nations Security Council, 2006).

By far the largest intervention in Somalia was Ethiopia's US-supported invasion of Somalia in December 2006 (Lefebvre, 2012). Despite external support, the TFG was on the verge of collapse under the advancing troops of the UIC when Ethiopia invaded Somalia to stop the UIC and to rescue the TFG. While Ethiopia's official justification for its intervention was that it was invited by the TFG, in reality it was an invasion, at least in part, aimed at pre-empting the formation of an Islamist government, which might rekindle the aspirations of creating 'Greater Somalia' as past Somali regimes.[40]

The involvement of the US was also born out of mistrust of Islamist movements and concern that an Islamist government would host and shelter terrorist elements.[41] Mobilizing most of the countries of the region to join the partnership in the war on terror and the training of Ethiopian troops were among the activities of US intervention, in addition to the occasional bombings of suspected terrorists. Ethiopian troops were being trained in infantry tactics by soldiers with the US Army's 1st Infantry Division's 1st Battalion, 16th Infantry Regiment at the Training Academy in Hurso as jets from the country bombed the Somali capital and ground forces invaded their eastern neighbour. The US Army had conducted training at the base at least since 2003.

The various external interventions contributed in radicalization of the insurgency in Somalia. The UIC, undoubtedly, was a mass organization that comprised groups and individuals of various political persuasions and competing visions. There were also internal frictions and tensions between groups with different objectives and agendas. External intervention, including US support to the warlords and Ethiopia's invasion that dislodged the UIC from power, however, strengthened the more fundamentalist wing of the organization. Al-Shebab, the more militant and fundamentalist wing of the UIC, for example, came to prominence after the UIC leaders were pushed out of the country. The intervention to destroy al-Shebab has also led to the declaration by some members of the leadership of al-Shebab on 9 February 2012 to join al-Qaeda. Along with the radicalization effect, external intervention has also led to splits within the Somali insurgency. After its defeat by Ethiopian troops, the UIC split into al-Shebab, ARLS-Djibouti and ARLS-Asmara. Under extensive external intervention and military setbacks, al-Shebab also seems to have split, with one wing joining al-Qaeda and another wing placing its focus entirely on domestic issues.

The defeat of the UIC by Ethiopian troops brought about a number of changes within the UIC and in the Somali political landscape. The UIC split into three groups, two of which were located outside Somalia. The UIC leadership, along with other opponents of the TFG, formed a new organization named the Alliance for the Re-liberation of Somalia (ARLS) in September 2007 in a conference that was held in Asmara, Eritrea. The principal aim of the organization was removing the Ethiopia-backed TFG. In May 2008, however, the ARLS split into two groups over holding peace talks with the TFG. One wing, led by Sharif Sheikh Ahmed, agreed to negotiate, while the other wing, led by Sheikh Hassan Dahir Aweys, rejected any negotiations before Ethiopian troops left Somalia. Meanwhile the insurgency within Somalia was radicalized as Ethiopia's occupation, along with US support, was viewed as a Christian invasion against Muslims. The Somalia-based insurgency forces came to be led by the more militant wing of the UIC, the al-Shebab, which emerged as the leader of the post-UIC insurgency in the country.

The negotiations between the TFG and the Sharif Sheikh Ahmed-led wing of the ARLS (ARLS-Djibouti), resulted in the formation of a new TFG consisting of the old TFG and the ARLS-Djibouti. Sharif Sheikh Ahmed, the former leader of the UIC, was elected by the parliament as president of Somalia (and the new TFG) and sworn in on 31 January 2009 in Djibouti. The Aweys-led ARLS (ARLS-Asmara) also returned to Somalia, renamed itself Hizbul Islam, and eventually joined al-Shebab, although the relationship was tenuous.

The reconciliation between the TFG and ARLS-Djibouti suggests that there was also an opportunity for the TFG and the UIC to reconcile and re-establish the Somali state in 2006 before the Ethiopian invasion. That window of opportunity was missed in large part due to external intervention. No doubt, there were fundamentalist Islamists within the UIC who were responsible for the introduction of some archaic policies, such as banning cinemas and soccer matches. Such policies were unpopular and there were possibilities that popular resistance could have turned against such policies weakening the militant and more fundamentalist wing of the UIC. As noted, *sufi* Islam in Somalia did not have much in common with some of the rigid policies introduced by the militant wing of the UIC. External intervention, however, did not allow for the internal struggle between the moderate and fundamentalist tendencies to take effect. A number of factors seem to have contributed to this missed opportunity. One factor is the subordination of the Somali interest of recreating their state to the US-led war on terror. Such prioritization did not allow the internal political process to sort things out and bring the UIC in line with the prevailing political and religious culture of society.

Another major factor was the concern of the Ethiopian regime over the possibility of a unified and militant Islamist state in Somalia supporting insurgency within the Somali population within its borders. One cannot be sure that the UIC-led Somali state would not support insurgency among Somali populations in neighbouring countries. However, this problem requires many more substantive changes that address the problem of partitioned ethnic groups rather than interference in Somali politics to obstruct recreation of the Somali state or to attempt to shape its nature, which is likely to backfire. A third factor seems to be that some regional governments and even regional organizations have been motivated to intervene in order to gain support from the US for partnering it in the war on terror rather than to address the regional problems in a manner that brings about sustainable regional stability.

In any case, at the time of writing the civil war, along with external intervention continues to rage. AMISOM has been strengthened and Kenya has also invaded Somalia. Ethiopian troops also continue to go back and forth into Somalia, and the US has continued to arm and provide political support to the TFG. Al-Shebab finds itself under considerable military pressure from greatly strengthened external forces, even though it still controls considerable portions of the country. At least one wing of al-Shebab has also declared itself to be part of al-Qaeda, even though affiliation with al-Qaeda and reliance on foreign fighters have alienated both its rank-and-file fighters as well as the broader population (Bruton, 2010). Even with al-Shebab's military setbacks, ending the conflict through a negotiated settlement seems unlikely since the US has placed the leaders of al-Shebab on its wanted list of terrorists and has offered financial rewards for information leading to their arrest. In the meantime there is little indication that the TFG has gained legitimacy or that it has become more effective.

Under the circumstances, it is difficult to predict the outcome. Doubtless, the intervention by various external actors has made it rather clear that the re-establishment of the Somali state would not be a Somali affair. External intervention, which picks winners in a country's identity-based civil war, as in Somalia, however, hardly produces a viable state. In such civil wars nation-building and state-building require negotiated political arrangements that accommodate the interests and values of the different identities within the population as well as the parties to the conflict. External military intervention, no doubt, can bring about change in the balance of forces among the various contenders for power and even register military victory. However, it is not likely that such an outcome will be sustainable, unless accommodation of the various groups, including the clans and sub-clans, accompanies the changes in the balance of power. A state built by the choice of external actors rather than by agreement among the conflicting identities is likely to be regarded as an external imposition that lacks legitimacy. As Fukuyama (2005) aptly notes, state creation by outsiders undermines the ability of domestic actors to create their own robust institutions and builds long-term dependence, and may ultimately come to be seen as illegitimate to the locals.

Al-Shebab and other insurgency groups, for instance, view the TFG as an external imposition. Former President Sharif Sheikh Ahmed, for his part, claimed that al-Shebab, which he sees to be the same as al-Qaeda, is 'a colonial power' and is trying to colonize Somalia (Khalif, 2012).

In addition, external intervention can intensify the animosity among the groups and extend the civil war even if it brings temporary military victory of the externally supported groups. It can also radicalize the groups that are victimized by external intervention and extend the circle of external intervention as the groups weakened by external intervention would likely invite new intervention. This may explain the reason why al-Shebab joined al-Qaeda, even though the decision may prove to be a fatal error.

Piracy and External Intervention

Another major regional development that contributed to external intervention in the post-Cold War era has been the problem of piracy. Over the last several years Somalia has been plagued by two types of piracy problems. One type (Somali piracy) involves the attacks on and hijackings of fishing and merchant ships by Somali pirates in the Gulf of Aden, the Gulf of Oman, the Arabian Sea, the Arabian Gulf, the Red Sea and parts of the Indian Ocean. The exact number of the attacks on vessels by Somali pirates is unknown and different sources give different figures. Nevertheless, table 6.2 gives a rough estimate of attacks and successful hijackings of vessels.

Somali piracy is said to have caused significant risks to seafarers and increases in the cost of shipping, although the amount of the costs is difficult to estimate. The One Earth Future Foundation (OEF), a non-profit organization studying piracy, puts the costs at roughly between $7 and $12 billion in 2010 and between $6.6 billion and $6.9 billion in 2011. About 80 per cent of the costs are said to be borne by the international shipping industry. According to the OEF, ransom payments to Somali pirates increased from an average of $150,000 in 2005 to an average of $5.4 million in 2010. The OEF estimates that the total ransom paid to Somali pirates for 2010 was about $238 million. The amount of ransom, obviously, constitutes a small portion (roughly 2.5 per cent) of the total cost associated with piracy.

The second type of piracy Somalia has experienced involves the pillage of its coastline by illegal, unreported and unregulated (IUU) fishing and illegal dumping on its coasts of waste,

Table 6.2. Estimates of attacks and hijackings of ships by Somali pirates

Year	Attacks	Successful hijackings
2004	10	–
2005	48	–
2006	10	–
2007	51	–
2008	111	41
2009	217	45
2010	219	49
2011	237	28
2012 (Jan.–Mar.)	36	7

Sources: ICC Commercial Crime Services, 2012; ICC International Maritime Bureau, 2011; One Earth Future, 2011; Bruton, 2010; United Nations Office on Drugs and Crime, http://www.unodc.org/documents/data-and-analysis/tocta/9.Maritime_piracy.pdf.

including toxic substances, by foreign vessels.[42] Somali pirates contend that they took up piracy in response to the plunder of their country's marine resources by pirates engaged in IUU fishing and the pollution of their coastline by waste dumped by foreign vessels (Report of the UN Secretary-General, S/2011/661 [UN Security Council, 2011]). In other words, Somali pirates see themselves acting as their country's coastguard, in the absence of a properly functioning state that protects the country's resources. Various reports confirm that a large number of foreign-flagged vessels have engaged in unlicensed and unregulated fishing in the area. A study by the University of British Columbia, for example, estimates that in 2002 about 30,000 tons of fish catches were taken by foreign-flagged vessels from the coasts of Somalia (UN Security Council, 2011). According to the High Seas Task Force and FAO, approximately 700 foreign-flagged trawlers were engaged in IUU fishing in and around Somali waters in 2005 (UN Security Council, 2011).

The UN Secretary-General's report (S/2011/661) notes that the surge in Somali piracy since 2004 led to a decrease in illegal fishing off Somalia's coast. The same document notes that the Security Council-authorized international naval operations to suppress Somali piracy have, according to some reports, inadvertently facilitated the resurgence of illegal fishing in Somali waters. In other words, the IUU fishing, which was restrained by the activities of Somali pirates, may have been intensified under the security umbrella provided by the Security Council-authorized naval operations against Somali pirates.

A more disturbing aspect of the IUU fishing is the attacks the unauthorized fishermen perpetrate against Somali fishermen who fish on their own coastline. Dershowitz and Paul (2012) and a 2005 UNEP report, for example, note that well-armed foreign fishing vessels have attacked and destroyed 'boats and equipment' of Somali fishermen (UNEP, 2005). The UN Secretary-General report (S/2011/661) also notes that Somali fishermen have claimed that they fear fishing 'beyond the horizon', alleging that the bodies of their peers have washed ashore with bullet wounds to the head, purportedly inflicted by operators of foreign-flagged vessels engaged in IUU fishing.

A number of reports substantiate the claim of dumping of waste and toxic materials off the Somali coastline (Dershowitz and Paul, 2012). The UN Secretary-General report (S/2011/661) notes that circumstantial evidence indicates that the dumping of illegal waste occurred during the 1990s. Surprisingly, however, the Secretary-General's report contends that verification has not been possible due to the security situation in Somalia as well as due to lack of funding. Neither funding nor security constraints has prevented investigations by other UN agencies, however, such as the Monitoring Group for Somalia and Eritrea, which investigates countries, groups and individuals that contravened the UN's arms embargo on Somalia or have any links with al-Shebab and its operations.[43]

The Secretary-General's report also notes the claims that the naval operations against Somali piracy may have sheltered the vessels engaged in IUU fishing. Yet, despite the gravity of the damage to Somalia, the Security Council has paid little attention to the illegal fishing and dumping of waste in Somali waters. The Council has also authorized no measures against the vessels engaged in IUU fishing.

Since the passage of Resolution 1816 on 2 June 2008 a Combined Maritime Forces, which is a US-led international naval coalition of 25 nations, has been engaged in a Maritime Intercept Operation (MIO) against Somali piracy in the Gulf of Aden, the Gulf of Oman, the Arabian Sea, the Arabian Gulf, the Red Sea and parts of the Indian Ocean. Individual countries, including India, China, Iran, Japan, Kenya, Saudi Arabia, South Africa and Yemen, have also deployed naval ships and/or aircraft to combat piracy in the region. There is little oversight and coordination over what measures such naval operations take against the Somali pirates. The Security Council authorizes the operations to include whatever measures necessary. As a result, some of the participants in the MIO have extended the fight against Somali pirates to land. The EU, for example, has allowed its maritime mission

ATALANTA to attack both sea and land targets against pirates, although it is unclear how to distinguish pirates from fishermen onshore.

Why the Region Has Failed to Curtail External Intervention

External intervention has had major adverse impacts on the socioeconomic landscape of the region. As noted, the post-Second World War geopolitical engineering of the region by western powers led to many chronic conflicts, including the Ogaden wars and the wars of Eritrea's independence. The various interventions during the Cold War and post-Cold War eras also intensified and extended the duration of many of the conflicts. Beyond the wars and conflicts, the interventions have produced a number of adverse impacts on the region. Among the most important of these are the following:

- The interventions have supported the autocratic political elite, hindering democratization and nation-building. Various human rights organizations have confirmed that the regimes in Eritrea, Sudan, Djibouti, Ethiopia and Uganda often suppress opposition groups and violate human rights. Yet, the regimes in the latter three countries have enjoyed extensive external financial, political and military support that fortifies their position against domestic opposition and thereby extends their tenure on power. External support has also allowed these regimes to be less reliant on popular support for their political lives. This relative independence from society, in turn, has allowed them to be unaccountable to their populations. The regimes which are out of favour with external (mostly western) powers, such as those in Eritrea and Sudan, are equally (if not more) despotic than those with western support. However, they utilize a different approach to stay in power. They claim to be victims of external meddling and isolation and appeal to nationalism to divert attention away from the atrocities they perpetrate upon their populations.

- External intervention has also hindered negotiated settlement of internal conflicts by strengthening the position of those who benefit from it. In so doing it has contributed to militarization of the region, thereby exacerbating the intensity of conflicts and extending their duration. In the Somali case, external intervention has essentially precluded negotiated settlement between the weak TFG and al-Shebab and other groups in the country (Elmi and Aynte, 2012). While the Somali situation is the most glaring example, it is by no means the only case in the region. Peaceful conclusion of the brutal Lord's Resistance Army saga in Uganda and other countries in the region has been hindered by the International Criminal Court's indictment of the LRA leaders. The ICC's refusal to revoke the indictment after a peace agreement was forged through traditional conflict resolution mechanisms has precluded the possibility of a peaceful end to that crisis. Regardless of the merits of the cases, the ICC indictments against Sudan's President and Defence Minister have also complicated the settlement of the various conflicts in that country. The charges of crimes against humanity levelled by the ICC against Kenya's presidential candidate Uhuru Kenyata and his running mate, William Ruto, is also likely to have serious complications on the country's March 2013 elections. The implications are likely to be even more serious if Mr Kenyata and his running mate win the election and are convicted by the ICC.

- External intervention has also contributed in hindering the settlement of inter-state conflicts in the region. As Liebl (2008) notes, there is little doubt that US support has encouraged Ethiopian intransigence in demarcating the border with Eritrea in line with the ruling of the Boundary Commission and ending that conflict. External meddling (both from within and from outside the region) has also become a factor in complicating the conflicts surrounding the various unresolved issues between Sudan and South Sudan in the aftermath of the break-up of the country. Issues such as boundary disputes and disputes about how to share oil revenue continue to threaten to thrust the two countries into a new cycle of destructive conflicts.

- External intervention has also contributed in weakening regional governance and in fragmentation of the region. IGAD has been unable to enhance the security of its members through effective conflict resolution or through warding off external interference. IGAD's inability to demand remedial measures from the Security Council for the pillaging of Somali's fish resources and the crime of dumping of waste materials on its coastline represents a failure to defend a defenceless member country. The inconsistency in the manner IGAD has responded to border problems between Djibouti and Eritrea and those between Ethiopia and Eritrea also shows the organization's lack of independence from external influence. IGAD was instrumental in subjecting Eritrea to Security Council imposed sanctions in part due to its border dispute with Djibouti. By contrast, IGAD has initiated no punitive measures against Ethiopia for its intransigence in demarcating the border with Eritrea. In large part, due to its excessive dependence on external financing of its operations, IGAD has largely become a conduit for external influence on the region rather than an agent for sheltering the region from external meddling.
- External intervention also hinders domestic and regional solutions to domestic and regional conflicts. External intervention is generally intended to promote solutions and policies that advance the interests of those intervening. As evident from the Somali case, external intervention hinders democratization of the process of conflict resolution by dictating or influencing decisions.
- In addition, intervention by external powers, which compete for control of the region's resources, has the potential to diminish the region's bargaining power in the global system. The region's interests lie in its ability to ensure competition among external actors for trade and

investments in the region. Militarization, which aims to establish monopolistic control of the region's resources through security arrangements, reduces the region's bargaining power. IGAD at the present time does not show that it is prepared to ward off interventions in the region that can undermine the region's bargaining power. In defence of IGAD, however, it does not possess the necessary level of autonomy from the member states to become effective.

Despite the identified adverse impacts of the avalanche of external intervention that has characterized the region, the Greater Horn states have failed to cooperate in curtailing self-serving external intervention and in addressing regional problems by themselves. A number of factors explain this paralysis. One relates to the structures of the state and nature of the political elite. As explained in chapter 4, the executive branch (the strongmen) dominates the state in these countries. In the absence of horizontal accountability among the organizations of the state and vertical accountability to the population, the autocratic leadership faces a plethora of violent and non-violent opposition from within their societies. In response the leadership often relies on external support for survival, thereby facilitating external intervention.

Another reason is poor inter-state relations. As, noted in chapters 2 and 4, the region has faced a number of inter-state conflicts. These conflicts have not only limited the countries' ability to cooperate in forming effective regional governance but also have encouraged them to invite external intervention. Economic vulnerabilities and reliance on external aid have hindered the countries of the region from ascertaining their independence by collaborating against external intervention.

The failure of the states of the region to strengthen IGAD and cultivate a strong system of regional governance is another factor that has hampered the region in warding off external intervention. As will be explained in chapter 8, among the principal goals of a regional integration scheme, such as IGAD, are to enhance the region's peace and security, to accelerate regional economic development through cooperation, and to ensure that an external agenda does not undermine regional interests. In other words, regional integration has a critical role in the advancement of collective security of the populations and states of member countries. The magnitude of the conflicts and external intervention that characterizes the region is a clear indication that regional governance has not been effective in the Greater Horn. IGAD's ineffectiveness, in turn, is a manifestation of the failure of the leaders of the region to build the capacity of the regional body by allowing the organization the necessary level of independence from the influences of individual member states.

The weakness of regional governance, in turn, is an indication that the region suffers from a deficit of statesmenlike leaders who are committed to building effective governance structures both at the national and regional level. As discussed in chapter 4, most of the leaders of the region have not engaged seriously in building institutions of governance at the national level. Instead they have often advanced personal rule. Given their failure to build institutions that would empower their populations, it would be hard to expect them to build institutions of regional governance. As the political elite's reliance on external forces for their survival in power deepens, their commitment to the advancement of national and regional interests declines and the agenda of their external supporters takes precedence over national and regional interests. The importance of regional cooperation and good neighbourliness, thus, declines, especially if they contravene the interests of the external supporters. In other words, as they lose sight of the importance of collective self-reliance, they also invest less effort in cultivating and developing regional relations. Under such conditions, even small differences among the region's leaders become causes of destructive conflicts. It would hardly be an exaggeration to suggest that the concept of 'the narcissism of minor difference' (Ignatieff, 1993) characterizes the behaviour of the region's leadership. How else would one explain how a dispute over a border of little significance led to the brutal two-year war, with over 70,000 in casualties, followed by a decade and half of absence of peace between Eritrea and Ethiopia? Similarly, the failure of Sudan and South Sudan to agree on sharing of oil revenue and demarcating their borders indicates how much they undervalue good relations between each other, even though it is vital to their socioeconomic development.

7 | Poor Resource Management and Environmental Degradation

Introduction

Whether there is a robust relationship between environmental degradation and conflict is a highly disputed issue. At least three points of view can be identified. One view claims that global warming increases the risk of civil wars in Africa. Burke et al. (2009) even claim that every 1°C increase in temperature above the norm is associated with 4.5 per cent increase in conflict incidence in the same year. According to their model, if temperatures kept rising, as predicted, the number of conflicts in Africa would increase by more than 50 per cent by 2030. A counter-view contends that there is no robust relationship between climate change and occurrence of civil wars (Buhaug, 2010; Buhaug et al., 2010). Buhaug et al. claim that their paper 'documents a wider set of sensitivity tests that provide further proof of the empirical disconnect between climate variability and civil war outbreak, incidence, and severity' (2010: 1). The study, however, is based on short-term effects of climate variability. Several of the articles in the special issue of the *Journal of Peace Research* (vol. 49, no. 1, 2012) also contend that there is little evidence to support that climate change is an important driver of conflict (Gleditsch, 2012).

A third view argues that climate change, by bringing about desertification and water scarcity, plays a large part in the origin and escalation of conflicts and usually acts in combination with other factors, such as poverty, economic decline, overpopulation and political instability (Spillmann, 1995). Claussen (2007) also notes that environmental degradation by creating scarcity of resources contributes to poverty, ethnic tensions and migration. These factors, in turn, are likely to contribute to the onset of various levels of conflicts, especially in the absence of proper management of diversity of identities by the state.

A number of factors help explain the sharp differences in views on the relations between environmental degradation and conflicts. Among them is lack of clarity in conceptualization as well as in differentiation of the various types of conflicts, including communal conflicts and civil wars. The relationships between environmental degradation and communal conflicts, for example, are much easier to establish than those between environmental degradation and civil wars or those between degradation and inter-state conflicts. Another issue in the disagreements relates to lack of clarity on whether climate change is a direct or indirect factor in provoking conflict. Many studies seem to test association between climate variability and conflicts rather than the association between the environmental degradation, manifested by scarcity of resources and the weakening of institutions that govern property rights and conservation measures, which are attributable to sustained climate change, and their relations with conflict. Survey respondents in three districts in each of three countries, Kenya, Ethiopia and Somaliland, for instance, identify the most common reasons for any conflicts their community might have had with neighbouring communities to be over disputes over land, water and cattle rustling (Kidane Mengisteab et al., 2011). The same survey also reveals that the scarcity of land and water, along with growing threat to livelihood, undermines the institutions of customary property rights and conservation measures. Testing the association between environmental degradation, which to a large extent is attributable to sustained climate change, and inter-communal conflicts is, thus, likely to produce more robust relations and more useful results than testing the association between undefined conflicts or civil wars and variability of temperature and precipitation over a short span of time.

The scarcity that environmental degradation creates, depending on its intensity, would be sufficient to cause communal conflicts, especially among pastoralists and between pastoralists and sedentary farmers, such as those in Darfur. In some cases the environmental degradation-induced scarcity of resources may hit groups which are marginalized and have already organized rebel groups against governments. In such cases the inter-communal conflicts and civil wars may converge. A good example is the case of the Ogaden and Ishaq Somali clans who fought over grazing land in the Ogaden region. The Ogaden clan supported the Western Somalia Liberation Front (WSLF), which fought against Ethiopia and was supported by the Republic of Somalia, while the Ishaq clan supported the Somali National Movement (SNM), which was supported by the Ethiopian regime and fought the Siad Barre regime in Somalia (Markakis, 1995).[44] As the Darfur case shows, identity groups do not engage in violent conflicts over grazing land when there is no scarcity of it and when customary property rights are adhered to. Under conditions of severe scarcity, however, institutions are violated and issues of who has access to what become contentious and may provoke violent conflicts. The more difficult question is whether environmental degradation's contribution to conflict is limited to communal conflicts or whether it also contributes to civil wars and inter-state wars.

As noted in chapter 1, the Horn of Africa has faced an alarming rate of environmental degradation manifested in the forms of frequent droughts, deforestation, loss of vegetation and biodiversity, increased soil erosion, desiccation and desertification. As shown in table 7.1, Ethiopia and Kenya endured at least ten major droughts each between 1980 and 2011. Djibouti and Uganda experienced eight droughts each, while Somalia and Sudan saw seven and six droughts respectively during the same period of time. While the causes for the worsening degradation may not be fully understood, they relate to global climatic changes and local (regional) environmental management practices. The actual effects and future

Table 7.1. Frequency of drought occurrences in the Greater Horn, 1980–2011

	Djibouti	Eritrea	Ethiopia	Kenya	Somalia	Sudan	Uganda
Total no. of droughts, 1980–2011	8.0	4.0*	10.0	10.0	7.0	6.0	8.0
Average no. of droughts/yr, 1980–2011	0.26	0.20	0.32	0.32	0.23	0.19	0.26
Average no. of people affected by each drought, 1980–2011 (000s)	155.7	–	6,465.0	4,720.0	1,850.0	4,558.3	690.0

* The number of droughts in Eritrea go back only to 1991, when the country gained independence. The number of people affected by the 2009 drought is also unknown.
Source: Calculated from EM-DAT, International Disaster Database, Centre for Research on the Epidemiology of Disasters, 2011, http://www.emdat.be/country-profile.

implications of the deepening crisis of degradation are also hard to map out accurately. However, there is little doubt that they have already produced cyclical droughts with devastating famines and massive socioeconomic dislocations, which foster conflicts in the region. Sudan's Darfur, for example, has endured conflicts at two levels, although they often converge. At one level is the inter-communal conflict over grazing land and water between the Rizeigat nomads of the northern part and their neighbours to the south, the farming communities from the Fur, Zaghawa, and Massleit ethnic groups. This level of conflict would be hard to explain fully without taking into account the environmental degradation which has produced acute scarcity of those vital resources, especially in the northern parts of Darfur (Ahmed, 2009). Climatic changes have forced the Rizeigat nomads to trek southwards and the farmers also to use extensive farming methods, bringing under cultivation areas that provided rich forage for herders. Such competition over resources transformed relations between the two groups into violent conflicts. Relations between the herders and farmers are said to have rarely involved violent conflicts before the environmental deterioration beginning in the 1970s (UNDP, 2006). The second level is the civil war, where rebel groups, such as the Justice and Equality Movement (JEM) and the Sudan Liberation Army (SLA), are fighting the Sudanese state. This level of the conflict is primarily attributable to grievances over socioeconomic marginalization of the region. The two levels of conflicts are closely intertwined with each other because the degradation intensifies the poverty and grievances caused by marginalization. Similarly, the vulnerability to scarcity of resources which are caused by environmental degradation is intensified by marginalization or neglect by the state. Land policy which disadvantages rural communities, especially pastoral groups, is another factor that connects the two levels of conflicts.

This chapter has four objectives. The first attempts to briefly describe some of the most common human activities within the region which, along with the global climatic changes, have led to the region's environmental crisis. The second part examines the massive socioeconomic dislocations which have resulted from the environmental degradation and have contributed to the region's conflicts and instability. The third part attempts to shed light on the future potential implications of the crisis if the countries of the region fail to take measures that would enable their populations to contain the worsening degradation process and to cope with its impacts. The last part briefly explores the issues that are likely to hinder the region's ability to control some of the factors that contribute to the environmental crisis and also to develop capability to cope with the effects of environmental degradation.

Factors for Environmental Degradation

As noted above, the Horn of Africa's environmental crisis is attributable to two broad factors. One relates to global climatic changes, which have affected many regions of the world, albeit differently. The second relates to human activities within the region, which contribute to various types of environmental degradation within the region, including deforestation, depletion of vegetation cover, soil erosion, soil contamination and water and air pollution. While there is much debate about the factors that cause global climatic changes, there has emerged a growing consensus that human activities are major culprits. A key factor in climate change is said to be the destruction of the ozone layer by emission of carbon dioxide (CO_2) and other ozone-depleting greenhouse gases, including methane, nitrous oxide and chlorofluorocarbons (CFCs). Economic activities, including industry, mining and agriculture, are all contributors to global warming through emission of the various greenhouse gases to the atmosphere. The burning of fossil fuels and global depletion of forests are among the leading factors in the increase in the emission of CO_2 to the atmosphere.

The continent of Africa is not a significant player in the production of the industrial emissions that generate global warming (Thornton et al., 2011). However, for a variety of reasons, including its already hot tropical climate, Africa is said to have been impacted more severely than other regions of the world by global warming (Christensen and Hewitson, 2003). Annual mean warming throughout the continent and in all seasons is higher in Africa (Christensen and Hewitson, 2003). It is estimated that Sub-Saharan Africa is warmer now than it was 100 years ago by 0.5°C (see figures 7.1 and 7.2

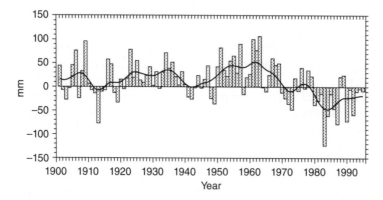

Figure 7.1. Changes in observed annual precipitation in Africa
Source: UNEP, *IPCC Special Report on the Regional Impacts of Climate Change*, 2000; ©GRID-Arendal.

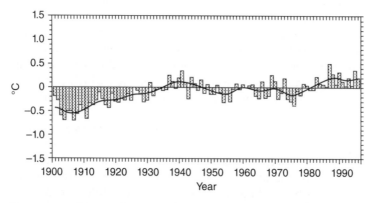

Figure 7.2. Observed annual temperature changes in Africa
Source: UNEP, *IPCC Special Report on the Regional Impacts of Climate Change*, 2000; ©GRID-Arendal.

for the trends). More importantly, the region's warming trend is expected to increase to an average of roughly 0.2°C per decade. According to some projections, the increase in the rate of warming is much higher and temperatures in Sub-Saharan Africa are estimated to be warmer by 4°C by 2060 (Thornton et al., 2011). The Horn of Africa, which contains large arid and semi-arid areas, is among the more vulnerable regions within Sub-Saharan Africa.

Rainfall trends vary from locality to locality. They are also difficult to predict, due to the variability of the many factors that determine them. While reliable data covering the whole region over a number of decades are not available, anecdotal data indicate a declining trend in at least parts of the region. The rate of decline for parts of the Horn is estimated at 30 mm per decade. For Kenya, for example, the observed decline between 1969 and 2009 is estimated at 100 mm (US Department of the Interior US Geological Survey, 2012). Projections of rainfall trend for the region are not reliable, as they vary from significant declines to modest increases. What seems certain is that the sharp fluctuations in rainfall and the resulting cyclical droughts, which have ravaged much of the region over the last several decades, are likely to remain the norm. The droughts have been major factors in the drastic changes in land-cover by contributing to deforestation, loss of vegetation, soil desiccation and desertification of the region. More importantly, they bring about devastations to crop-farming and livestock husbandry, resulting in chronic food shortages and periodic famines. In addition, they lead to severe decline in export earnings from livestock products, which constitute a significant portion of export earnings of the countries of the region.

Under rising temperatures, the region also faces an increasing trend in the evaporation rate, which, according to some studies, is expected to increase between 5 and 10 per cent by 2050. Any possible decline in rainfall is, thus, certain to be worsened by the higher evaporation rate, while any increase in rainfall might be offset by it (Herrero et al., 2010). Higher temperatures, along with higher evaporation rates, are also certain to exacerbate the region's shrinking supply of water and declining vegetation cover (for projected decline in water supply in the region, see table 7.2).

Beyond the global climatic changes, various human activities within the region have contributed to different kinds of environmental degradation. Rapid change in land-cover has occurred in much of the region through removal of vegetation by land clearing, harvesting of trees and overgrazing. Rapid population growth, land policy which disregards the way of life of the majority of the population and generates poverty, development approaches that foster mismanagement of land, and poorly conceived expansion of commercial farming and extractive industries are among the human activities contributing to the region's environmental degradation.

Population

The region's population has grown roughly 2.4-fold since the early 1960s (see table 2.1 in chapter 2). As a result, notable changes have taken place in the rate, extent and intensity of land-use and land-cover. More land is cleared for agriculture and more trees are cut for construction and firewood. Although reliable data are not available, it is also reasonable to assume that livestock population has increased with

Table 7.2. Declining trend in the region's water supply (in cubic metres (m³)/person/year)*

	1990	2050
Sudan	Over 4,500	Less than 2,500
Uganda	Over 3,500	Roughly 1,500
Ethiopia	Over 2,000	Roughly 1,000
Somalia	Over 1,000	Less than 500
Kenya	Roughly 750	Less than 250
Djibouti	Roughly 500	Less than 250

* 2,000 m³/person/year is classified as vulnerability; 1,000 m³/person/year is considered stress; and below 1,000 m³/person/year is viewed as scarcity.
Source: ILRI, 2006.

increases in human population. IGAD countries are home to an estimated 68 million livestock units. Ethiopia and Sudan (North and South) are said to have 28.4 million and 22.3 million livestock units respectively (Sandford and Ashley, 2008). With growing population and increasing size of livestock and longer and more frequent droughts, overgrazing, soil erosion, declining land fertility and shortages of quality pasture have become serious problems in many parts of the region. Given the climatic trends, if the population continues to grow at current (or near current) rates,[45] and the region's economic systems, especially the subsistent agriculture and pastoral sectors, fail to undergo fundamental changes, then the adverse changes in land-use and land-cover can be expected to intensify and reduce large parts of the region into a wasteland.

Land Policy and Development Approaches

Land tenure policy is another major factor in the region's environmental degradation. Agriculture-based economies, such as those of the Horn of Africa, require effective management of land and resources, especially given the environmental adversity and rapid population growth they face. Land tenure policy in the region hardly promotes effective management of land resources, however. The land tenure system is characterized by parallel tendencies. One is the policies of governments to promote private holdings and to give land concessions to large-scale commercial farmers and to investors in extractive industries. The other is the struggles of subsistent farmers, agro-pastoralists and pastoralist communities to maintain customary communal tenure systems. These conflicts between customary land tenure systems and land policy have contributed to land degradation in a number of ways.

Land tenure systems in the region are highly diverse. Communal ownership was the most common tenure system historically but it has undergone notable incursions under both the colonial and post-colonial states.[46] The colonial state transferred ownership of large portions of communal land to the state, especially in Kenya and Eritrea. In some cases, Kenya and Uganda in particular, the British colonial state even declared that all communal land belonged to the state in order to be able to expropriate any land it wanted at any time without giving any compensation to customary holders. Crown Land Ordinances in those two countries, thus, reduced customary holders of land to tenants at the will of the crown. Land expropriations forced communities to be concentrated in substantially reduced areas, where they generally overexploited land resources. In some cases, as in Eritrea and Sudan, land appropriations also allowed the colonial state to give logging licences, which led to extensive deforestation. Some communities who lost their land to these expropriations by the colonial state, such as the Maasai of Kenya, continue to demand that the post-colonial state restores their lost land. Instead, the post-colonial state has continued the policy of land-taking, failing to distinguish itself from the colonial state in this regard.

Ethiopia

In the case of Abyssinia (present-day Ethiopia), which was successful in foiling colonization, a different kind of land expropriation took place. As noted in chapter 2, with its expansion southward in the late nineteenth and early twentieth centuries, the empire expropriated much of the land of the defeated natives and redistributed it among its troops and administrative staff in lieu of salaries. The land grants were inheritable and created a new class of landlords, who were essentially non-native to the localities. The native peasants in the newly incorporated territories were also subdivided among the new landlords to work the land as share-cropping tenants (Pankhurst, 1966). Although the magnitude is unknown, it is certain that the influx of northern settlers along with the expropriation of land led to impoverishment of the local population and to the clearing of considerable land for farming.

In the northern parts of the country (Abyssinia proper) the tenure system was mostly *rist* (kinship ownership) of farmland and communal ownership of pastoral areas. At different periods in the country's history, large tracts of land were given to the Orthodox Church by monarchs and regional leaders in various parts of the country. In the post-Second World War era the monarchy gave considerable land to the *arbenoch* (leaders of the resistance to Italian occupation, 1936–41) mostly but not exclusively from land used by pastoralists that was suitable for farming. The monarchy also gave land to investors in large-scale commercial farming in various parts of the country, especially in riverine areas. The Awash River valley in the Afar region and the Tana Beles project in the Gumuz areas, in the western part of the country, were among the most notable in terms of their adverse impacts on local rural communities. The starvation of thousands of Afar nomads in the mid-1970s is largely attributed to the fact that they were pushed away to dry areas from their customary grazing areas along the banks of the Awash River (Lundstrom, 1976). The government also alienated land for game parks, including in the Awash Valley exerting further pressure on the Afar nomads.

Ethiopia's 1975 land reform abolished the landlord–tenant relations which were predominant in the southern parts of the country, and restored usufructuary rights to land to the tillers (the tenants) while the state assumed ownership and control of all land. The country's latest (1994) constitution also vests the right to ownership of rural and urban land, as well as of all underground natural resources, exclusively in the state. However, in a contradictory manner, the constitution provides peasants and pastoralists the right to free land for cultivation and grazing as well as the right not to be displaced from the land they hold. The right not to be displaced has remained hollow, as it has been trampled by development concerns. The state has actively promoted foreign investments in commercial farming by giving a growing number of land concessions (see table 7.3).

Kenya

Kenya endured the most significant land-taking by the colonial state in the region. According to some estimates, Kenyan

Table 7.3. Rough estimates of land concessions given to commercial farmers

Country	Minimum estimate (ha 000s)	Maximum estimate (ha 000s)
Ethiopia	2,892	3,524
Sudan*	3,171	4,899
Uganda	1,874	1,904
Kenya	135.0	150.0

* Includes both North and South Sudan.
Source: Global Land Project, 2010.

communities lost about 5 per cent of the country's total arable land (Adams and Turner, 2006). This is a small proportion relative to the expropriations that took place in the settler economies, such as South Africa, Zimbabwe and Namibia. Nevertheless, land expropriations have remained a major source of conflict, especially since the post-colonial state's land policy allowed land-takings to continue. The country's Land Act (amended 1964) empowered the president to allocate land to anyone, irrespective of whether the land was occupied or not (Alao, 2007: 87). Land alienation and transfer of ownership through various means, including corrupt mechanisms, characterized post-colonial Kenya's land policy (APRM, 2006). The system also allowed land clearing of forest areas for settlement with considerable damage to the environment. The 2010 constitution has withdrawn the power of the president in allocating land. The constitution also makes a provision that land belongs to communities. The application of this provision, however, remains to be seen. How communities are defined and who they include and exclude are also yet to be clarified.

Uganda
Uganda also did not recognize the rights of customary holders of communal land until the ratification of its 1995 constitution. Communal land holders were simply regarded as tenants in crown land who could be evicted with three-months' notice

and with compensation for any developments on land only (Mwebaza, 1999). With the 1995 constitution a Land Act was promulgated in 1998. The Act was primarily designed to promote a freeholder system and a land market (Coldham, 2000). Nevertheless, it also attempted to reduce the insecurity of tenure of customary holders of communal land by recognizing communal ownership. The Act gave communal holders the option of registering their holdings either as a freehold or as a communal holding. The Act, however, allows the state to retain rights to land-based natural resources. Land holders can thus be evicted in the event that mineral resources are discovered on the land or even if the land is deemed needed to promote development.

Sudan

The British colonial administration introduced three types of tenure systems in Sudan. One type was private property of land recognized through the Titles to Land Ordinance of 1899. This Ordinance recognized as private property the continuously cultivated lands in northern and central riverine Sudan (UNDP, 2006). The second system was government land subject to no right and was confined mainly to the northern and central riverine regions, including the deltas of Tokar and Gash in eastern Sudan. Both the colonial and post-colonial states allotted land to local and expatriate investors from these areas essentially at the expense of local communities, such as the Hadendawa, who were pushed out of the fertile Tokar and Gash deltas to the marginal lands of the Red Sea hills (UNDP, 2006). The third class of tenure was government land where customary usufruct rights of communities, such as villages, clans and ethnic groups, were recognized but not registered. This tenure system applied to Darfur in the west, the entire North Kordofan, the Nuba Mountains, as well as the whole South. The usufruct rights of communities were not secure in this system and withdrawing of usufruct rights occurred throughout the colonial period. With the 1930 Land Acquisition Ordinance the colonial state was free to acquire any land that is likely to be required for any public purpose (UNDP, 2006).

The post-colonial state did not change the colonial legacy of land tenure systems in the country. The Unregistered Land Act of 1970 reaffirmed that all unregistered land belonged to the state. The state allocates leases from such land mostly to commercial farmers without reference to the rural communities who are actually living on the land (de Waal, 2006).

Eritrea

The colonial state had declared state ownership (*demaniale*) of most of the land in the country's lowlands, mainly inhabited by nomadic communities. It also gave pockets of land to Italian settlers in the highlands, despite protests and rebellions by the native communities. One such rebellion was led by a notable by the name of Bahta Hagos, who mobilized resistance to land-taking by saying that 'once a white snake bites (white settlers occupy our land) you cannot find a cure for it' (Tekeste Negash, 1986). In 1994 the post-colonial Eritrean state outdid the colonial state by declaring state ownership of all rural and urban land. The country's constitution, which was ratified by the National Assembly in May 1997 but has yet to be implemented, also endorses state control of all land. The Land Reform proclamation has not yet been fully implemented. The state has, however, taken land for urban development in peri-urban areas and for commercial farming and expansion of mining in different parts of the country. The 1994 Land Reform proclamation enables the state to take any land but it also obligates it to pay a fair compensation in kind or in cash, determined by courts, to customary holders whose holdings it takes. Yet, contrary to the provisions of the Land Reform proclamation, the government has engaged in land-taking without giving any compensation.

Somalia

In Somalia the Siad Barre regime introduced a new land registration law in 1975. All land was considered as previously unclaimed and state property. The registration process, however, became a mechanism of redistribution of communal land in favour of the most influential segments of society. The most valuable farming land was grabbed by businessmen, politicians and civil servants (Deherez, 2009). With the registration law land also became a resource for rewarding political loyalty and some clans became more privileged than others in access to land. Pastoralists and smallholders, who did not have the resources, connections and information and often did not understand the need for registration, were severely disadvantaged by the new land policy. Pastoral communities, in particular, were dispossessed of their traditional grazing land by land registration.

Djibouti

Djibouti's main exports are livestock and hides, although only a quarter of the population lives in rural areas (outside Djibouti city and other urban areas), mostly as herders. Two customary tenure systems operate in the country. In the Issa areas of the south land is essentially under communal ownership. In the Afar areas of the north, by contrast, land is held under the trusteeship of the sultan and allocated among members of the community. There is little agricultural land outside the privately owned irrigated garden plots used for vegetable production in smaller urban areas. As a result, unlike the other countries of the region, Djibouti has not seen any major national land legislation that displaces pastoralist communities. Some property laws were enacted in 1991 in order to establish agricultural centres, to manage natural reserves, to take protective measures for sites and monuments, to establish water points, to undertake irrigation projects and to acquire vacant lands. These laws, however, did not have significant effects on pastoralists. Moreover, due to droughts and loss of livestock, there has been an increasing trend towards sedentary life in the urban areas by pastoralists (Bohrer, 1998).

Expansion of Commercial Farming and Extractive Industries

Despite the apparent reforms to improve the security of land tenure of customary holders, as in Ethiopia and Uganda, the priority of the region's governments has been to promote private holdings and to grant land concessions to foreign investors in order to entice investors. Oblivious to the land and water constraints many of their populations face, the governments of the region have engaged in rapid acquisition of land from pastoralists and subsistence farmers in order to give concessions to foreign investors in large-scale commercial farming as well as in extractive industries.

Growing food markets in the land- or water-deficit Middle Eastern and Asian countries, rising global food prices and growing demand for bio-fuels are some of the factors that have stimulated investments in farmlands in the region, as in many other parts of Africa as well as other countries in the developing world.[47] Middle Eastern countries, including Saudi Arabia, the United Arab Emirates, Qatar and Kuwait, along with China, India, South Korea and Egypt are among the newcomers to investing in farmland in the Greater Horn region. Investors from western countries, especially Western European, have also made notable investments in commercial farming in the region. Unlike investors from the Middle Eastern and Asian countries, investors from western countries mostly invest in the production of bio-fuels, sugar and industrial products, such as rubber and cotton.

Data on the magnitude of land concessions awarded to commercial farmers and on the fate of those stripped of their lands are not easy to assemble, partly because the transactions lack transparency and partly because the process of land-taking is still unfolding. Anecdotal data, however, suggest that land grabs and the resulting evictions of peasants and pastoralists are taking place at a rapid rate (see table 7.3 for estimates).

Often the land concessions granted to commercial farmers, usually on ninety-nine-year lease bases, are either in riverine areas or in areas where water availability is reasonably secure. The customary users of the appropriated lands are, thus, deprived not only of land but also of water. The figures also do not include the land grabs taking place by local small-scale commercial farmers as well as by government officials and other influential individuals. Such practices have taken place in all the countries of the region, although the magnitude is difficult to determine.

As Cotula (2011) notes, no prior and informed consent of local land holders are required before land is allocated to an investor. The land lease fees, which are generally kept low in order to encourage investors, also accrue to governments and not to the former owners or holders of land. When compulsory acquisition of land takes place, in most cases compensation is only given for loss of improvements and not for the value of the land, although the Ethiopian governments gives as compensation the value of an estimated ten-year produce from the land.

Governments justify the land leases by pointing to the potential development impacts of the investments. They argue that the investments generate revenue and contribute to food security, infrastructure development and job creation. In some cases, they also argue that the land that is given as concession is generally unused or underutilized land. Often, however, governments simply conceal the land concessions they have awarded. President Museveni of Uganda is said to have declared that foreign investors should not be allocated huge chunks of land because such land should be owned by Ugandans. Yet, it is reported that Uganda has offered over 840,000 hectares (ha) of farmland, roughly 2.2 per cent of the country's total land area, to Egypt to produce wheat and corn to feed its population (Butagira, 2008). Uganda has also given 18,000 acres to Bidco, a manufacturer of edible oils, to grow oil palms. A German agro-investor, NKG Tropical Management, was also given 2,500 acres. Uganda is also said to have leased 10,000 acres to around 300–400 Chinese farmers.

The terms of the lease, although they vary from one country to another are, however, unlikely to generate much revenue. In most cases they range between $1/ha per year to $5/ha/ year (Cotula, 2011). It is highly likely that the farms will displace more jobs than they create, since large-scale farming is often mechanized. The jobs that might be created are also likely to be seasonal, due to the nature of agriculture. The contributions of the foreign investors in commercial farming to food security of host countries are also suspect since the products of such investors are essentially geared towards foreign markets. Their impacts on infrastructure development are unclear but it not likely that they will invest in areas without the necessary infrastructure.

The argument that the land that is given as concession is generally unused or underutilized land is made by Ethiopian officials. But this argument is not convincing for a number of reasons. According to Ethiopia's Ministry of Mines and Energy, the country is said to have 23.3 million ha of land suitable for the production of oil-rich jatropha. The same Ministry's study has also indicated that 700,000 ha of land is available for sugarcane production. It is not very convincing that the country would have such amounts of land that are lying unused. More importantly, the land that investors want is prime land with availability of water. This is also the land that local producers want to keep. It is not very likely that such prime lands are there unclaimed or unused. Another reason why such an argument is not convincing is that some of the areas where concessions are made, such as Gambela, are characterized by land-based conflicts. Furthermore, Ethiopia is a country with a rapidly growing population, which is expected to reach 150 million by 2050. The demand for land is likely to rise sharply over the coming decades. It is unclear if policy-makers are considering the future employment opportunity that may be lost when they grant the land leases, which are mostly for ninety-nine years.

Concessions to Extractive Industries

In addition to the land concessions to foreign investors in large-scale commercial farming, the governments in the region have also engaged in granting land concessions to investors in extractive industries. This sector is presently rather small in the region; however, considerable effort is being made by every country to attract foreign direct investment into the sector by liberalizing economic policies and by putting in place generous incentive packages for investors. According to the country's Minister of Mines, Ethiopia, for instance, aims to expand the sector to contribute 10 per cent of GDP by 2016 from its contribution of 4 per cent in 2011.

Although the size of land concessions to extractive industries remains unknown, there is little doubt that it has been growing, since the industry has seen notable expansion over the last decade or so, especially in Ethiopia, Eritrea, Sudan and Uganda. Like the commercial farming sector, the ability of the extractive industry to create jobs is rather limited due to its capital-intensive nature. Although there is little empirical evidence, it is likely that the extractive industry sector, like the commercial farming sector, displaces more people than it employs. Thus, it is likely that it may exacerbate poverty through displacements as well as through its adverse impacts on the environment, even as it contributes to economic growth. Extractive industries through spillage and emission of chemicals pollute both surface and underground water. This is especially true with the oil industry in Sudan and South Sudan. Through emissions of dust and CO_2 it also pollutes the air and may contribute to health problems. Some of the mines that Eritrea is developing are near population centres, such as the capital city, Asmara, and may produce serious health problems.

In part due to its impacts on poverty, the industry also stimulates artisanal mining, which has damaging impacts on the environment. Moreover, like the commercial farms, extractive industries contribute to deforestation both directly and indirectly. Directly, they bring about the clearing of forests. Indirectly, through their impacts on poverty they contribute to land denudation by impoverished rural residents who clear marginal land for farming and engage in charcoal-making to sell in the urban areas. A short drive to the outskirts of major towns in any of the countries of the region gives a good indication of the daily flow of thousands of sacks of charcoal from rural to urban areas. Under such conditions it will not be long before the region's forests are completely wiped out. There is little doubt that the traditional conservation measures in rural areas have fallen apart under pressure from declining standards of living. Unfortunately, as the forests vanish and soil erosion worsens, poverty rates get worse.

Socioeconomic Dislocations and Conflicts Related to Environmental Degradation

The region's alarming environmental degradation has produced severe socioeconomic disruptions and various kinds of conflicts. Among the most conspicuous and serious impacts have been chronic food insecurity and periodic famines resulting from droughts and erratic rains. At the time of writing the region is again being ravaged by a severe drought and millions of people are at risk of starvation. News headlines such as the BBC's 'Horn of Africa Drought: "A Vision of Hell" ' (8 July 2011) give an indication of the severity of the situation. Another headline in *The Telegraph* (4 July 2011), which reads 'East Africa Drought: Africa Must do More to Help Itself', suggests the chronic nature of the problem. The largest country in the region, Ethiopia, faced the region's most devastating famines that shocked the international community in 1974. Droughts and famine devastated large parts of the country again in 1984. Ethiopia has continued to face major droughts at an average of one every three years since the early 1980s. In 2009 the Ethiopian government appealed for urgent food aid to feed 6.2 million people. At the time another 7 million people were on government-run foreign-funded food-for-work schemes (Malone, 2009; Pflanz, 2011). In 2011, the country, along with the rest of the region, was again hit by another cycle of drought and famine. Some reports warn that in Somalia, which is the hardest hit, up to 750,000 people could perish (BBC News, 2011). Beyond the large-scale famines that attract global attention, however, pastoralist and peasant populations throughout the region regularly face hunger and malnutrition, along with livestock starvation. The 2012 Global Hunger Index scores of the countries of the region are Eritrea 34.4, Ethiopia 28.7, Djibouti 21.7, Sudan 21.5, Kenya 19.3 and Uganda16.4 (IFPRI, 2012).[48]

With droughts and famines the region has also faced a growing number of climate refugees and internally displaced people. Persistent droughts are forcing peasants and nomads to flock to cities or refugee camps to avoid starvation. The numbers of climate refugees and displacements are difficult to estimate since there are other factors, such as conflicts, that cause displacements. UN officials in 2009 estimated that about 10 per cent of the nearly 300,000 Somali refugees at the Dadaab refugee camp in northern Kenya were climate refugees (Sanders, 2009). The number of the refugees in the Dadaab camp has swollen to over 400,000 since then (Dar, 2011).

Environmental Degradation and Violent Conflicts

As already noted, the relationship between environmental degradation and conflict is often disputed (Buhaug, 2010; Salehyan, 2008). A careful look at the various conflicts in the Horn of Africa, however, provides compelling evidence that environmental degradation has contributed to the conflicts. There is little doubt, for instance, that scarcity of resources such as land and water has undermined the institutional mechanisms that govern access to such resources in the region. With shortage of farmland peasant farmers often clear marginal lands for farming against the conservation norms and rules of their communities. In times of drought livestock herders also graze their hungry herds in places where they do not have the right of access, thereby triggering conflicts. There is, thus, little doubt that many conflicts such as those in Darfur are at least in part triggered by land and water shortages. Scarcity of resources generally intensifies competition for access to resources and also undermines adherence to existing institutions of property rights and allocation of resources. Under conditions of severe scarcity of vital resources communities and even states attempt to acquire access to the scarce resources through various means, including violence.

It is impossible to deny that the frequent droughts that have ravaged the region have brought about desertification, and decline in land quality and water availability creating scarcity of these vital resources. It is also hard to dispute that environmental degradation, such as extended and frequent droughts, is in itself sufficient condition for bringing about scarcity. Often, however, rapid population growth and the land policies of governments have complemented the environmental degradation in engendering the problem of scarcity.

In light of these circumstances it is prudent to recognize that environmental degradation creates scarcity, which often fosters conflicts. The relationship between environmental degradation and conflict is, however, mostly indirect. Since several factors contribute to creating scarcity, it also needs to be recognized that environmental degradation contributes to conflicts often in conjunction with other factors, although it can create scarcity of resources by itself. The fact that the contribution of environmental degradation to conflict is mostly indirect and that it occurs in the presence of other factors does not diminish its contribution to conflicts, however. In the next few pages we identify examples of different types of conflicts in the Greater Horn that have been caused, at least in part, by scarcity of resources, which was caused by a set of factors, including environmental degradation.

Communal Conflicts

The Horn of Africa has seen violent conflicts that are related to scarcity of resources. The conflicts are often of three types. Some are inter-communal conflicts, where communities engage in conflict over land, due to overcrowding, exacerbated by environmental degradation and rising demographic density. Among such conflicts are inter-communal conflicts that occur among ethnic or clan identities. Some of these conflicts occur over access to grazing or farming land and over access to water. In some cases violent conflicts are also fought over livestock theft, which may be triggered by efforts to restock herds depleted by droughts. Examples of inter-communal conflicts related to land and water scarcity are many (see table 2.6 in chapter 2). The conflicts among various ethnic identities in Darfur and South Sudan are among the most obvious examples. Scarcity-related inter-communal conflicts in Ethiopia include those between the Borona and Guji, the Ogaden and Ishaq Somali clans, and between the Nuer and Anuak in the Gambela region. Conflicts, such as those between the Kalenjin and Kisii in Kenya's Rift Valley are other examples. Cattle rustling has also led to many inter-communal conflicts in the region, including those between the Lou Nuer and Murle groups in the Jonglei area of Southern Sudan and various ethnic groups, such as the Turkana, Pokot and Karamoja, in northern Kenya and northern Uganda. Recent field research in parts of Ethiopia, Kenya and Somaliland shows that inter-communal conflicts are over land, water and cattle theft about 95 per cent of the time in Ethiopia, 87.5 per cent in Kenya and 39.8 per cent in Somaliland (Kidane Mengisteab et al., 2011).

Cross-Border Communal Conflicts

Environmental degradation is also a major factor in cross-border communal conflicts in the region. Incursions by pastoralists across customary communal and international boundaries in search of water and pasture have become common occurrences and have led to various clashes in the region (see table 7.4). Cattle rustling is also a major factor in the cross-border inter-communal conflicts in the region. Such conflicts are common in the boundaries between Ethiopia and South Sudan, Ethiopia and Kenya, between Kenya and Uganda, and between South Sudan and Uganda and Kenya. The conflicts between the Turkana, Pokot and Karamoja and

Table 7.4. Incidents of cross-border community conflicts (May 2003–November 2009)

	Violent incidents	Human deaths
Ethiopia	319	517
Kenya	842	1,072
Uganda	1,912	2,852
Total	3,073	4,441

Source: Computed from Wulf and Debiel, 2009.

those between Pian Karimojong and Bokora ethnic groups in Kenya and Uganda are among the examples.

Civil Wars

Civil wars are the third kind of conflict that is impacted by environmental degradation. As indicated in chapter 1, civil wars are those fought between the state and armed political entities, often ethnic, clan or religious-based. The relationships between environmental degradation and civil wars are complicated and more difficult to establish, however. The land and water scarcity created by environmental degradation does not, in itself, trigger a war against the state. However, environmental degradation contributes to civil wars in situations where there is already a rebellion against the state by a given identity (or identities) over its poverty and real or perceived marginalization. Environmental degradation sharpens the scarcity of resources and poverty of the disaffected group, thereby intensifying its grievances and the group's support for the rebellion. The Darfur and Ogaden civil wars seem to have been intensified by the environmental degradation. Often the rebels also attack establishments that they consider to contribute to the scarcity of resources or exploit their resources. The Ogaden National Liberation Front (ONLF), for example, attacked a Chinese oil company on 24 April 2007 killing some 74 people. Among the reasons the Front allegedly gave was that the company was clearing land making it more difficult for local pastoralists to feed their livestock. In such cases the rebellion is over broader issues of marginalization and deprivation but they are intensified by the scarcity that environmental degradation sets off. The conflicts in the Nuba Mountains and the Red Sea region of Sudan also revolve around land issues and scarcity largely brought about by land policy. However, in these cases too, the environmental degradation has contributed to the conflicts by intensifying the scarcity.

Inter-State Conflicts

As noted in chapter 2, most of the countries of the region have territorial and boundary disputes. But such problems are not related to resource scarcity propelled by environmental degradation. There are, however, some tensions related to water scarcity and the sharing of water from rivers. The Omo River, which flows from southern Ethiopia to Lake Turkana in northern Kenya is one of the points of tension. Ethiopia is currently building the Gibe III Dam, diverting water from the river for the stated goal of generating hydroelectric power. The dam is anticipated to generate 6,500 GW/year contributing to Ethiopia's ambition of becoming a major hydroelectric power exporter earning about $407 million annually. Ethiopia has also built dams on the Tekezé River, a tributary of the Nile. Once the hydropower projects are fully operational, earnings from power exports are expected to surpass those from coffee. There are fears, however, that the Gibe III Dam will dramatically alter the Omo River's flood cycle adversely affecting over 200,000 agro-pastoralists who depend on the river's annual flood to support riverbank cultivation and livestock grazing. Various animal and bird species and biodiversity of the Lower Omo Valley, which is a UNESCO World Heritage Site, may also be destroyed. It is also feared that Kenya's Lake Turkana, which receives roughly 90 per cent of its water from the Omo River, will be affected by the dam for a number of reasons. First filling the dam with a holding capacity of 11.75 billion m^3 will take over two years, during which time the volume of water flowing into the lake will be severely reduced. The lake has already been shrinking and the dam could expedite the process. Second, the dam is likely to cause a loss of a significant amount of water due to evaporation and underground leakage through cracks that are likely to be caused by shifting ground (Avery, 2012; International Rivers, 2013). Finally, Ethiopia is likely to develop irrigation projects once the dam is complete, further reducing the flow of water to Lake Turkana. There have been protests by the communities in the Lower Omo Valley, environmentalists, such as the Friends of Lake Turkana, and some of Kenya's parliamentarians. UNESCO has also expressed objections to the construction of the dam due to its implications to the Lower Omo habitat. It is not clear, however, if the Kenyan government has expressed overt opposition to the construction of the dam.

Tensions over the Nile Waters

Another major source of inter-state tension is the sharing of the waters of the Nile. Eleven countries, including Burundi, the DRC, Egypt, Eritrea, Ethiopia, Kenya, Rwanda, South Sudan, Sudan, Tanzania and Uganda, have some claim to the Nile waters. But a series of colonial era treaties allot the right to use the Nile waters to only two countries, Egypt and Sudan. One of the treaties is the 15 May 1902 treaty between Great Britain and Emperor Menelik II of Ethiopia. According to that treaty, the Ethiopian emperor committed himself not to construct or allow to be constructed any work across the Blue Nile, Lake Tana or the Sobat, which would arrest the flow of their waters, except in agreement with the government of Great Britain.

Another treaty that determined the allotment of the Nile waters is the 7 May 1929 agreement between Egypt and the Anglo-Egyptian Sudan. This treaty gave a near monopoly, roughly 92 per cent, of the Nile's water to Egypt and the remaining, roughly 8 per cent, was allotted to Sudan. The upstream states were denied any rights to control or claim any of the Nile's waters. Moreover, that treaty empowered Egypt to veto any projects by upstream countries that would impinge on its share of the waters of the Nile.

Understandably, the upper riparian states have now challenged the colonial era treaties, which they consider grossly unfair. In May 2010, six upstream states, Ethiopia, Kenya, Burundi, Tanzania, Rwanda and Uganda, signed a Cooperative Framework Agreement to seek more water from the River Nile. Egypt and Sudan are however opposed to the new framework. The upper riparian states have also begun to construct projects that utilize water from the Nile. The Ethiopian government has built the Tekezé Arch Dam, which will add 300 megawatts (MW)/year to Ethiopia's power grid. Another project in the Nile Basin is the Tana Beles hydropower plant, which will generate 460 MW. Ethiopia's Grand

Renaissance Dam, which currently is under construction, is the largest and has already created tensions between Ethiopia and Egypt. The East African Community (EAC) countries, including Kenya, Tanzania, Uganda, Rwanda and Burundi, have committed themselves to develop their agriculture through irrigation schemes as well as to develop hydroelectric power generation capacity. The Bujagali Hydroelectric Power Station is among the projects in the EAC area exploiting the Nile waters. The Ugandan government is also said to be developing a national twenty-five-year master plan on irrigation to respond to droughts which have affected the country's food security. Burundi, Rwanda, Tanzania and Uganda have joined together to exploit the Kagera River, which feeds into Lake Victoria.

No doubt, the projects constructed by the upper riparian countries would have some impact on the volume of the Nile water that flows to Sudan and Egypt. The colonial era treaties are, however, unsustainable, since the upstream countries, which are being ravaged by cyclical droughts, are no longer willing to abide by the colonial era treaties, which deny them access to the waters of their rivers. A fairer new agreement will not be easy to reach, however, since Egypt and Sudan are likely to resist giving up much of the quota they have enjoyed. Tensions are, thus, likely to grow until an agreement is reached. Direct violent conflicts over the Nile waters are not likely, however, since the problem cannot be settled by violence.

Future Potential Implications of Unmitigated Environmental Degradation

According to many experts, the warming trend of the region's temperature is expected to accelerate and the frequency of the droughts is likely to at least continue in a similar trajectory as the last forty or so years. The population growth rate is also not expected to decline significantly. As noted, Ethiopia's population is, for example, expected to reach 150 million by 2050. Under such a scenario the Horn of Africa would find itself in a cataclysmic crisis in a matter of decades. The economic sectors that employ over 70 per cent of the region's population, pastoral and subsistence farming systems, would likely be unsustainable. If every three or four years a new cycle of drought destroys their livestock, pastoral and agro-pastoral communities would be likely to abandon that mode of production. Subsistence farmers also do not have the level of productivity that would enable them to accumulate surplus and ride over the drought cycles. They too are likely to abandon the system in droves. The question is where these population groups go to earn a living since the rest of the economy is not expanding rapidly enough to absorb them. Indeed, this is a frightening scenario because it can lead to total regional chaos.

The adverse impacts of the droughts are not limited to the rural communities. They bring about serious economy-wide disruptions since they affect the water and energy supply of the whole region. During the 2009 drought, for example, newspapers in Kenya reported that Lake Kamnarok in Kenya's Rift Valley had dried up (Kiprotich, 2009). The death of the lake brought about the doom of wildlife including an estimated 10,000 crocodiles. Water points in Lake Nakuru National Park also dried up while Lake Naivasha shrank considerably. Nairobi's three reservoirs, including those at Ndakaini, Sasumua and Mombasa were also dangerously low causing water crisis in Nairobi. In addition, the critical hydro-electric stations on the Tana River in Kenya had to be shut down due to a fall in its dam's water levels causing power shortages. Some factories had to shut down in Nakuru, including Flamingo Bottlers, Coil Products Kenya Limited and Kapi Limited, due to water shortages.

During the same period Ethiopia also witnessed the death of Lake Haramaya in the Oromia region. The country had to engage in water and electricity rationing, due to low water levels in power-generating dams. The water shortage and power outages are likely to have affected the country's overall economy. The water and energy crisis in 2009 was not limited to Kenya and Ethiopia. Eritrea, Somalia, Sudan and even parts of Uganda also faced serious drought problems. The dry river bed that cuts through Hargeisa, in Somaliland, gives no indication that the city of roughly 900,000 inhabitants was once blessed with a river flowing through its middle.

Water shortages will continue to intensify shortages of arable land and land for pasture. Such shortages are likely to increase the scarcity-driven conflicts. They will also be a major threat to the coexistence of humans and wildlife, as they have to compete for the same resources. Wildlife will be the loser in such conflicts. However, as the animals vanish, the lucrative tourist industry in the region may also be irreparably damaged.

In addition to the consequences for economic production and conflicts, the water and power shortages will have serious health implications. Water shortages result in sanitation problems creating conditions for epidemics, such as cholera. These problems are likely to be particularly serious in crowded cities with large slums, such as Nairobi and Addis Ababa.

Can the Region Control the Degradation and its Impacts?

As pointed out at the outset of this chapter, the Horn of Africa's environmental degradation is attributable to global climatic changes and regional human activities. Reversing the global factors, even if possible, is beyond the region's control. However, controlling regional human activities which contribute to the degradation by changing land-use and land-cover patterns is within the region's reach since there are many policy options that could make a positive difference in the region with regard to these issues. Development policy geared towards transforming the subsistence farmers and pastoralists could, for example, reduce poverty and thereby the overexploitation of land and forest resources by impoverished rural communities. Abandoning large-scale land-takings, which concentrate rural communities in smaller farming and grazing areas, would also help in reducing overexploitation of land resources by increasing the availability of land. Alternatively, the communities whose land is given to investors could be made partners in the commercial farms (as shareholders or rent collectors) since they are contributing their land to the projects. Such measures would reduce the poverty triggered by evictions. Land-cover could also be gradually restored by controlling overgrazing and felling of trees as well as through large-scale reforestation activities. Rural electrification is another measure that could help reduce reliance on wood energy and the cutting of trees for fuel.

Reversing the degradation process will be neither easy nor quick; nevertheless, policies such as those identified above could slowly begin to rehabilitate the environment. The restorative process, however, requires the political commitment by the states of the region to reorient their development strategy. It also requires their ability to coordinate the efforts of all stakeholders. Failure by a single country, especially one of the larger ones, such as Ethiopia, to implement restorative policies would undermine the efforts of all the rest, since the effects of environmental degradation cannot be confined to national boundaries. Whether the region's alarming degradation process is reversed or the region continues in its present trajectory will, thus, depend on the political will of the states of the region to reorient their development strategies and to coordinate their restorative measures.

Given the prevailing neglect of rural communities by the governments in the region, however, one can hardly be optimistic that the measures necessary for reversing the degradation process will be undertaken. Moreover, as the earlier chapters have shown, environmental degradation is not the only crisis the Greater Horn is facing. The security and economic crises are the other components of the region's general problems. Since environmental, security and economic crises are closely intertwined and mutually reinforcing, the governments of the region would need a comprehensive approach to deal with them all. Unfortunately, there is little indication that such a comprehensive policy approach is in the works.

Prospects for Democracy, Integration and Stability

Introduction

At the outset of this book a number of categories of factors which have collectively rendered the Greater Horn of Africa a zone of conflict were identified. One set of factors relates to the conflict-engendering contexts left behind by pre-colonial and colonial empires. Among the key aspects of these legacies were the nature of the relations the empires established with different segments of the populations; the partitioning of various ethnic groups into several countries; the economic and institutional fragmentation of the region's societies; the uneven, economic, political and cultural relations that were cultivated among various identities; and the poorly delineated inter-state boundaries. The impacts of such legacies have continued to engender inter-state, state–identity and inter-identity conflicts in the region.

A second category of factors relates to the nature of the post-colonial state, including the divergence of its economic and institutional systems from those adhered to by large segments of society. Excessive concentration of power in the executive branch of government is another critical deformity in the structures of the state. This problem arises from the absence of checks and balances and accountability within the various organizations of the state, mainly due to an insufficient level of independence of the constituent organizations of the state from the executive branch of government. This absence of a well-developed system of checks and balances within the structures of the state engenders various state–society and inter-elite conflicts, hinders democratization as well as effective state-building and fosters pandemic corruption by the functionaries of the state.

Another category of factors relates to the poor management of diversity by the state and the ensuing crisis of nation-building. Failure to develop institutional systems of governance that accommodate equitably the interests and cultural values of the disparate ethnic, clan, religious or regional identities within the population has rendered the state ineffective in promoting nation-building. As a result, state–identity conflicts have remained pervasive throughout the region.

A fourth category of factors relates to various forms of intervention by state and non-state actors from outside the region. The region's strategic location, along with the insecurity of autocratic leaders, who often rely on external support to stay in power, and the failure of regional governance to coordinate foreign policies of member states in a manner that mitigates external meddling in the region's affairs, have exposed the region to endless external intervention, which often intensifies and in some cases initiates conflicts.

A fifth category of factors is the alarming rate of environmental degradation, which, along with rapid population growth, has culminated in land and water scarcity, widespread economic and social dislocations and rampant resource-based conflicts. The failure of the states of the region to develop long-term strategies to address this unfolding crisis and to cooperate in combating environmental degradation and in coordinating resource utilization has contributed to the cyclical catastrophic famines and various conflicts that beset the region.

This chapter attempts to explain how a contextualized comprehensive approach to democratization, along with a broad-ranging regional integration, can help the region extricate itself from being one of the hottest conflict zones in the global system by enabling it to address many of the identified conflict-generating socioeconomic categories of factors. A contextualized democratization and effective regional integration can also help the region in reducing unwanted external intervention and in coping with the environmental crisis. The chapter is organized into four parts. The first part aims to explain briefly why the current election-centred liberal approach to democratization in the region is unlikely to lead to substantive democratization, which could mitigate conflicts and address the problems of diversity management by ensuring equitable citizenship rights to all segments of the population. The second part introduces what a contextualized comprehensive approach to democratization would entail and how it could address many of the identified conflict-fostering factors in the region. The third part of the chapter attempts to explain how a multifaceted integration scheme could complement a contextualized comprehensive democratization in transforming the conflict factors in the region. The last part examines the prospects for a successful implementation of a contextualized comprehensive democratization and regional integration in the region in the near future.

Limitations of the Existing Approach to Democratization

The countries of the region, with the notable exception of Eritrea, have all implemented some of the institutions of liberal democracy. Most of them have undertaken steps in liberalizing the press, despite periodic clampdowns when it becomes threatening to regime stability. Most of them have also established multiparty systems. Kenya allowed a multiparty system in 1991, followed by Djibouti in 1992 and Ethiopia in 1995. Uganda also followed suit in 2005. Most of these countries have also conducted several rounds of elections, although they are hardly contested on a level playing field. Often dominant parties put in place various types of restrictions on opposition parties in order to undermine their ability to become effective contenders.[49] Moreover, the elections are often marred by irregularities.

While not insignificant, these liberalization efforts, which are often donor-driven, have not produced substantive democratization which could transform the socioeconomic conditions of citizens. The substance of democracy, which is supposed to result from the procedures of democracy, empowers the general population to control decision-making in the public sphere. Such empowerment of the general population in the African context is likely to produce policies that alleviate poverty, safeguard human rights, end the marginalization of various segments of society, bring about peaceful settlement of conflicts and make public services, such as health care, education and information, accessible to the general populace, including the segment that operates under the traditional economic systems.

Under the existing approach to democratization some of the elections have resulted in violent conflicts instead of resolving conflicts. The 2007 election in Kenya and the 2005 election in Ethiopia were the most violent ones within the region. Elections, while essential, have often become worrisome enterprises because of their potential to foster violent conflicts. More importantly, the election-centred approach has not addressed the broader obstacles to substantive democratization. As a result, it has made little difference in reducing the region's conflicts or in improving the quality of life of the populations. Human rights violations remain rampant throughout the region, as various reports by human rights groups indicate. Abject poverty and deprivation also remain widespread. Lack of progress in substantive democratization in the region raises two important questions. One is why elections tend to lead to violent conflicts instead of to peaceful succession to power. The second is if the region's democratization process in its present form has the necessary requisites to succeed in producing substantive democratization.

The existing election-centred democratization approach faces a complex set of problems that render it highly unlikely to lead to substantive and sustainable democracy in much of Africa. One critical problem relates to the dichotomy of economic and institutional systems in the region. Liberal democracy is a form of democracy that requires a capitalist economic system to function properly. The countries that practise liberal democracy are countries where the capitalist system is the dominant mode of production. In many cases these countries were capitalist economies before they implemented liberal democracy. The countries of the Greater Horn, like much of the rest of Africa, are, however, still transitional societies with the parallel existence of capitalist and non-capitalist (traditional) economic and institutional systems. As noted in chapter 1, the overwhelming majority of the region's population is engaged in the traditional subsistence farming and pastoral economic systems. This segment of the population largely adheres to traditional institutional systems of governance that correspond with their economic systems.[50] Liberal democracy faces a number of problems operating under such dichotomous socioeconomic systems. Some of the capitalist property rights norms and resource allocation mechanisms it advances are largely incompatible with the existing modes of production and their corresponding institutional systems and the cultural values of the populations in the traditional economic system. In much of traditional (mostly rural) Africa allegiances are often based on ethnic links, decisions are generally made in a consensual manner and conflicts are resolved in a reconciliatory non-adversarial manner. Competitive elections that produce winners who monopolize the power of policy-making do not fit well with this cultural context. Under the circumstances, liberal democracy would need to undergo major modifications in order to become relevant to the populations in the non-capitalist traditional economic sectors.

Two decades ago, Claude Ake (1993) initiated enquiry into democratization under fragmented modes of production. Unfortunately, much work remains to be done on what approaches to democratization would be operable under conditions of parallel economic and institutional systems of transitional societies. The consociational model of democracy (Lijphart, 1969, 1977) attempts to adjust the democratization approach in order to deal with divided societies. Among the key elements of the consociational approach are grand coalitions to include rival groups in government, autonomy for ethnic groups, proportional representation and minority rights to a veto on vital issues. The consociational model represents a significant adjustment of liberal democracy to make it operable in conditions where nation-building is not well developed. It does not, however, deal with conditions of fragmented modes of production.

Another critical obstacle to the success of the election-centred democratization approach relates to the structures of the African state. As explained in chapter 4, the state embodies a set of interlocking institutions that collectively organize socioeconomic life in a given country. Among the component institutions of the state are: the bureaucracy, the military, the judiciary and constitutional court, the central bank, the electoral commission and the government (with the executive and legislative branches), which coordinates and manages the activities of the other constituent institutions. Building a sustainable democratic system requires that the component institutions of the state enjoy a measure of independence from each other, and especially from the executive branch of government, so that they act as checks and balances on each other. Such a structural arrangement allows accountability within the component institutions of the state and safeguards a space for civil society to engage in the political process. Independence of the judiciary and constitutional courts, for example, is expected to protect the rights of citizens from possible transgressions by the executive as well as the legislature, which may pass laws that may infringe on the rights of citizens in general or certain segments of the population. Independence of the legislature also aims to ensure representation of citizens in decision-making. If the legislature is a rubberstamp of the executive branch of government, as usually is the case in the Greater Horn region, it can hardly represent the interests of its constituency and there would hardly be separation of powers between the executive and the legislative branches of government. Needless to say, independence of the electoral commission is also essential so that it protects the integrity of elections. Concentration of power within the executive and autocratic leadership is the likely outcome when the component institutions of the state lack the necessary level of independence from each other and from the executive organ of government. Under such conditions multiparty systems and competitive elections are unlikely to advance the cause of democracy. Instead, they will, at best, become a mechanism for rotating ruling parties and leaders without diminishing the concentration of power in the hands of the executive or strongmen who dominate the executive branch of government. In other words, elections become a means of legitimization of autocracy even if they bring about changes of leaders and ruling parties.[51]

Another critical requisite for establishing a sustainable democratic system is building a community of citizens under shared institutions (nation-building) by erecting institutions of governance that manage diversity by accommodating the interests, values and aspirations of the various identities that comprise the citizenry. Democracy is generally understood to be a political system that allows the general population through its elected representatives to control decision-making in the public sphere. Under conditions where the general population is fractured along various diversity fault-lines, including modes of production, the institutions of governance and ethnicity, religion and region, however, the general population can hardly form a community of citizens that can control decisions. In the absence of proper diversity management, some identities may be left out while others may engage in active conflict against the state or against other identities. Given such societal fragmentation, political parties are also likely to be formed along identity lines, as in Ethiopia and Kenya. In these situations elections, especially those that are based on winner-takes-all arrangements, can hardly legitimize outcomes and promote a democratic system. Rather, they are likely to be associated with societal polarization and violent conflicts.

In the absence of accommodating institutions of diversity management, identity-related conflicts are likely to undermine the processes of nation-building and state-building, as well as democratization. Elections carried out in the absence of shared institutions of diversity management merely attempt to give legitimacy to the winners to monopolize power and to rule without the consent of identities with grievances.

Elections, under such conditions, tend to create or sharpen conflicts rather than resolve them.

The countries of the Greater Horn, like those in much of the rest of Africa, suffer from the prevalence of the identified obstacles to the success of liberal democracy. They are all characterized by (1) dichotomous economic and institutional systems, especially between rural and urban areas;[52] (2) the deformities in state structures, which concentrate power within the executive and blur the distinction between government and state; and (3) the absence of institutions of diversity management resulting in low levels of nation-building, which are reflected by high levels of diversity-related conflicts. In such a context, substantive democracy is not likely to be attained by merely establishing multiparty systems and conducting elections. The approach to democratization would need to be reconceived in order to address the above identified obstacles and thereby establish the structural requisites for a democratic system of governance.

A Contextualized and Comprehensive Approach to Democratization

The analysis in the foregoing section has shown that successful democratization of the countries of the Greater Horn, as well as of the rest of Africa, is highly unlikely under the existing liberal approach to democratization. This section proposes an alternative approach that takes into account the conditions and challenges that prevail on the ground. More specifically, it is suggested that the approach and institutions of democratization need to reconcile the fragmented economic and institutional systems so that they are relevant for both socioeconomic spaces. The new approach also needs to be comprehensive enough to address simultaneously the key democracy-hindering conditions, including the deformities in the structures of the state and the problems of diversity management and nation-building. Needless to say, the new approach has also to establish the institutions of democracy, including civil liberties, and the institution of representation through credible elections. Figure 8.1 attempts to sketch a contextualized and comprehensive approach to substantive democratization.

As the figure illustrates, a comprehensive democratization approach, which produces substantive democracy (components listed in the box E), needs to incorporate all the measures represented in the boxes labelled A through D. As noted already, the presence of parallel and unequal economic and institutional systems with different property rights laws, distinct decision-making systems and different conflict resolution practices impedes democratization by fostering unequal access to participation in the political process by the segments of the population in the parallel socioeconomic systems. For a variety of reasons, the population in the traditional sector has limited access to participation. This same segment of

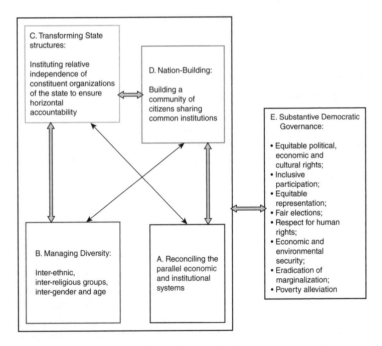

Figure 8.1. A contextualized and comprehensive approach to democratization

the population also faces serious economic and cultural marginalization.

Reconciling the fragmented socioeconomic systems and addressing the marginalization of the traditional sector are among the most challenging aspects of diversity management. Yet, it would be unrealistic to expect a sustainable democratic system when the overwhelming majority of the population operates largely outside the state's formal institutions of governance with limited influence on policy and under a precarious subsistence economy. Facilitating the participation in the democratization process of the population in the subsistence sector entails a number of changes. Among them are reconciliation of the parallel socioeconomic systems, which includes: (1) granting legal recognition to customary property rights laws, especially land rights by rural communities; (2) establishing administrative structures that ensure the participation of leaders of rural communities in local governance, from which they can influence both local and national policies including those pertaining to allocation of public services and other resources; (3) supporting the transformation of the subsistence sector of the economy; (4) reforming traditional institutions to safeguard women's rights; and (5) recognizing customary judicial systems, which already adjudicate large proportions of disputes, especially in rural areas, as shown in chapter 2.

Another critical requisite for successful democratization is nation-building, i.e. building a community of citizens who share common institutions. It is hard to conceive successful democracy in divided communities that frequently engage in violent conflicts. A system of institutions that manages diversity properly by accommodating the interests and cultural values of diverse identities within the citizenry needs to be established in order to promote a peaceful process of nation-building. Building appropriate institutions of diversity management is a rather complex process because it requires the participation and consent of the complex web of diverse groups in establishing them. In other words, building a workable democratic system requires a participatory process of establishing the guiding institutions and principles upon which nation-building is founded. A properly functioning democratic system would, in turn, strengthen the institutions of diversity management.

State structures which do not allow relative independence of the constituent institutions of the state impede democratization by concentrating power in the hands of the executive organ of government. As noted earlier, absence of horizontal accountability hinders the establishment of a political space where civil society engages in the political process. Under such state structures, multiparty elections, even if they are held regularly, essentially serve to rotate parties and the political elite in power without democratizing the system of governance. A contextualized democratization approach would have to transform such democracy-hindering state structures by establishing the necessary level of independence of the different organizations of the state to ensure checks and balances and accountability.

Why a Contextualized Comprehensive Approach Would Enhance Democratization

The contextualized comprehensive approach to democracy proposed here is an approach that builds the institutions of democracy in a manner that reflects the socioeconomic context that exists in the region. It is also an approach that attempts to promote democratization in the context of parallel socioeconomic systems, for which the existing election-centred approach to democratization is ill-suited. Moreover, it is comprehensive enough to address simultaneously the various challenges that hinder democratization. In other words, building the necessary requisites for democracy becomes part of the democratization process rather than an exogenous activity. Transforming the traditional socioeconomic system and reconciling fragmented institutions, for example, become an integral part of the democratization process rather than a separate policy issue. Diversity management and nation-building are also part of the process of establishing a democratic system since they are the foundations for a sustainable process of democratic governance.

The contextualized comprehensive approach to democratization has a number of advantages over the existing election-centric approach in promoting substantive democratization and in addressing many of the conflict-engendering factors in the region. One of its advantages is that it attempts to build the foundations for democratic governance instead of attempting to establish democratic institutions where the foundations for their success do not exist. Reconciling the dichotomous economic and institutional systems is perhaps the most critical component of the contextualized comprehensive approach. As noted, it is difficult to conceive successful democratization under dichotomous economic and institutional spaces. Without reconciling the parallel socioeconomic spaces, it also becomes hard to bring into the political process the populations that operate within the marginalized subsistence sector and its corresponding institutional systems. The contextualized approach, by pursuing policies that transform the traditional system and empower the population in the subsistence sector, would be more likely to bring all segments of society into the political process and thereby make the democratic system relevant to all segments of the citizenry.

Given the pandemic problem of uneven development and marginalization of various ethnic and religious groups and women and youth in the Greater Horn region, effective diversity management would be essential in order to bring such groups into the political process and to broaden the scope of democracy beyond elections. As explained in chapter 4, state–identity conflicts are largely triggered by grievances and disagreements about the terms of incorporation of identity groups into the state and about uneven distribution of citizenship rights (access to political and economic opportunities and cultural privileges) among identity groups. Building institutions that ensure equitable access to all rights that citizenship awards, including participation so that the terms of nation-building are agreed upon by all, enhances the prospects of success of peaceful nation-building as well as of substantive democratization. Such agreements would also mitigate election-related violence by lowering the costs of losing elections to contestants and their supporters.

Transforming the structures of the state by ensuring the relative independence of the different constituent institutions of the state is another critical strength of the contextualized and comprehensive approach. Such transformation of the structures of the state creates the potential to:

- Reduce the concentration of political power in the hands of the executive and to safeguard against despotic rule;
- Enhance horizontal accountability within the constituent organizations of the state;
- Safeguard the political space for civil society;
- Enhance legitimacy of the state and promote synergy in state–society relations and thereby reduce state–society conflicts;
- Enhance legitimacy of elections and reduce post-election conflicts;
- Reduce corruption through greater accountability;
- Reduce the insecurity of the political elite and thereby reduce the need for them to rely on their ethnic roots and external actors.

As argued so far, an integrated approach to reconciling the dichotomous economic and institutional spaces, creating institutions of diversity management and transforming the structures of the state promotes substantive democratization. As figure 8.1 depicts, substantive democratization, in turn, strengthens the foundations of democracy propelling an upward spiral. In other words, substantive democratization would enhance the reconciliation process of the parallel socioeconomic spaces, strengthen the institutions of diversity management and solidify the democracy-fostering structures of the state. Such an upward spiralling of the democratization process can also be expected to mitigate the pandemic ethnic and post-election conflicts that ravage the region. As the institutions of diversity management become more effective, the intra-state conflicts are likely to be reduced substantially. The inter-state conflicts and tensions, which often spill over from intra-state conflicts, are also likely to decline. The stability gains, along with the progress in democratization, can also be expected to produce economic gains, which, in turn, are likely to strengthen the stability as well as the democratization process.

Regional Integration and its Potential Contributions

Regional integration is a mechanism which has the potential to complement the contextualized approach to democratization in addressing many of the conflicts in the Greater Horn. There is a general consensus that, appropriately designed and implemented, regional integration has the potential to foster regional peace and promote socioeconomic development of member countries. Although the performance of most African regional integration schemes, including IGAD (Intergovernmental Authority of Development), does not match the positive expectations of regional integration, the underperformance of these schemes rests more on poor implementation and on the conditions under which they operate rather than on the integration mechanism itself.

Some argue that 'regional economic integration in Africa is often poorly conceived and in some regions suffers from chronic duplication, whilst the economic and political bases for it are often woefully lacking' (Draper and Qobo, 2007: 4). Views are highly polarized on what the appropriate design and scope of African integration schemes should be and on why the motivation and commitment of leaders to properly implement the integration agreements are weak. Some contend that regional integration schemes should be outward looking (open and export promoting) to serve as a gateway for the integration of African economies with the global economic system (Niekerk, 2005). Others view unregulated openness as endangering regional economic diversification and suggest that industrial policy coordination along with measures to reduce transaction costs are more appropriate designs. These debates reflect the long-standing disagreements about the appropriate roles of the market and policy. A regional integration that aims to address both conflicts and economic problems cannot be merely market-driven. Policy has also a critical role to play in promoting peace and stability, diversifying the economy and developing infrastructure. Market and policy partnership would, thus, be indispensable. The policy, however, has to be a product of democratic decision and aimed at advancing broad social interests to become effective.

Despite these debates about the appropriate type of design, the benefits of regional integration are rarely disputed. This section of the chapter attempts to explain how regional integration, in concert with contextualized democratization, could promote peace and stability as well as economic transformation in the Greater Horn region.

Potential Benefits of Regional Integration

Regional integration is a set of multidimensional formal and informal agreements that tie the component member countries in some form of cooperative partnership, creating new forms of supra-state organization, which coexists with the traditional state-led form of organization (de Lombaerde and van Langenhove, 2005). While the goals of informal integration may vary widely, depending on the interests of the non-governmental actors involved, the general goals of formal integration include: (1) maintaining peace, (2) attaining greater multipurpose capabilities, such as enhancing economic development, (3) accomplishing a range of specific tasks and (4) gaining a new self-image and role identity (Deutsch, 1968).

The Greater Horn's formal integration scheme, IGAD, was established in 1986 initially to coordinate regional cooperation in combating drought. Accordingly, the original name of the organization was the Intergovernmental Authority on Drought and Development. However, it upgraded itself into a multidimensional integration scheme in 1996. Among the specific goals of IGAD are promoting regional peace and stability, enhancing economic development, managing environmental problems, promoting food security, coordinating complementary transportation infrastructure and reducing dependency of member countries on external powers.

Regional integration schemes vary in orientation and scope and often are based on different approaches. The original founding of IGAD was essentially based on the neo-functionalist approach to integration. This approach operated on the assumption that success of cooperation in specific areas or projects among states leads to a gradual spillover to cooperation in more areas, with the possibility of ultimately culminating in full integration. Neo-functionalism recognizes that integration is likely to fail if the supra-state or intergovernmental authority, which leads the integration, wrongly guides member states. However, neo-functionalism largely fails to consider the possibilities of stagnation or even reversal of the integration process, due to various factors, including political conflicts among the member states. There are various other general theories of integration, including liberal intergovernmentalism and international relations, and comparative politics approaches. For our purposes, however, the organizational analysis theory (approach) is more suitable.

From the angle of organizational theory, organizations, such as those of regional integration, flourish so long as they create value for various groups or stakeholders, who join and stay active members provided that the inducements they receive are attractive. Sometimes, it is possible that member states will forgo the benefits from integration under conditions of hostilities with other members of the integration scheme. If the stakeholders are expanded beyond states, however, withdrawals might be less likely to happen since the organization creates value to a greater array of stakeholders and thereby expands the social forces that serve to perpetuate it. Moreover, under broad membership if withdrawals take place, they are less likely to undermine the organization, given the greater size of supportive stakeholders. From this perspective it seems to be imperative that IGAD broadens its constituency by working with civil society organizations, professional associations, identity leaders, etc. In other words, the approach to the region's integration needs to be both top-down as well as bottom-up. Needless to say, the supra-state body also needs to surround itself with competent and effective technocrats, who realize that only success justifies the existence of the organization.

As noted throughout this book, devastating conflicts, grinding poverty, alarming rates of environmental degradation and unrelenting external intervention are among the most crucial problems the Greater Horn countries face. Regional integration can play an indispensable role in tackling these problems. A brief look at IGAD shows that it has not been effective in dealing with most of these challenges, despite the organization's potential to make considerable difference.

There are broadly six types of conflict that plague the Greater Horn, as outlined in chapter 1. Two are domestic and cross-border inter-identity (inter-communal) conflicts that largely, although not exclusively, revolve around resource scarcity aggravated by environmental degradation. The third type of conflict is inter-state conflicts, which in most cases are fought through proxies. The fourth type is state–identity conflicts, which are manifestations of poor diversity management and low levels of nation-building and state-building. The fifth type of conflict is the one-sided atrocities perpetrated against civilians by governments and armed opposition groups. The last type is the conflicts among rebel groups.

An effective regional integration scheme which commands the mandate of its member states and their populations can help in addressing most of these conflicts. However, it can only do so when member states create the political atmosphere that allows the supra-state body the necessary level of authority to establish codes of conduct that binds its members. A regional integration scheme is likely to be ineffective in the absence of the necessary level of authority and/or in the absence of commitment by leaders of member states to cooperate in addressing the conflicts in line with the directives of the regional body. When member states have the political will to resort to peaceful means of resolving conflicts, in accordance with established norms of the supra-state organization, however, regional integration becomes a major enabling resource.

Through its Protocol of a Conflict Early Warning and Response Mechanism (CEWARN), which was established in January 2002, IGAD has made some progress in at least developing early warning mechanisms. However, CEWARN's role is essentially limited to cross-border conflicts among pastoral communities. Its activities have been mostly in the areas of livestock rustling, conflict over grazing and water points, smuggling and illegal trade, nomadic movements, refugees, landmines and banditry. These cross-border inter-communal conflicts, which are in the purview of CEWARN, constitute only a small portion of the inter-communal conflicts in the region. However, addressing such conflicts is not insignificant. Moreover, CEWARN's early warning system can also be applied to addressing domestic-level inter-communal conflicts that revolve around the problems of resource scarcity.

Despite the potential gains effective regional integration makes possible, IGAD has not been successful in dealing with the most challenging types of conflicts that devastate the region. One type of conflict that a regional integration scheme is expected to be effective in resolving is inter-state conflicts. One of the key factors for this type of conflict in the Greater Horn is border disputes. Over 70,000 people perished in the 1998–2000 border war between Eritrea and Ethiopia. Border disputes between the two Sudans also have the potential to explode into highly destructive and enduring wars. IGAD has yet to develop mechanisms for resolving border disputes before they erupt into violent conflicts, even though all of the countries of the region face border disputes of various magnitudes.

Most of the inter-state conflicts in the region are fought through proxies. The countries of the Greater Horn have intervened in each other's internal conflicts, mostly by supporting each other's rebel groups, but also by cooperating with friendly regimes in suppressing rebellions. As already noted, Sudan, for example, supported the Eritrean People's Liberation Front (EPLF) and the Tigray People's Liberation Front (TPLF) against the Mengistu regime of Ethiopia. Ethiopia reciprocated by supporting the Sudan People's Liberation Movement (SPLM) against the Sudanese regime. Ultimately, both countries ended up losing their wars and two new states, Eritrea and South Sudan, emerged as the region's new states. Eritrea currently supports various Ethiopian rebel groups against the Ethiopian regime, while the Ethiopian regime also supports some Eritrean rebel groups. Uganda and Sudan have supported each other's rebellions and Sudan and South Sudan have already begun to engage in proxy wars against each other. Interventions by Ethiopia and Kenya in Somalia in support of the Transitional Federal Government against the Union of Islamic Courts (UIC) and al-Shebab are much more direct. Again, an effective regional integration scheme can regulate the behaviour of member states so that they don't unilaterally interfere, either directly or through proxies, in the conflicts of member states. It can also establish effective mechanisms that settle peacefully inter-state conflicts, such as border disputes, so that member states do not resort to violence.

IGAD's failure in dealing with direct and proxy inter-state conflicts is rather conspicuous. Yet, resolving inter-state conflicts remains an area where a regional integration scheme can play a critical role by establishing and implementing protocols for resolving conflicts between member states. Failing to resolve such conflicts can also be detrimental to the regional body itself. Conflicts among member states undermine the very existence of an integration scheme, since member countries who are engaged in conflict with each other are unlikely to remain under the same tent of an integration scheme, let alone cooperate in building it up. Suspension of Eritrea's IGAD membership in protest of the organization's failure to oppose Ethiopia's direct intervention in Somalia in 2006 and Ethiopia's refusal to allow reinstatement of Eritrea's membership in the organization has weakened IGAD. It also sets a precedent for possible similar cases in the future. There is little doubt that the organization needs to establish clear laws to govern such issues and it also needs to be governed by the rule of law and not by ad hoc decisions which are influenced by short-term political goals of member states.

State–identity conflicts are the most common of the conflicts in the region. Often these conflicts also become fertile ground for proxy wars among states causing economic destruction and disruption, gross human rights abuses, and refugee flows and internal displacements of large numbers of people. Regional integration has the potential to become a positive force in dealing with these conflicts also. Many of the state–identity conflicts in the region involve identities that are partitioned into two or more countries. Dynamic integration with open borders can allow identities that are split by national boundaries to have the freedom for greater interaction with their kinsmen across state lines. Such freedom, in turn, is likely to reduce their grievances with the states, which they regard as symbolizing their fragmentation. Identities, such as the Somalis, Afar, Beja and many others, which are often involved in conflicts against their respective states, would benefit from regional integration that has arrangements for free mobility of people across borders.

An effective integration scheme can also reduce state–identity conflicts by developing mechanisms of diversity management that govern member states and by overseeing their proper implementation. Moreover, the supra-state organization that guides the integration scheme can become a neutral mediator in such conflicts, to the extent that it can assert its independence and establish a record of capable leadership.

Similarly, effective regional integration can reduce one-sided atrocities against civilians, especially those committed by the state but also those committed by non-state actors. It can put political and economic pressure or even coordinate various other measures (incentives and disincentives) against states or rebel groups that commit atrocities against civilian populations. Membership in an integration scheme requires adhering to certain codes of behaviour that govern member states. If the supra-state organization fails to regulate the behaviour of its member states and remains silent when they abuse their civilian populations, then it loses popular legitimacy. Erosion of legitimacy, in turn, undermines its ability to promote integration as it fails to build a constituency for integration among the general population of the region.

IGAD presently suffers from a lack of constituency within civil society and has yet to build popular social forces which would propel the integration of the region.

Warding off external intervention and reducing dependency on external actors is another potential benefit a regional integration scheme can offer weak states, such as those of the Greater Horn of Africa. Regional integration can achieve these goals by integrating the markets and pulling together the resources of member countries and by coordinating their economic and foreign policy. Success in these aspects, of course, assumes that the supra-organization is committed to regional independence and that it is able to wield influence on member countries to refrain from pursuing unilateral policies that undermine the collective interests and goals. Such coordination of policy would allow the regional grouping to achieve goals that member countries would not be able to attain individually. Despite such a potential, IGAD, so far, has not distinguished itself as a promoter of regional independence or as a defender of the region from external intervention. It has particularly failed to coordinate the foreign policy of its members. At least three reasons can be identified. One reason seems to be that the leaders of member countries often obtain notable security and economic assistance from external powers and are unwilling to risk losing such benefits for untested security to be provided by the regional body. In other words, some leaders may be unwilling to sacrifice short-term gains for possible long-term regional gains. This, of course, reveals leadership deficit, since the perpetuation of dependency for short-term gains undermines the path to long-tern regional independence. Another reason is IGAD's inability to build popular social forces that defend and promote its goals. In the absence of popular support, IGAD becomes ineffective when it fails to secure the commitment of leaders of member states. A third reason is the organization's financial dependence on external actors. IGAD is hardly in a position to act as a defender of the region from external meddling and intervention as it relies on external funding for its own operations. Some of the programmes of IGAD, such as the IGAD Capacity Programme against

Terrorism (ICPAT) seem to be more a reflection of external funding than regional priority.

Poverty Alleviation and Economic Development

It is well established in the literature that promoting economic development is another potential contribution of regional integration. Given the resource and market constraints of the economies of the individual countries in the Greater Horn, economic integration and collective self-reliance are likely to mitigate constraints, enhance the region's economic development and help alleviate the crushing poverty large segments of the region's populations endure. Faster economic development and poverty reduction, in turn, can contribute to conflict reduction in a variety of ways. Economic development can, for example, give governments the ability to address grievances of marginalized identities and regions.

Integration can enhance the development of the economies of the Greater Horn region through a number of mechanisms. One is through better management of the environment and bringing under control the alarming rate of land degradation the region has faced over the last several decades. Needless to say, the deepening environmental crisis has adversely affected the region's economies in various ways, as explained in chapter 7. The environmental crisis is unlikely to be effectively addressed by individual countries. A regional approach, along with a regional body that coordinates the management activities, is likely to render far better results. IGAD has played a notable role in the areas of climate prediction and early warning systems of droughts and food insecurity. It can also contribute in various other ways, including developing drought-resistant crops and vegetation to reduce the devastating impacts of cyclical droughts.

Another mechanism through which regional integration can promote regional economic development is the establishment of development-fostering projects. IGAD has been engaged in projects such as cross-border control of HIV/AIDS (IGAD Regional HIV and AIDS Partnership), malaria and tuberculosis; the development of infrastructure including roads, railway and energy; and the establishment of a disaster preparedness facility, to name a few. The economic and social implications of reducing HIV/AIDS infections and controlling malaria and TB would be enormous. Infrastructure development is also likely to have significant impacts on economic development and on the quality of life of millions of people. IGAD's Livestock Policy Initiative also has the potential to provide significant assistance to the region's pastoral communities.

Promotion of intra-region trade is another mechanism through which integration can enhance economic development. While there are notable differences among integration schemes, the growth rates of intra-region trade in Africa have been hugely disappointing so far. Poor intra-state relations, poor transportation systems and weak financial infrastructure are among the factors that undermine the development of intra-region trade. Lack of diversification and complementarity of the economies are other factors that undermine trade-based integration schemes in Africa. However, integration, especially one that incorporates some level of regional industrial policy and promotes joint investments in carefully selected areas, can contribute in diversifying the region's economies and promote their complementarity. Moreover, although not fully developed yet, there are several economic sectors in the Greater Horn that can promote complementarity of the region's economies. Among such sectors are agriculture, energy, transportation and communication, and electricity and water supply. Three of the countries of the region, Ethiopia, South Sudan and Uganda, are landlocked and can benefit from close cooperation and integration in the areas of transportation and communication, while infrastructure development can stimulate trade and growth throughout the region. These three countries have notable potential in agricultural development as they have significant water resources and could stabilize the region's food security. They also have the potential to develop electricity resources that can benefit the whole region. Although still in early development, some of the countries of the region, including South

Sudan, Uganda and Kenya, also have oil, which would enable them to meet the energy needs of the region. With the development of these various sectors, complementarity of the region's general economies can be forged leading to enhanced intra-region trade and interdependence.

Prospects for Implementation of Contextualized Democracy and Effective Regional Integration

The foregoing discussion has argued that contextualized democratization, along with effective regional integration, has the potential to reduce conflicts and enhance economic development in the Greater Horn. It is further contended that the two processes can contribute in freeing the populations of the region from political repression and economic deprivation. However, given the failure to contextualize the democratization approach so far and the failure of IGAD to implement effective regional integration, a number of questions can be raised about the likelihood of a contextualized democratization approach and effective integration materializing in the region in the near future. Among the major questions are: (1) whether the region has the social forces that could drive these two critical changes; (2) who the champions of the changes would be; and (3) what the prospects are that these changes would take place within an intermediate time frame (roughly a decade or so).

These are difficult questions to answer, especially the question dealing with the time frame for the change. There is little doubt, however, that the dynamics and social forces for the change are building up in the region. Despite existing democratization efforts, political repression, economic, political and cultural marginalization of large segments of the population, crippling conflicts, unchecked external meddling and devastating environmental degradation continue to ravage the region. As explained in chapter 7, subsistence farming and pastoral economies, which employ the overwhelming majority of the population in the region, are fast becoming unsustainable. There is also little indication that an alternative source of employment is being created fast enough to absorb this population, which is facing displacement. Even within urban areas, the economies of the region are increasingly failing to create jobs to absorb high school and college graduates. This trend of deepening crisis has created general social dissatisfaction and various social groups who have the potential to become forces for change. Among such groups are the youth (students and high school and college graduates) and women, who bear the brunt of the unemployment and marginalization problems; pastoral and subsistence farming communities, who increasingly find their livelihoods unsustainable; ethnic groups, whose marginalization receives little attention; workers, who face stagnant wages and poor working conditions; people in the media, who find their right to a free press regularly trampled; the intelligentsia, who find the oppression and misery of their populations unbearable; and democracy and human rights activists. External support can also boost the cause of democracy by strengthening the forces of democracy. However, there are two risks with external support. One is that external actors are likely to push for types of democracy that are not compatible with realities in the region. A second risk is that democracy entails self-determination in decision-making, and external support is likely to subvert such self-determination either inadvertently or intentionally.

Champions for Change

Even in the presence of potential social forces, bringing substantive change requires an organized leadership that articulates the type of changes that could address the prevailing general crisis and can organize social forces to propel the change. In the Horn countries the leadership for change is unlikely to come from governments or ruling political parties. Ruling parties and autocratic leaders are not likely to spearhead changes that would transform the structures of the state because such changes place checks on the power of the executive and ruling parties. It is not impossible for ruling parties and state leaders to implement defensive changes when they face pressure from the forces of social change. They are not likely to serve as vanguards of change, however. Leaders have also failed to champion regional integration and have often obstructed it for political expediency.

Opposition parties have the potential to serve as champions of change. So far, however, there has not been a clear indication that opposition parties have articulated the path for change that is capable of reversing the region's general crises. Instead of building platforms that articulate the necessary change and mobilizing the social groups that would be forces for change, opposition parties have been, by and large, preoccupied with taking power to trade places with ruling parties. Instead of championing policy independence they also compete with ruling parties for external patronage. If they do not articulate the path to change while in opposition and put pressure on ruling parties and mobilize populations around platforms of change, they are not likely to bring about significant change if and when they take over power. If and when in power they are likely to defend their power rather than curtail it. A good example of such failure of an opposition party in developing a platform for change was the Coalition for Unity and Democracy (CUD) or Kinijit (in Amharic) in Ethiopia. The party did surprisingly well in the country's 2005 election, winning (officially) 21.9 per cent of the 547-seat Lower House of People's Representatives. The party claimed it won the election and accused the ruling party, the Ethiopian People's Revolutionary Democratic Front (EPRDF), of stealing the election. In protest at the alleged rigging of the election, Kinijit refused to sit in parliament, giving up the opportunity to articulate a path for change within the legislature and use its parliamentary position to mobilize the social forces for change and put pressure on the government. Since boycotting the parliament the coalition has broken down and the party has fragmented.

The conspicuous failure of existing opposition parties in articulating a clear path for change does not, however, preclude that they can transform themselves. It is also possible that new opposition parties, whose primary aim is to articulate the needed changes and mobilize the forces for change, rather than trading places with ruling parties, may come into being. Without an organized leadership that articulates the necessary change, however, it is difficult to envision change taking place in the near future. Protests, riots and revolts by the disaffected social forces may take place at increasing frequency. Nevertheless, such activities do not necessarily lead to the desired type of change. In the medium-term, however, it is possible for new parties with a clear vision about the needed changes to emerge and to lead the social forces that would support such change. But if this does not occur, the region's conflicts are likely to remain high and perhaps even intensify.

Notes

1. Sudan's independence in 1956 represents the beginning of the era of decolonization of the countries of the region. The post-decolonization era in this study, thus, refers to the time period between the mid-1950s and the present.
2. Eritrea suspended its membership in IGAD due to disagreements over IGAD's support of Ethiopia's intervention in Somalia's civil war by invading the country in 2006. At the time of writing, Eritrea's membership has remained suspended, although the country has applied for reinstatement.
3. The boundaries between the different types of conflicts are not always clear. Civil wars and one-sided wars, for example, are generally differentiated by the size of casualties anti-government forces are able to inflict upon government forces. Casualty figures are, however, rarely accurate if available at all. Inter-state wars and civil wars also are not always clearly distinguishable, since states often fight other states through proxies and also the territorial identity of states is often disputed.
4. Different data sets, such as the Correlates of War (COW) and the Uppsala Conflict Data Programme (UCDP) International, use different casualty thresholds. According to UCDP definitions war implies at least 1,000 battle-related deaths per year. Minor armed conflict involves at least 25 battle-related deaths per year but fewer than 1,000 deaths during the course of the conflict. Intermediate armed conflict, on the other hand, entails at least 25 battle-related deaths per year and a total of at least 1,000 total deaths but fewer than 1,000 deaths in any given year (Gleditsch et al., 2002). The distinction based on arbitrary

casualty figures is problematic for various reasons. Estimates of casualty figures are also often unreliable.

5. The Front's aim was to separate the Ogaden from Ethiopia and join it to Somalia. The Front was often supported by the Somali state, which aspired to bring all Somali people, who were partitioned by colonialism, under one state.

6. It is not clear if moderate refers to less Islamic fundamentalism or more accommodating to external demands. But the wing of the ARLS led by Sharif Sheikh Ahmed is often referred to as moderate, especially by American policy-makers.

7. Al-Shebab, also known as Harakat al Shebab al Mujahideen, wants to establish a fundamentalist Islamic state in Somalia. The group was designated as terrorist by the US government in February 2008.

8. The Algiers Treaty also established a neutral Claims Commission with the mandate to decide through binding arbitration all claims for loss, damage and injury by one government against the other.

9. Eritrea had refused mediation proposed by the UN and western powers alleging that those bodies had prejudged the conflict by condemning Eritrea as the aggressor before conducting any serious investigation of the factors for the conflict.

10. Civil wars of small magnitude, where opponents inflict on the state fewer than 100 casualties per year, are generally referred to as civil conflicts.

11. According to survey respondents in a recent study, 95 per cent of inter-communal conflicts in Ethiopia and 87.5 per cent in Kenya revolve around land, water and livestock theft (Kidane Mengisteab et al., 2011).

12. A number of problems are raised with the casualty figures-based determination of civil wars, including the threshold. Sambanis (2002b), for example, questions whether the threshold figure of 1,000 should be per year, for the first year of the war, or for the total duration of the war. He also suggests that the absolute figure of 1,000 would exaggerate the number of wars in large countries compared to countries with small populations. Other important questions raised about the threshold is whether it should be limited to battle deaths of combatants or if it should include direct and indirect civilian casualties.

13. Ethnic-based rebel groups also receive various forms of support from members of their ethnic group in a neighbouring country

even if they don't get support from states. Somali rebels in Ethiopia or Kenya, for example, can count on support from Somalis in Somalia even if the Somali state does not support them. Zaghawa rebels in Darfur's Justice and Equality Movement (JEM) also receive support from the Zaghawa community in Chad. Similarly, Oromo Liberation Front (OLF) rebels from Ethiopia get support from Kenya's Oromo community.

14. Within the Ethiopian federal state (1991–present), the region is now known as the Somali state or Region 5.

15. In some cases inter-communal conflicts are spillovers from civil conflicts. The 2007 post-election violence in Kenya, for instance, spilled over into inter-ethnic violence among ethnic groups supporting the different candidates for the country's presidency.

16. The government of Sudan strongly disagrees with these estimates. Its own estimate is in the tens of thousands only.

17. According to a local commissioner in Pibor County in the Jonglei state, 2,182 women and children and 959 men were killed, 1,293 children were abducted and 375,186 cows were stolen when armed Luo Nuer fighters attacked Murle villages in December 2011 (Gettleman, 2012). These figures may be inflated but they show how deadly guns have made communal conflicts.

18. The Abyssinian empire played a double role in the slave trade. It curtailed the slave trade by the Oromo kingdoms, which it conquered in the late 1880s, giving relief to the victims of those kingdoms in the southern parts of the country. At the same time, however, it engaged in slave trade itself.

19. The tradition in many cases does not disallow women from participation and there are indications of women increasing their participation, but their participation remains at a much lower rate than men (see Kidane Mengisteab et al., 2011).

20. There are widespread arguments that ethnic conflicts are essentially caused by entrepreneurial elite who mobilize ethnic groups to further their own political interests. These arguments, however, tend to overstate the case. In many cases, ethnic groups rebel against the state because they face marginalization. In such instances the conflict cannot be simply attributed to political entrepreneurs.

21. The name Abyssinia comes from the term Habesha, which collectively refers to various identity groups in Ethiopia and Eritrea who speak Semitic languages. While ancient empires, such as

that of Axum may have been built by the Habesha, the Abyssinian empire usually refers to the empire which came into existence in present-day central Ethiopia in the early thirteenth century AD. That empire largely disintegrated into small kingdoms in the eighteenth century and was reconstituted in the mid-nineteenth century and expanded southwards incorporating large groups of non-Habesha populations into the empire. The name of the country was changed from Abyssinia to Ethiopia in the aftermath of the Second World War to reflect the new demographic composition of the empire.

22. The need for autonomy of the different organs of the state from the government is easy to understand during elections. Political parties competing to unseat the party in power clearly would not like to see the electoral commission, the central bank, the military, the constitutional court and the bureaucracy serving as agents for the re-election of the government. The expectation of neutrality is based on the recognition that the state and the government are not the same thing and that the different organs of the state need to have autonomy from the government.

23. The forms of the nationalist struggle and the contents of their agenda differed from country to country but liberation from oppression and deprivation were at the core of all of them. Among the most well-known nationalist struggles in the Greater Horn are the Mau Mau rebellion in Kenya, the patriotic resistance against colonization in Ethiopia in the late 1930s and the long struggle from successive foreign rule in Eritrea. However, the anti-colonial nationalist struggles in the region were also accompanied by sub-nationalist internal struggles. In Ethiopia and Sudan, where the Abyssinian and the Mahdiya empires had subjugated many identities, sub-nationalist struggles were rife. Even in Uganda, where the Buganda kingdom was unhappy about its position in post-colonial Uganda, sub-nationalist sentiments were widespread.

24. A third layer of institutions consists of the informal societal norms that may vary from one community to another on the basis of ethnicity, religion, mode of production and many other factors.

25. There is some controversy over what constitutes traditional institutions. Present-day African traditional institutions largely originate from formal institutions of governance under pre-colonial African political systems. With the introduction of

alien institutions of governance by the colonial state traditional institutions were relegated to the sphere of informality, although they continued to operate, in part, due to the indirect rule system of colonialism. Traditional institutions have continued to evolve and it has become a point of debate whether or not they can be regarded as genuinely traditional, given the changes they have undergone. The reason why we refer to them as traditional is, however, not because they continue to exist in an unadulterated form as they did in Africa's pre-colonial past. Rather, we regard them as traditional because they are largely indigenous and are adhered to principally, although not exclusively, by the population in the traditional sectors of the economy. *Traditional institutions may be considered to be informal institutions in the sense that they are not state sponsored. They are otherwise formal within the communities that operate under them.*

26. The traditional sector's lack of access to policy is evident in its relative deprivation in access to public services throughout the continent. The traditional sector, which is largely a subsistence economy, no doubt engages in the market system. However, in many cases, its production system is largely motivated by subsistence needs (use value) rather than exchange and profit (exchange value).

27. Another danger with the lack of separation between the state and the government is that when a government falls, for a variety of reasons the whole state falls with it, since the subversion of the state by the government does not allow the building of the institutions of the state.

28. As noted in chapter 1, the era of decolonization refers to the period between 1956, when Sudan gained its independence, to approximately the early 1960s, when Somalia, Uganda and Kenya attained their independence. The era after the mid-1960s (roughly) is referred to as post-colonial. The terms decolonization and post-colonial do not apply directly to Ethiopia but the terms are used to refer to the time periods and are not intended to suggest that they apply to all the countries of the region.

29. The line of demarcation between the two categories is not always clear, however. The reason is, in part, due to the fact that individuals and groups can change their identity over time. Membership of a social class, for example, can be both ascribed (primordial) and attained. When people change their religion

also, the new religion, which is adopted by choice, blurs the line of demarcation between primordial and social identities.

30. Bride price is often viewed as a practice that facilitates the oppression of women since they cannot abandon bad marriages for fear that the parents would be forced to return the bride-wealth. However, some survey research also shows that bride-wealth is viewed as a mechanism that elevates the importance of women in society. Bride-wealth is also generally not returnable if the marriage has resulted in children.

31. It appears that one of the potential implications of the greed theory is that, regardless of how equitable the distribution of economic, political and cultural power is, wars are likely to occur so long as there are lucrative payoffs and the constraints to engaging in wars are weak.

32. A recent four-country study shows that the overwhelming majority of conflicts in rural areas are taken to the traditional institutions for settlement (Kidane Mengisteab et al., 2011). According to survey respondents in rural and peri-urban areas the proportion of conflicts handled by traditional institutions are: 65 per cent in Kenya, 59.2 per cent in Somaliland and 78.7 per cent in Ethiopia.

33. Mussolini is said to have boasted of nearly uniting all Somali people under one state when Italy annexed British Somaliland as well as Jubaland and Somali inhabited Kenyan areas from the British in 1940. Between 1897 and 1908, Italy made agreements with Ethiopia and Britain that marked out the boundaries of Italian Somaliland. Italy also took the Ogaden area from Ethiopia by the late 1920s.

34. Sudan's alleged support of the Lord's Resistance Army (LRA) was essentially in retaliation for Uganda's support of the Sudan People's Liberation Movement (SPLM).

35. Even non-state actors, including mercenary outfits, have intervened in the region. The South Africa-linked private military company Saracen International has, for example, trained and operated a private army in Somalia, in violation of UN Security Council resolutions (Pretorianews.co.za/private-firm-flouts-unembargo-in-somalia-1.1242748, 27 February 2012). Saracen is said to be linked to a former head of Blackwater and a former Mogadishu CIA bureau chief.

36. There are allegations that there were individuals within movements, such as the AIAI, who had some level of link with al-Qaeda. However, there were hardly any organizations with

a known agenda of transnational terrorism. Groups that struggle against regimes are, however, often labelled terrorists by the elite in power regardless of the legitimacy of their agenda. The Oromo Liberation Front (OLF) and the Ogaden National Liberation Front (ONLF) are, for example, terrorist groups, according to the Ethiopian regime. The Union of Islamic Courts (UIC) was also labelled as such by the US as well as by the Transitional Federal Government of Somalia.

37. An Amnesty International report (2008), for example, notes that abuses by Ethiopian and African Union forces in the country included rape, kidnapping, mortar fire on civilian hospitals and media houses, and indiscriminate shelling of civilian crowds in response to insurgent attacks.

38. An additional complication is that stateless Somalia has also seen criminal groups engage in kidnapping and hostage taking. Such criminal activities by unknown groups also contribute to intensify the atrocities committed against the civilian population in the country. They also make it difficult to identify the perpetrators of terrorist attacks. The murder of a nun outside a Mogadishu hospital on 17 September 2006 as well as the 30 November bombing on the outskirts of Baidoa were, for example, condemned by the Union of Islamic Courts, although US officials accused the UIC of killing nuns and children (Bourbaki, 2006).

39. Secretary-General Kofi Annan told reporters at a news conference on 15 June 2006 that, 'it was wrong for the United States government to support warlords in Somalia. "I would not have recommended to the UN or the Security Council to support warlords," Mr. Annan said. "I don't know much about the Islamic Court group. What I can say is that the people of Somalia are totally fed up with the warlords, that I suspect that most Somalis, except those with vested interests [sic], will say good riddance." ' (Shabazz, 2006).

40. The rhetoric of some of the UIC leaders no doubt included references to the 'Greater Somalia' but it is not clear that this was a formal policy of the group.

41. US officials were concerned that the UIC would offer safe haven to al-Qaeda and other radical Islamic groups, as the Taliban did after it took control of Afghanistan (Shabazz, 2006).

42. The High Seas Task Force refers to illegal, unreported and unregulated fishing (IUU) as poaching and piracy (http://www.illegal-fishing.info/uploads/HSTFFINALweb.pdf).

43. The MG is accused by some of making false and unsubstantiated claims in linking groups and individuals to al-Shebab (Samatar, 2012).

44. It is possible that in some cases the marginalized groups may redirect their grievances against the state and avoid intercommunal conflicts. Eritrean independence movements were, for example, able to prevent inter-communal conflicts through mediation.

45. The rate of growth of the population is not expected to decline markedly over the next several decades. Ethiopia's population is, for example, expected to reach 150 million by 2050.

46. Communal ownership of land refers to ownership of land by a village or kinship group. In this system all members of the community are entitled to obtain use rights to land but they generally cannot sell land.

47. World Bank data compiled from blogs between October 2008 and August 2009 show that 48 per cent of investment projects covering some two-thirds of the total area (32.0 million ha) involve Sub-Saharan Africa (World Bank, 2010).

48. The Global Hunger Index is the average of three indicators: the proportion of the population that is undernourished (in per cent), prevalence of underweight in children under five (in per cent) and proportion of children dying before the age of five.

49. The People's Rally for Progress (RPP) in Djibouti has been in power since 1979, while the Ethiopian People's Revolutionary Democratic Front (EPRDF) has been in power in Ethiopia since 1991. In Sudan the National Congress Party has been in power since 1998 and in Uganda the National Resistance Movement (NRM) has been in power since 1986.

50. The ratio of the region's subsistence sector, including the population in the pastoral economic system, is among the highest in the world.

51. No doubt, separation of powers with checks and balances among the organizations of the state is an essential aspect of liberal democracy. Unfortunately, in the transitional societies, such as those of the Greater Horn of Africa, elections are emphasized even when the separation of powers is barely established.

52. The rural–urban distinction is not merely in terms of physical location. Rather, rural refers to segments of the population that operate primarily in the traditional subsistence segment of the economy, while urban refers to the population in the capitalist mode of production.

Bibliography

Abbink, Jon (2003) 'Ethiopia-Eritrea: Proxy Wars and Prospects of Peace in the Horn of Africa', *Journal of Contemporary African Studies* 21(3): 407–25.

Abdi, Ali A. (1997) 'The Rise and Fall of Somali Nationalism: From Traditional Society to Fragile "Nationhood" to Post-State', *Horn of Africa* 15(1/4): 34–80.

Abdulle, Sahal (2006) 'Somalis Rally against US Peacekeeping Plan', Reuters (4 December).

Adams, Martin (1982) 'The Baggara Problem: Attempts at Modern Change in Southern Darfur and Southern Kordofan (Sudan)', *Development and Change* 13(2): 259–89.

Adams, Martin and Stephen Turner (2006) 'Legal Dualism and Land Policy in Eastern and Southern Africa', CAPRI, *Land Rights for African Development*, pp. 6–8; http://www.capri.cgiar.org/pdf/brief_land-02.pdf

Addis Hiwet (1975) *Ethiopia: From Autocracy to Revolution.* London: Review of African Political Economy, Occasional Publication, No. 1.

Adejumobi, Said (2001) 'Citizenship, Rights, and the Problem of Conflicts and Civil Wars in Africa', *Human Rights Quarterly* 23(1): 148–70.

African Development Bank (2012) *African Economic Outlook.* Abidjan, Côte d'Ivoire.

Ahmed, Abdel Ghaffar M. (2009) 'Climate Change as a Crucial Factor in the Darfur Crisis', in Marcel Leroy (ed.) *Environment and Conflict in Africa: Reflections on Darfur.* Addis Ababa: University of Peace.

Ake, Claude (1991) 'Rethinking Democracy', *Journal of Democracy* 2(1): 32–44.

Ake, Claude (1993) 'The Unique Case of African Democracy', *International Affairs* 69(2): 239–44.

Alao, Abiodun (2007) *Natural Resources and Conflict in Africa: The Tragedy of Endowment*. Rochester Studies in History and the African Diaspora. New York: University of Rochester Press.

Amare Tekle (1996) 'International Relations in the Horn of Africa (1991–96)', *Review of African Political Economy* 23(70): 499–509.

Amnesty International (2008) 'Routinely Targeted Attacks on Civilians in Somalia', AI Index: AFR 52/006/2008 (6 May).

Amutabi, Maurice N. (2005) 'Transient, Mobile "Nations" and the Dilemma of Nationhood in the Horn of Africa: Interrogating Nomadic Pastoralists, Insecurity and the Uncertainty of Belonging', in F.A. Yieke (ed.) *East Africa in Search of National and Regional Renewal*, pp. 103–33. Dakar: Codesria.

Anonymous (2002) 'Government Recognition in Somalia and Regional Political Stability in the Horn of Africa', *Journal of Modern African Studies* 40(2): 247–72.

APRM (African Peer Review Mechanism) (2006) *Country Review Report of the Republic of Kenya* (May). Addis Ababa.

APRM (African Peer Review Mechanism) (2009) *Country Review Report of the Republic of Uganda* (January). Addis Ababa.

APRM (African Peer Review Mechanism) (2011) *Country Review Report: Federal Democratic Republic of Ethiopia* (January). Addis Ababa.

Asiwaju, Anthony I. (1985) 'The Conceptual Framework', in Anthony I. Asiwaju (ed.) *Partitioned Africans: Ethnic Relations Across Africa's International Boundaries, 1884–1984*, pp. 1–18. New York: St. Martin's Press.

Auvinen, Juha and Wayne Nafziger (1999) 'The Sources of Humanitarian Emergencies', *Journal of Conflict Resolution* 43(3): 267–90.

Avery, Sean (2012) 'Lake Turkana and the Lower Omo: Hydrological Impacts of Major Dam and Irrigation Developments', Report, African Studies Centre, vol. 1, University of Oxford (October); http://www.africanstudies.ox.ac.uk/sites/sias/files/documents/Vol%20I.pdf

Awuondo, Odegi C. (1992) *Life in the Balance: Ecological Sociology of Turkana Nomads*. Nairobi: ACTS Press.

Ayittey, George (1993) *Africa Betrayed*. New York: St. Martin's Press.

Ayittey, George (1998) *Africa in Chaos*. New York: St. Martin's Press.

Aynte, Abdi (2010) 'The Anatomy of Al-Shebaab', *Horn of Africa Journal* 29; http://www.scribd.com/doc/34053611/The-Anatomy-of-Al-Shabaab-by-Abdi-Aynte

Ayoade, John A.A. (1998) 'State without Citizens: An Emerging African Phenomenon', in Donald Rothchild and Naomi Chazan (eds) *The Precarious Balance: State and Society in Africa*, pp. 100–18. Boulder, CO: Westview Press.

Ballentine, Karen and Heiko Nitzschke (2003) 'Beyond Greed and Grievance: Policy Lessons from Studies in the Political Economy of Armed Conflict', International Peace Academy, Program on Economic Agendas in Civil War (EACW), IPA Policy Report (October).

Ballentine, Karen and Heiko Nitzschke (2005) 'The Political Economy of Civil War and Conflict Transformation', Berghof Research Centre for Constructive Conflict Management; http://www.berghof-handbook.net

Bard, Mitchell G. (1988/9) 'The Evolution of Israel's Africa Policy'; http://www.jewishvirtuallibrary.org/jsource/Politics/africa.html

Bariagaber Assefaw (2006) *Conflict and the Refugee Experience: Flight, Exile, and Repatriation in the Horn of Africa*. Aldershot: Ashgate.

Barletta, Michael (1998) 'Chemical Weapons in the Sudan: Allegations and Evidence', *The Nonproliferation Review* (Fall): 115–36.

Barnes, T. Sandra (2005) 'Global Flows: Terror, Oil, and Strategic Philanthropy', *African Studies Review* 48(1): 1–23.

BBC News (1999) 'Sudan Demands Factory Bombing Inquiry' (20 August); http://news.bbc.co.uk/2/hi/africa/425552.stm

BBC News Africa (2011) 'Horn of Africa Drought: "A Vision of Hell"' (8 July); http://www.bbc.co.uk/news/uk-14078074

Berdal, Mats (2005) 'Beyond Greed and Grievance – And Not Too Soon . . . A Review Essay', *Review of International Studies* 31(4): 687–98.

Belshaw, D. and M. Malinga (1999) 'The Kalashnikov Economies of the Eastern Sahel: Cumulative or Cyclical Differentiation between Nomadic Pastoralists'. Paper presented at the first workshop of the Study Group on Conflict and Security of the Development Studies Association, South Bank University/University of East Anglia.

Bereket Habte Selassie (1989) *Eritrea and the United Nations and other Essays*. Trenton, NJ: Red Sea Press.

Bereketeab Redie (2009) 'The Eritrea–Ethiopia Conflict and the Algiers Agreement: Eritrea's March Down the Road to Isolation', in Richard Reid (ed.) *Eritrea's External Relations: Understanding its Role and Foreign Policy*. London: Chatham House/Brookings Institution Press.

Berhe Tadesse and Yonas Adaye Afar (2007) *The Impact of Local Conflict on Regional Stability*. Tshwane, Pretoria: Institute for Security Studies.

Beshir, Mohamed Omer (1986) *The Southern Sudan: Background to Conflict*. London: Hurst.

Besley, Timothy and Marta Reynal-Querol (2012) 'The Legacy of Historical Conflict: Evidence from Africa', CEPR Discussion Paper, No. DP8850 (February).

Blas, Javier and A. England (2008) 'Foreign Fields: Rich States Look Beyond their Borders for Fertile Soil', *Financial Times* (FT.com) (19 August).

Bohrer, Kevin (1998) 'Djibouti Country Profile', in John W. Bruce (ed.) *Country Profiles of Land Tenure: Africa, 1996*, pp. 160–3. Madison: Land Tenure Center, University of Wisconsin.

Bollig, M. (1990) 'Ethnic Conflicts in North-West Kenya: Pokot–Turkana Raiding 1969–1984', *Zeitschrift für Ethnologie* 115: 73–90.

Bond, Doug and Patrick Meier (2006) 'Resource Scarcity and Pastoral Armed Conflict in the Horn of Africa'. Paper presented at the annual meeting of the International Studies Association, Town and Country Resort and Convention Center, San Diego, California (22 March); http://www.allacademic.com/meta/p98844_index.html

Bondestam, Lars (1974) 'People and Capitalism in North Eastern Ethiopia', *Journal of Modern African Studies* 12(3): 432–9.

Bourbaki, N. (2006) 'Inside the Somali Civil War and the Islamic Courts' (22 December); http://cryptome.org/wikileaks/inside_somalia_v5.doc

Brons, Maria (2001) *Society, Security, Sovereignty and the State in Somalia: From Statelessness to Statelessness*. Utrecht: International Books.

Bruchhaus, Eva-Maria (ed.) (2006) *Trading Places: Alternative Models of Economic Co-operation in the Horn of Africa*. Uppsala: Life and Peace Institute.

Bruton, Bronwyn E. (2010) 'Somalia: A New Approach', Council on Foreign Relations, Center for Preventive Action, Special Report, No. 52 (March).

Buhaug, Halvard (2010) 'Climate not to Blame for African Civil Wars', *Proceedings of the National Academy of Sciences* 107(38): 16477–82.

Buhaug, Halvard, Havard Hegre and Havard Strand (2010) 'Sensitivity Analysis of Climate Variability and Civil War', Peace Research Institute, Oslo (17 November); http://www.prio.no/Publications/Publication/?x=4683

Burke, Marshall B., Edward Miguel, Shanker Satyanath et al. (2009) 'Warming Increases the Risk of Civil War in Africa', *Proceedings of the National Academy of Science* 106: 20670–4.

Butagira, Tabu (2008) 'Ambassador Speaks Out on Egypt's 2m acre Land Claim', *The Monitor* (30 September).

Cabral, Amilcar (1969) *Revolution in Guinea: An African People's Struggle.* London: Monthly Review Press.

Callaghy, Thomas (1987) 'The State as Lame Leviathan: The Patrimonial Administrative State in Africa', in Zaki Ergas (ed.) *The African State in Transition*, pp. 87–116. New York: St. Martin's Press.

Caporaso, James (1982) 'The State's Role in Third World Economic Growth', *Annals of the American Academy of Political and Social Science* 459 (January): 103–11.

Chau, Donavan C. (2007) 'Political Warfare in Sub-Saharan Africa: U.S. Capabilities and Chinese Operations in Ethiopia, Kenya, Nigeria, and South Africa', U.S. Strategic Studies Institute (March); http://www.StrategicStudiesInstitute.army.mil/

Christensen, Jens H. and Bruce Hewitson (2003) 'Regional Climate Projections'; http://www.ipcc.ch/pdf/assessment-report/ar4/wg1/ar4-wg1-chapter11.pdf

Clapham, Christopher (1995a) 'The Horn of Africa: A Conflict Zone', in Oliver Furley (ed.) *Conflict in Africa*, pp. 72–91. London: Tauris Academic Studies.

Clapham, Christopher (1995b) 'The Politics of Post-Insurgency', in John A. Wiseman (ed.) *Democracy and Political Change in Sub-Saharan Africa*, pp. 116–36. London: Routledge.

Clapham, Christopher (1996) 'Boundary and Territory in the Horn of Africa', in Paul Nugent and A.I. Asiwaju (eds) *African Boundaries: Barriers, Conduits and Opportunities*, pp. 237–50. London: Frances Pinter.

Clapham, Christopher (1998) 'Introduction: Analysing African Insurgencies', in Christopher Clapham (ed.) *African Guerrillas*, pp. 1–18. Oxford: James Currey.

Claussen, Eileen (2007) Speech by Eileen Claussen, President, Pew Center on Global Climate Change, American Colleges and University Presidents Climate Commitment Summit, Washington, DC (12 June).

Claussen, Eileen (n.d.) 'Environment and Security: The Challenges of Integration'. Address to Woodrow Wilson Environment and Security Discussion Group; http://www.wilsoncenter.org/sites/default/files/ECSP1.pdf

Cliffe, Lionel (1999) 'Regional Dimension of Conflict in the Horn of Africa', *Third World Quarterly* 20(1): 89–111.

Cliffe, Lionel (2004) 'Regional Impact of the Eritrea–Ethiopia War', in Dominique Jacquin-Berdal and Martin Plaut (eds) *Unfinished Business: Ethiopia and Eritrea at War*. Trenton, NJ: Red Sea Press.

Cliffe, Lionel and Philip White (2002) 'Conflict Management and Resolution in the Horn of Africa', in Ciru Mwaura and Susanne Schmeidl (eds) *Early Warning and Conflict Management in the Horn of Africa*. Trenton, NJ: Red Sea Press.

Cobham, Alex (2005) 'Causes of Conflict in Sudan: Testing the Black Book', QEH Working Paper, No. 121 (January).

Cohn, Julie (2010) 'Terrorism Havens: Somalia', Council on Foreign Relations (June); http://www.cfr.org/somalia/terrorism-havens-somalia/p9366

Coldham, Simon (2000) 'Land Reform and Customary Rights: The Case of Uganda', *Journal of African Law* 44(1): 65–77.

Collier, Paul and Anke Hoeffler (2002) 'Greed and Grievance in Civil War', World Bank, CSAE WPS/2002-01 (13 March); http://128.118.178.162/eps/dev/papers/0409/0409007.pdf

Cotula, Lorenzo (2011) *Land Deals in Africa: What is in the Contracts?* London: International Institute for Environment and Development.

Cramer, Christopher (2006) *Civil War is not a Stupid Thing: Accounting for Violence in Developing Countries*. London: Hurst and Company.

Cranna, M. (ed.) (1994) *The True Cost of Conflict*. London: Saferworld.

Daily Nation (2008) 'Role of Media in Kenya's Post Election Violence' (3 March).

Dagne Theodros (2000) 'The Horn of Africa: Another Humanitarian Crisis?', *Mediterranean Quarterly* 11(3): 116–28.

Dagne Ted and Bathsheaba Everett (2004) 'Sudan: The Darfur Crisis and the Status of the North–South Negotiations', Congressional Research Service (22 October).

Daniel Kendie (1999) 'Egypt and the Hydro-Politics of the Blue Nile River', *Northeast African Studies* NS 6(1–2): 141–69.

Daniel Kendie (2003) 'Problems and Prospects for a Horn of Africa Confederation/Federation', *Horn of Africa* 21: 1–19.

Dar, Osman (2011) 'The Dadaab Camps – the Daemon in the Detail', Chatham House, The Worldtoday.org (October); http://www.chathamhouse.org/sites/default/files/TWT1011p18Dadaab.pdf

Davidson, Basil (1992) *Black Man's Burden*. London: James Currey.

Debessay, Hedru (2003) 'Eritrea: Transition to Dictatorship, 1991–2003', *Review of African Political Economy* 30(97): 435–44.

Deen, Thalif (2012) 'Somalia's Rich Maritime Resources Being Plundered, Report Says', Terraviva (1 April); http://ipsnews.net/newsTVE.asp?idnews=106842

Deherez, Dustin (2009) 'The Scarcity of Land in Somalia: Natural Resources and their Role in the Somali Conflict', Occasional Paper, Bonn International Centre for Conversion.

Deininger, Klaus (2003) 'Causes and Consequences of Civil Strife: Micro-level Evidence from Uganda', *Oxford Economic Papers* 55: 579–606.

De Lombaerde, Philippe and Luk van Langenhove (2005) 'Indicators of Regional Integration: Methodological Issues', IIIS Discussion Paper, No. 64 (March).

Deng, Francis Mading (2008) *Identity, Diversity, and Constitutionalism in Africa*. Washington, DC: United States Institute of Peace Press.

Deng, Francis Mading (2010) *Self-Determination and National Unity: A Challenge for Africa*. Lawrenceville, NJ: Africa World Press.

Dershowitz, Suzanne and James Paul (2012) 'Fishermen, Pirates and Naval Squadrons: The Security Council and the Battle over Somali's Coastal Seas', Global Policy Forum (February); http://www.globalpolicy.org/images/pdfs/Security_Council/GPF_Somalia_illegal_fishing.pdf

Deutsch, Karl W. (1968) *The Analysis of International Relations*. Englewood Cliffs, NJ: Prentice-Hall.

De Waal, Alex (2005) *Islamism and its Enemies in the Horn of Africa*. London: Hurst.

De Waal, Alex (2006) 'Sudan: The Question of Land', AllAfrica.com (14 July); http://allafrica.com/stories/200607140762.html

Dia, Mamadou (1996) *Africa's Management in the 1990s and Beyond: Reconciling Indigenous and Transplanted Institutions*. Washington, DC: World Bank.

Doom, Ruddy and Koen Vlassenroot (1999) 'Kony's Message: A New Koine? The Lord's Resistance Army in Northern Uganda'. *African Affairs* 98(390): 5–36.

Dowd, Robert and Michael Driessen (2006) 'Ethnically Dominated Party Systems and the Quality of Democracy: Evidence from Sub-Saharan Africa'. Paper presented at the annual meeting of the American Political Science Association, Philadelphia, PA (31 August–3 September).

Dowden, Richard (2008) *Africa: Altered States, Ordinary Miracles*. London: Portobello Books.

Draper, Peter and Mzukisi Qobo (2007) 'Rabbits Caught in the Headlights? Africa and the "Multilateralizing Regionalism" Paradigm'. Paper presented at the conference on Multilateralizing Regionalism, sponsored and organized by the WTO–HEI and the Centre for Economic Policy Research, Geneva, Switzerland (10–12 September).

Dunn, Kevin C. (2004) 'Killing for Christ? The Lord's Resistance Army of Uganda', *Current History* 103(673): 206–10.

East African Community (1999) 'Treaty Establishing the East African Community', Arusha.

Ehrenreich, Rosa (1998) 'The Stories We Must Tell: Ugandan Children and the Atrocities of the Lord's Resistance Army', *Africa Today* 45(1): 79–102.

Eiobu, Angonu (2000) 'Teso Gets Guns from Museveni', *The Monitor* (22 March): 3.

Eisenstadt, Samuel N. (1968) 'Social Institutions: The Concept', in D.L. Sills (ed.) *International Encyclopedia of Social Sciences*. New York: Macmillan.

El-Battahani, Atta (2007) 'Tunnel Vision or Kaleidoscope: Competing Concepts on Sudan Identity and National Integration', *African Journal on Conflict Resolution* 7(2): 37–61.

Elischer, Sebastian (2008) 'Ethnic Coalitions of Convenience and Commitment: Political Parties and Party Systems in Kenya', GIGA Research Programme: Violence, Power and Security, No. 68 (February).

Elmi, Afyare Abdi and Abdi Aynte (2012) 'Somalia: The Case for Negotiating with al-Shebaab', Al Jazeera Centre for Studies (16 January); http://studies.aljazeera.net/ResourceGallery/media/Documents/2012/2/16/20122161343144443734Somalia_The%20Case%20for%20Negotiating%20with%20al-Shabab.pdf

Elnur, Ibrahim (2008) *Contested Sudan: The Political Economy of War and Reconstruction*. Durham Modern Middle East and Islamic World Series. London and New York: Routledge.

El-Tom, Abdullahi Osman (2006) 'Darfur People: Too Black for the Arab-Islamic Project', in Salah M. Hassan and Carina E. Ray (eds) *Darfur and the Crisis of Governance in Sudan*, pp. 84–102. Ithaca, NY and London: Cornell University Press.

EM-DAT (2011) The International Disaster Database, Centre for Research on the Epidemiology of Disasters (CRED); http://www.emdat.be/country-profile

Englebert, Pierre (1997) 'The Contemporary African State: Neither African nor State', *Third World Quarterly* 18(4): 767–75.

Englebert, Pierre (2000) *State Legitimacy and Development in Africa*. Boulder, CO: Lynne Rienner.

Enzensberger, Hans Magnus (1994) *Civil Wars: From L.A. to Bosnia*. New York: The New Press.

Esteban, Joan and Debraj Ray (1994) 'On the Measurement of Polarization', *Econometrica* 62 (July): 819–51.

Ethiopia, Federal Democratic Republic (2004) *Statistical Abstracts*.

Ethiopia, Federal Democratic Republic (1994) *Constitution of the Federal Democratic Republic of Ethiopia*. Addis Ababa: Government Printers.

FAO (2009, 2012) *The State of Food Insecurity in the World*. Rome.

Faris, Stephen (2007) 'The Real Roots of Darfur', *Atlantic Monthly* (April).

Fayemi, Ademola Kazeem (2009) 'Towards an African Theory of Democracy', *Thought and Practice: A Journal of the Philosophical Association of Kenya* NS 1(1): 101–26.

Fernyhough, Timothy Derek (2010) *Serfs, Slaves and Shifta: Modes of Production and Resistance in Pre-Revolutionary Ethiopia*. Addis Ababa: Shama Books.

Finnstrom, Sverker (2006) 'Wars of the Past and War in the Present: The Lord's Resistance Movement/Army in Uganda', *Africa: The Journal of the International African Institute* 76(2): 200–20.

Finnstrom, Sverker (2008) *Living with Bad Surroundings*. Durham, NC: Duke University Press.

Freedom House (2010) 'Eritrea', in *Freedom in the World: The Annual Report of Political Rights and Civil Liberties*, pp. 218–20; http://www.freedomhouse.org/research/#reports

Fukui, Katsuyoshi and John Markakis (eds) (1994) *Ethnicity and Conflict in the Horn of Africa*. London: James Currey/Athens: Ohio University Press.

Fukui, Katsuyoshi and David Turton (eds) (1979) 'Warfare among East African Herders', Senri Ethnological Series, No. 3. Osaka: National Museum of Ethnology.

Fukuyama, Francis (2005) 'Building Democracy after Conflict: "Stateness" First', *Journal of Democracy* 16(1): 84–8.

Fulford, Robert (2003) 'Idi Amin's Crimes Can't be Counted', *The National Post* (26 July).

Gaim Kibreab (2009) 'Eritrean–Sudanese Relations in Historical Perspective', in Richard Reid (ed.) *Eritrea's External Relations: Understanding its Regional Role and Foreign Policy*. London: Chatham House.

Gebrewold K. and S. Byrne (2005) 'Small Arms and Light Weapons in the Horn: Reducing the Demand', in Dorina A. Bekoe (ed.) *East Africa and the Horn*, pp. 11–20. New York: International Peace Academy.

Gebru Tareke (2000) 'The Ethiopia–Somalia War of 1977 Revisited', *The International Journal of African Historical Studies* 33(3): 635–67.

Gebru Tareke (2009) *The Ethiopian Revolution*. New Haven, CT: Yale University Press.

Geertz, Clifford (1963) *Old Societies and New States: The Quest for Modernity in Asia and Africa*. Glencoe, IL: Free Press.

Genet Mersha (2009) 'Experts Worry about Negative Consequences: International Agricultural Land Deals Award Ethiopian Virgin Land to Foreign Companies' (12 August); http://www.addistimes.com/opinion.html

Gennaioli, Nicola and Ilia Rainer (2007) 'The Modern Impact of Pre-Colonial Centralization in Africa', *Journal of Economic Growth* 12(3): 185–234.

Gertzel, Cherry J., Maure Goldschmidt and Don Rothchild (eds) (1969) *Government and Politics in Kenya: A Nation Building Text*. Nairobi: East African Publishing House.

Gettleman, Jeffrey (2012) 'Accounts Emerge in South Sudan of 3,000 Deaths in Ethnic Violence', *The New York Times* (5 January).

Gibert, Marie (2006) 'The European Union in the IGAD-Subregion: Insights from Sudan and Somalia', *Review of African Political Economy* 33(107): 142–50.

Gleditsch, Nils Petter (2008) 'Armed Conflict and the Environment', in Ronald B. Mitchell (ed.) *International Environmental Politics*, vol. IV, pp. 273–58. London: Sage.

Gleditsch, Nils Petter (2012) 'Whither the Weather? Climate Change and Conflict', *Journal of Peace Research* 49(1): 3–9.

Gleditsch, Nils Petter, Peter Wallensteen, Mikael Eriksson et al. (2002) 'Armed Conflict 1946–2001: A New Dataset', *Journal of Peace Research* 39(5): 615–37.

Global Land Project (2010) *Land Grab in Africa: Emerging Land System Drivers in a Teleconnected World.* Copenhagen: University of Copenhagen, Department of Geography; http://www.globallandproject.org/arquivos/GLP_report_01.pdf

Gros, Jean-Germain (1996) 'Towards a Taxonomy of Failed States in the New World Order', *Third World Quarterly* 17(3): 455–71.

Groves, Jason (2011) 'Cameron Warns Africans over the "Chinese Invasion" ', *Daily Mail Online* (20 July).

Gulliver, P.H. (1955) *The Family Herds: A Study of Two Pastoral Tribes in East Africa: The Jie and Turkana.* London: Routledge and Kegan Paul.

Gurr, Ted Robert (1970) *Why Men Rebel.* Princeton, NJ: Center of International Studies, Princeton University Press.

Gurr, Ted (1993) *Minorities at Risk: A Global View of Ethnopolitical Conflicts.* Washington, DC: United States Institute for Peace Press.

Hadley, H. Jenner (1997) *Pastoralist Cosmology: The Organizing Framework for Indigenous Conflict Resolution in the Horn of Africa.* Harrisonburg, VA: Eastern Mennonite University.

Hamer, John (2007) 'Decentralization as a Solution to the Problem of Cultured Diversity: An Example from Ethiopia', *Africa* 77(2): 207–25.

Hammond, Laura C. (2003) 'Obstacles to Regional Trade in the Horn of Africa: Borders, Markets, and Production', Clark University (February).

Hansson, Cote (2003) 'Building New States: Lessons from Eritrea', in Tony Addison (ed.) *From Conflict to Recovery in Africa.* Oxford: Oxford University Press.

Harbeson, John W. (1978) 'Territorial and Development Politics in the Horn of Africa: The Afar of the Awash Valley', *African Affairs* 77(309): 479–98.

Hartley, Joanna (2009) 'Qatar Signs Food for Port Deal with Kenya', *Arabian Business* (13 January).

Hassan, Salah M. and Carina E. Ray (eds) (2006) *Darfur and the Crisis of Governance in Sudan.* Ithaca, NY and London: Cornell University Press.

Healy, Sally and Martin Plaut (2007) *Ethiopia and Eritrea: Allergic to Persuasion*. London: Chatham House.

Helmke, Gretchen and Steven Levitsky (2004) 'Informal Institutions and Comparative Politics: A Research Agenda', *Perspectives on Politics* 2(4): 725–40.

Hendrickson, Dylan, Robin Mearns and Jeremy Armon (1996) 'Livestock Raiding among the Pastoral Turkana of Kenya', *IDS Bulletin* 27(3): 17–30.

Henry, Neil (1991) 'Mengistu Leaves Ethiopia in Shambles; Civil Wars, Famine and Political Terror Marked 17-Year Rule by Marxist President', *The Washington Post* (22 May).

Herrero, Mario, Claudia Ringler, Jeannette van de Steeg et al. (2010) *Climate Variability and Climate Change and their Impacts on Kenya's Agricultural Sector*. Nairobi: International Food Policy Research Institute.

Homer-Dixon, Thomas (1999) *Environment, Scarcity, and Violence*. Princeton, NJ: Princeton University Press.

Human Rights Watch/Africa (1997) *The Scars of Death*. New York: Human Rights Watch.

Hyden, Goran (1983) *No Shortcuts to Progress: African Development Management in Perspective*. Berkeley: University of California Press.

Hyden, Goran (1996) 'Rethinking Theories of the State: An Africanist Perspective', *Africa Insight* 26(1): 26–35.

ICC Commercial Crime Services (2012) 'Piracy Attacks in East and West Africa Dominate World Report' (19 January); www.icc-ccs.org/news/711-piracy-attacks-in-east-and-west-africa-dominate-world-report

ICC International Maritime Bureau (2011) 'The Human Cost of Somali Piracy 2011' (22 June); http://www.icc-ccs.org/?start=8

ICG (International Crisis Group) (2006) 'Can the Somali Crisis be Contained?', Africa Report, No. 116 (10 August). Nairobi and Brussels.

ICG (International Crisis Group) (2008) 'Beyond Fragile Peace between Ethiopia and Eritrea: Averting New War', Africa Report, No. 141 (17 June). Nairobi and Brussels.

IFPRI (International Food Policy Research Institute) (2012) 'Global Hunger Index 2012'; http://www.ifpri.org/publication/2012-global-hunger-index

IGAD (Intergovernmental Authority for Development) (2007) *IGAD Environment and Natural Resources Strategy* (April). Djibouti.

Ighobor, Kingsley (2013) 'China in the Heart of Africa: Opportunities and Pitfalls in a Rapidly Expanding Relationship', *Africa Renewal* (January): 6–8.

Ignatieff, Michael (1993) *Blood and Belonging: Journeys into the New Nationalism*, pp. 21–8. New York: Farrar, Straus and Giroux.

ILRI (International Livestock Research Institute) (2006) *Mapping Climate Vulnerability and Poverty in Africa*. Report to the Department for International Development, Nairobi (May).

International Rivers (2013) 'The Downstream Impacts of Ethiopia's Gibe III Dam' (January); http://www.internationalrivers.org/files/attached-files/impact_of_gibe_3_final.pdf

Iyob Ruth and Edmond J. Keller (2005) 'US Policy in the Horn: Grappling with a Difficult Legacy', in Dorina A. Bekoe (ed.) *East Africa and the Horn*, pp. 101–25. New York: International Peace Academy.

Jackson, Robert (1990) *Quasi-States: Sovereignty, International Relations and the Third World*. Cambridge: Cambridge University Press.

Jackson, Robert H. and Carl G. Rosburg (1982) 'Why Africa's Weak States Persist: The Empirical and Juridical in Statehood', *World Politics* 35 (October): 1–24.

Jacquin-Berdal, Dominique (ed.) (2005) *Unfinished Business: Ethiopia and Eritrea at War*. Trenton, NJ: Red Sea Press.

Johnson, Douglas (2002) *The Root Causes of Sudan's Civil Wars*. London: James Currey.

Jok, Madut Jok (2007) *Sudan: Race, Religion, and Violence*. Oxford: Oneworld Publishers.

Kabwegyere, Tarsis B. (ed.) (1995) *The Politics of State Formation and Destruction in Uganda*. Kampala: Fountain Publishers.

Kaldor, Mary (1999) *New and Old Wars: Organized Violence in a Global Era*. Stanford, CA: Stanford University Press.

Kaldor, Mary (2000) 'Cosmopolitanism and Organised Violence'. Paper prepared for Conference on 'Conceiving Cosmopolitanism', Warwick (27–29 April).

Kaldor, Mary (2009) 'Mary Kaldor on Framing War, the Military-Industrial Complex, and Human Security', Theory Talk, No. 30 (16 May); http://www.theory-talks.org/2009/05/theory-talk-30.html

Kalyvas, Stathis (2001) '"New" and "Old" Civil Wars: A Valid Distinction?', Research Note, *World Politics* 54 (October): 99–118.

Kanet, Roger E. (2006) 'The Superpower Quest for Empire: The Cold War and Soviet Support for "Wars of National Liberation"', *Cold War History* 6(3): 331–52.

Karl, Terry Lynn (1999) 'The Perils of the Petro-State: Reflections on the Paradox of Plenty', *Journal of International Affairs* 53(1): 31–48.

Kasfir, Nelson (2005) 'Sudan's Darfur: Is it Genocide?', *Current History* 104(682): 195–202.

Kaufman, Michael T. (2003) 'Idi Amin, Murderous and Erratic Ruler of Uganda in the 70's, Dies in Exile', *The New York Times* (17 August).

Kenworthy, Joan M. (1998) 'Resource Conflict in the Horn of Africa', *African Affairs* 97: 579–80.

Khalif, Abdulkadir (2012) 'Somalia: Mogadishu Brands Al-Qaeda "Colonialists"', AllAfrica (14 February); http://allafrica.com/stories/201202140053.html

Kidane Mengisteab (1999) 'Democratization and State Building in Africa: How Compatible are They?', in Kidane Mengisteab and Cyril Daddieh (eds) *State Building and Democratization in Africa*, pp. 21–39. Westpoint, CT: Praeger.

Kidane Mengisteab and Cyril Daddieh (1999) 'Why State Building is Still Relevant in Africa and How it Relates to Democratization', in Kidane Mengisteab and Cyril Daddieh (eds) *State-Building and Democratization in Africa*, pp. 1–17 Westport, CT: Praeger.

Kidane Mengisteab and Okbazghi Yohannes (2005) *Anatomy of the African Tragedy: Political, Economic and Foreign Policy Crisis in Post-Independence Eritrea*. Trenton, NJ: Red Sea Press.

Kidane Mengisteab, Gerard Hagg, Ikubolajeh Logan et al. (2011) 'Reconciling Africa's Fragmented Institutions of Governance: A New Approach to Institution Building', Research Report submitted to the IDRC (September).

Kiprotich, Alex (2009) 'Residents Suffer Nature's Wrath as Lake Dries up' (5 July); http://www.standardmedia.co.ke/?articleID=1144018602&story_title=Residents-suffer-nature%E2%80%99s-wrath-as-lake-dries-up

Klugman, Jeni (2000) 'Kenya: Economic Decline and Ethnic Politics', in E.W. Nafziger, F. Stewart and R. Vayrynen (eds) *Weak States and Vulnerable Economies: Humanitarian Emergencies in the Third World*. Oxford: Oxford University Press.

Knaup, Horand and Juliane von Mittelstaedt (2009) 'Foreign Investors Snap up African Farmland', *Spiegel* (30 July).

Kornprobst, Markus (2002) 'The Management of Border Disputes in African Regional Subsystems: Comparing West Africa and the Horn of Africa', *Journal of Modern African Studies* 40(3): 369–93.

Koser, Khalid (2008) 'Internal Displacement in Kenya'. Statement by Khalid Koser, Deputy Director, Brookings-Bern Project on Internal Displacement (14 March).

Laitin, David and Said S. Samatar (1987) *Somalia: Nation in Search of a State*. Boulder, CO: Westview Press.

Larick, Roy (1986) 'Age Grading and Ethnicity in the Style of Loikop (Samburu) Spears', *World Archaeology* 18: 269–83.

Lassey, Allan (2000) 'Mining and Community Rights – The Tarkawa Experience'. Seminar paper on Human Rights Violations in the Extractive Sector, organized by Foundation for Human Rights, Port Harcourt, Nigeria (29 October–5 November).

Leenco Lata (2003) 'The Ethiopia–Eritrea War', *Review of African Political Economy* 97: 369–88.

Leenco Lata (2004a) 'Ethiopia: The Path to War, and the Consequence of Peace', in Dominique Jacquin-Berdal and Martin Plaut (eds) *Unfinished Business: Ethiopia and Eritrea at War*, pp. 37–56. Trenton, NJ: Red Sea Press.

Leenco Lata (2004b) *The Horn of Africa as Common Homeland: The State and Self-Determination in the Era of Heightened Globalization*. Waterloo, ONT: Wilfred Laurier University Press.

Lefebvre, Jeffrey A. (1991) 'Globalism and Regionalism: U.S. Arms Transfers to Sudan', *Armed Forces and Society* 17(2): 211–27.

Lefebvre, Jeffrey A. (1987) 'Donor Dependency and American Arms Transfers to the Horn of Africa: the F-5 Legacy', *The Journal of Modern African Studies* 25(3): 465–88.

Lefebvre, Jeffrey (2012) 'Choosing Sides in the Horn of Africa: *Wikileaks*, the Ethiopia Imperative, and American Responses to Post-9/11 Regional Conflicts', *Diplomacy and Statecraft* 23(4): 704–27.

Lewis, Ioan M. (ed.) (1983) *Nationalism and Self Determination in the Horn of Africa*. London: Ithaca Press.

Lewis, Ioan M. (1998) *Peoples of the Horn of Africa: Somali, Afar and Saho*. London: Haan Publishers.

Lewis, Ioan M. (2002) *A Modern History of Somalia: Nation and State in the Horn of Africa*. London: Longman.

Lewis, Joanna (2000) *Empire State-Building: War and Welfare in Kenya 1925–1952*. Eastern African Studies. Oxford: James Currey.

Lewis, M. Paul (ed.) (2009) *Languages of the World* (16th edn). Dallas, TX: SIL International; http://www.ethnologue.com/country_index.asp?place=Africa

Liebl, Vernie (2008) 'Military Policy Options to Revise the French Military Presence in the Horn of Africa', *Comparative Strategy* 27(1): 79–87.

Lijphart, Arend (1969) 'Consociational Democracy', *World Politics* 21(2): 207–25.

Lijphart, Arend (1977) *Democracy in Plural Societies: A Comparative Exploration*. New Haven, CT: Yale University Press.

Livingston, Ian (1986) 'The Common Property Problem and Pastoralist Economic Behaviour', *Journal of Development Studies* 23(1): 5–19.

Lotuai, D. (1997) 'The Causes and Consequences of Cattle Rustling among Pastoralist Communities', APA Paper, No. 47/97. Nairobi: KIA.

Lundstrom, Karl J. (1976) *North Eastern Ethiopia: Society in Famine*. Research Report, No. 34. Uppsala: Scandinavian Institute of African Studies.

MacInnes, Charles M. (ed.) (1950) *Principles and Methods of Colonial Administration*. London: Butterworth Scientific Publications.

Mackay, James (1982) 'An Explanatory Synthesis of Primordial and Mobilizationist Approaches to Ethnic Phenomena', *Ethnic and Racial Studies* 5 (October): 395–420.

Malone, Barry (2009) 'Why is the West still Feeding Ethiopia?', Reuters (23 October); http://blogs.reuters.com/africanews/2009/10/23/why-is-the-west-still-feeding-ethiopia/

Mamdani, Mahmood (1996) *Citizen and Subject: Contemporary Africa and the Legacy of Late Colonialism*. Kampala: Fountain Publishers/Cape Town: David Phillip/London: James Currey.

Mamdani, Mahmood (2012) 'Mamdani on Kony 2012 video' (13 March); http://www.chimpreports.com/index.php/people/blogs/4111-mamdani-on-kony-2012-video.html

Markakis, John (1987) *National and Class Conflict in the Horn of Africa*. Cambridge: Cambridge University Press.

Markakis, John (1989) 'The Ishaq–Ogaden Dispute', in Anders Hjort af Ornäs and M.A. Mohamed Salih (eds) *Ecology and Politics: Environmental Stress and Security in Africa*, pp. 157–68. Uppsala: The Scandinavian Institute of African Studies.

Markakis, John (ed.) (1993) *Conflict and the Decline of Pastoralism in the Horn of Africa*. London: Macmillan.

Markakis, John (1995) 'Environmental Degradation and Social Conflict in the Horn of Africa', in Kurt Spillmann and and Gunther Bachler (eds) *Environmental Crisis: Regional Conflicts and Ways of Cooperation.* Environment and Conflict Occasional Papers, No. 14 (September), pp. 109–14. Zurich: Centre for Security Studies and Conflict Research.

Markakis, John (1998) *Resource Conflict in the Horn of Africa.* Oslo: International Peace Research Institute/London: Sage.

Martin, Denis-Constant (1995) 'The Choices of Identity', *Social Identities: Journal for the Study of Race, Nation and Culture* 1(1): 5–20.

Maxted, Julia and Abebe Zegeye (2002) 'Human Stability and Conflict in the Horn of Africa', *African Security Review* 11(1): 55–9.

Mazrui, Ali (1975) *Soldiers and Kinsmen in Uganda: The Making of a Military Ethnocracy.* Beverly Hills, CA: Sage.

Mburu, Nene (1999) 'Contemporary Banditry in the Horn of Africa: Causes, History and Political Implications', *Nordic Journal of African Studies* 8(2): 89–107.

Mekuria Bulcha (1994) 'The Language Policies of Ethiopian Regimes and the History of Written Afaan Oromoo: 1844–1994', *Journal of Oromo Studies* 1(2): 91–115.

Menkhaus, Ken (2002) 'Political Islam in Somalia', *Middle East Policy* 9(1): 109–23.

Metelis, Claire (2004) 'Reformed Rebels? Democratization, Global Norms and the Sudan People's Liberation Army', *Africa Today* 51(1): 64–82.

Michalopoulos, Stelios and Elias Papaioannou (2011) 'The Long-Run Effects of the Scramble for Africa', National Bureau of Economics Research, Working Paper 17620 (November).

Mkutu, Kennedy (2000) 'Banditry, Cattle Rustling and the Proliferation of Small Arms, the Case of Baragoi Division of Samburu District', Arusha Report. Nairobi: African Peace Forum.

Mkutu, Kennedy (2005) 'Pastoralism and Conflict in the Horn of Africa', Africa Peace Forum/Saferworld/University of Bradford.

Mkutu, Kennedy and M. Marani (2001) *The Role of Civic Leaders in the Mitigation of Cattle-Rustling and Small Arms: The Case of Laikipia and Samburu.* Nairobi: African Peace Forum.

Mohammed Hassen Ali (1990) *The Oromo of Ethiopia: A History 1570–1860.* Cambridge: Cambridge University Press.

Möller, Björn (2008) 'The Horn of Africa and the US "War on Terror" with a Special Focus on Somalia', *Post-Conflict*

Peace-Building in the Horn of Africa, Research Report in Social Anthropology, No. 1. Lund.

Morrison, J. Stephen (2002) 'Somalia's and Sudan's Race to the Fore in Africa', *The Washington Quarterly* 25(2): 191–205.

Mousseau, Demet Y. (2001) 'Democratization with Ethnic Divisions: A Source of Conflict', *Journal of Peace Research* 38(5): 547–67.

Mudoola, Dan M. (1993) *Religion, Ethnicity and Politics in Uganda*. Kampala: Fountain Publishers.

Mutibwa, Phares (2008) *The Buganda Factor in Ugandan Politics*. Kampala: Fountain Publishers.

Mwaura, Ciru and Susanne Schmeidl (eds) (2002) *Early Warning and Conflict Management in the Horn of Africa*. Lawrenceville, NJ and Asmara, Eritrea: Red Sea Press.

Mwaura, Ciru, Gunther Baechler and Bethuel Kiplaga (2002) 'Background to Conflicts in the IGAD Region', in Ciru Mwaura and Susanne Schmeidl (eds) *Early Warning and Conflict Management in the Horn of Africa*, pp. 31–42. Lawrenceville, NJ and Asmara, Eritrea: Red Sea Press.

Mwebaza, Rose (1999) 'Integrating Statutory and Customary Tenure Systems in Policy and Legislation: The Uganda Case'. Paper presented at a workshop on Land Tenure Policy in African Nations, Sunningdale, UK.

Nafziger, Wayne and Juha Auvinen (2002) 'Economic Development, Inequality, War, and State Violence', *World Development* 30(2): 153–63.

Nafziger, E. Wayne, Frances Stewart and Raimo Vayrynen (eds) (2001) *War, Hunger, and Displacement: The Origins of Humanitarian Emergencies* (vol. 1: Analysis, vol. 2: Case Studies). Oxford: Oxford University Press.

Ndegwa, Stephen N. (2003) 'Kenya: Third Time Lucky?', *Journal of Democracy* 14(3): 145–58.

Ngoga, Pascal (1998) 'Uganda: The National Resistance Army', in C. Clapham (ed.) *African Guerrillas*, pp. 91–106. Oxford: James Currey.

Niekerk, Lolette Kritzinger-van (2005) 'Regional Integration: Concepts, Advantages, Disadvantages and Lessons of Experience'. Paper presented at a seminar in Maputo, organized by Banco de Mocambique and World Bank.

Noll, Christian (2010) 'The Betrayed: An Exploration of the Acholi Opinion of the International Criminal Court', *Journal of the Third World Studies* 26(1): 99–119.

North, Douglas C. (1991) 'Institutions', *The Journal of Economic Perspectives* 5(1): 97–112.

Nugent, Paul and Anthony Ijaola Asiwaju (1996) *African Boundaries: Barriers, Conduits and Opportunities*. London: Pinter.

Nunn, Nathan and Leonard Wantchekon (2009) 'The Slave Trade and the Origins of Mistrust in Africa', *American Economic Review* 101(7): 3221–52.

Nyaba, Peter Adwok and Peter Otim (2001) *Conflicts in Pastoral Areas along Borders: The Kenya, Uganda, and Sudan*. CEWARN Consultancy Report. London: FEWAR.

Nyang'oro, Julius E. (1999) 'Civil Society, Democratization and State Building in Kenya and Tanzania', in Kidane Mengisteab and Cyril Daddieh (eds) *State Building and Democratization in Africa*, pp. 183–99. Westpoint, CT: Praeger.

Ofcansky, Thomas P. (1996) *Uganda: Tarnished Pearl of Africa*. Boulder, CO: Westview Press.

Okbazghi Yohannes (1991) *Eritrea: A Pawn in World Politics*. Gainesville: University of Florida Press.

Okbazghi Yohannes (1997) *The United States and the Horn of Africa: An Analytical Study of Pattern and Process*. Boulder, CO: Westview Press.

Olsen, Johan P. (2007) 'Understanding Institutions and Logics of Appropriateness: Introductory Essay', ARENA, Working Paper, No. 13 (August).

One Earth Future Foundation (2011) 'The Economic Cost of Somali Piracy 2011', Working Paper; http://oceansbeyondpiracy.org/sites/default/files/economic_cost_of_piracy_2011.pdf

Osamba, Joshia O. (2000) 'The Sociology of Insecurity', *African Journal on Conflict Resolution* 1(2): 11–37.

Ottaway, Marina (1999) 'Nation Building and State Disintegration', in Kidane Mengisteab and Cyril Daddieh (eds) *State Building and Democratization in Africa*, pp. 84–97. Westpoint, CT: Praeger.

Ouma, Gilbert (2008) 'Food Security and Climate Change in Africa: Are Existing Climate Risk Management Mechanisms Adequate to Sustain Food Security in Africa? Case of the Greater Horn of Africa', IGAD Climate Prediction and Application Centre.

Pan-African African Parliament, African Union (2011) http://au.int/en/sites/default/files/111Draft%20Protocol%20on%20PAP%20-%20EN%20-%20REVISED%20VERSION%20OF%2019%20Sept%202011%20-%20FINAL.pdf

Pankhurst, E. Sylvia (1952) *Eritrea on the Eve: The Past and Future of Italy's 'First-born' Colony, Ethiopia's Ancient Sea Province.* Woodford Green: New Times and Ethiopia New Books.

Pankhurst, E. Sylvia and Richard Pankhurst (1953) *Ethiopia and Eritrea: The Last Phase of the Reunion Struggle, 1941–1952.* Woodford Green: Lalibela House.

Pankhurst, Richard (1966) *State and Land in Ethiopian History.* Addis Ababa: Oxford University Press.

Pankhurst, Richard (1968) *Economic History of Ethiopia: 1800–1935.* Addis Ababa: Haile Selassie I University Press.

Patrick, Erin (2005) 'Intent to Destroy: The Genocidal Impact of Forced Migration in Darfur, Sudan', *Journal of Refugee Studies* 18(4): 410–29.

PBS NewsHour (2012) 'Who Was Behind Kidnapping, Rescue in Somalia?' (25 January); http://www.pbs.org/newshour/bb/military/jan-june12/somalia2_01-25.html

Pflanz, Mike (2011) 'East Africa Drought: Africa Must do More to Help Itself', *The Telegraph* (4 July).

Plaut, Martin (2005) 'The Eritrea Opposition Moves Towards Unity', *Review of African Political Economy* 32(106): 638–43.

Pleitgen, Fred and Mohamed Fadel Fahmy (2011) 'Slaves Freed After CNN Documentary', CNN (17 November).

Poluha, Eva (1998) 'Ethnicity and Democracy: A Viable Alliance?', in Margaret A. Mohamed-Salih and John Markakis (eds) *Ethnicity and the State in Eastern Africa*, pp. 30–41. Uppsala: Scandinavian Institute of African Studies.

Pool, David (2001) *From Guerrillas to Government: The Eritrean People's Liberation Front.* Oxford: James Currey.

Potekhin, Ivan I. (1963) 'Land Relations in African Countries', *Journal of Modern African Studies* 1(1): 39–59.

Pruine, Gerard (2007) *Darfur: The Ambiguous Genocide* (rev. edn). Ithaca, NY: Cornell University Press.

Quam, Michael D. (1996) 'Creating Peace in an Armed Society: Karamoja, Uganda', *African Studies Quarterly* 1(1): 15.

Qugnivet, Noelle (2006) 'The Report of the International Commission of Inquiry on Darfur: The Question of Genocide', *Human Rights Review* 7(4): 38–68.

Reid, Richard (2001) 'The Challenge of the Past: The Quest for Historical Legitimacy in Independent Eritrea', *History in Africa* 28: 239–72.

Reid, Richard (2003) 'Old Problems in New Conflicts: Some Observations on Eritrea and its Relation with Tigray, from Liberation Struggle to Inter-State War', *Africa* 73(3): 361–401.

Reid, Richard (2011) *Frontiers of Violence in North-East Africa: Genealogies of Conflict since c. 1800.* Oxford: Oxford University Press.

Renner, Michael (1996) *Fighting for Survival: Environmental Decline, Social Conflict, and New Age of Insecurity.* New York: W.W. Norton.

Rex, John (1995) 'Ethnic Identity and the Nation State: The Political Sociology of Multi-Cultural Societies', *Social Identities: Journal for the Study of Race, Nation and Culture* 1(1): 21–34.

Reynal-Querol, Marta (2002) 'Ethnicity, Political Systems, and Civil Wars', *Journal of Conflict Resolution* 46(1): 29–54.

Richardson, Philip (2011) 'Avoiding Civil War in South Sudan', *African Policy Watch* 7 (January–March): 1–14.

Ross, Michael (2003) 'Oil, Drugs, and Diamonds: The Varying Roles of Natural Resources in Civil War', in Karen Ballentine and Jake Sherman (eds) *The Political Economy of Armed Conflict: Beyond Greed and Grievance*, pp. 47–70. Boulder, CO: Lynne Rienner.

Rothbard, Murray (2002) *For a New Liberty: The Libertarian Manifesto* (rev. edn). New York: Collier Macmillan.

Rothchild, Donald (2001) 'The U.S. Foreign Policy Trajectory on Africa', *SAIS Review* XXI(1): 179–211.

Rotherg, Robert and I. Battling (eds) (2005) *Terrorism in the Horn of Africa.* Washington, DC: Brookings Institution Press.

Rubenson, Sven (1962) 'The British in Eritrea', *The Journal of History* III(1): 528–30.

Sachs, Jeffrey D. and Andrew M. Warner (2001) 'The Curse of Natural Resources', *European Economic Review* 45(4–6): 827–38.

Salehyan, Idean (2008) 'From Climate Change to Conflict? No Consensus Yet', *Journal of Peace Research* 45(3): 315–26.

Salih, Mohamed M.A. (1999) 'Other Identities: The Politics of Sudanese Discursive Narratives', *Identities: The Journal of Global Culture and Power* 5(1): 1–27.

Salih, Mohamed (2005) 'Understanding the Conflict in Darfur', Occasional Paper, Centre for African Studies, University of Copenhagen.

Samatar, Abdi Ismail (2012) 'An Odious Affair: The UN in Somalia', Aljazeera.com (3 April); http://www.aljazeera.com/indepth/opini on/2012/04/2012417050577774.html

Samatar, Abdi Ismail and Ahmed Samatar (2002) 'Introduction', in Abdi Samatar and Ahmed Samatar (eds) *The African State: Reconsiderations*, pp. 1–16. Portsmouth, NH: Heinemann.

Samatar, Abdi Ismail and Ahmed Samatar (2005) 'Transition and Leadership: An Editorial', *Bidhaan* 5: 1–16.

Samatar, Abdi Ismail and Waqo Machaka (eds) (2006) 'Conflict and Peace in the Horn of Africa: A Regional Approach', in *Quest for a Culture of Peace in the IGAD Region*, pp. 26–55. Nairobi: Heinrich Boll Foundation.

Samatar, Said (2002) 'Unhappy Masses and the Challenge of Political Islam in the Horn of Africa', *Horn of Africa* 20: 1–10.

Sambanis, Nicholas (2002a) 'A Review of Recent Advances and Future Directions in the Literature on Civil War', *Defence and Peace Economics* 14(3): 215–43.

Sambanis, Nicholas (2002b) 'Defining and Measuring Civil War: Conceptual and Empirical Complexities'. Paper presented at the 43rd Annual Convention of the International Studies Association, New Orleans, LA (24–27 March).

Sambanis, Nicholas (2004) 'What is Civil War? Conceptual and Empirical Complexities of an Operational Definition', *Journal of Conflict Resolution* 48(6): 814–58.

Sanders, Edmund (2009) 'Changing Climate, Changing Lives: Fleeing Drought in the Horn of Africa', *The Los Angeles Times* (25 October).

Sandford, Judith and Steve Ashley (2008) 'Livestock, Livelihoods and Institutions in the IGAD Region', IGAD, LPI Working Paper, No. 10-08.

Scherrer, Christian P. (ed.) (1997) *Ethiopia, Eritrea and Sudan between Change and Civil War* (vol. 1: Horn of Africa: The Authentic Voice of Ethno-Nationalists, Insurgents and the Democratic Opposition, vol. 2: Ethiopia versus Oromia: The Empire Strikes Back). Moers: Institut zur Forderung der Ethnizitatsforschung und Konfliktbearbeitung (IFEK/IRECOR).

Schlee, Gunther (2003) 'Redrawing the Map of the Horn: The Politics of Difference', *Africa/International African Institute* 73(3): 343–68.

Schraeder, Peter J. (1992) 'The Horn of Africa: U.S. Foreign Policy in an Altered Cold War', *The Middle East Journal* 46(4): 571–93.

Scimia, Emanuele (2012) 'Europe Enters the New Scramble for Africa', *Asia Times* (4 April); http://www.atimes.com/atimes/global_economy/nd04dj04.html

Seekers of Truth and Justice (2006) 'The Black Book: Imbalances of Power and Wealth in Sudan, Part 1', in Salah M. Hassan and Carina E. Ray (eds) *Darfur and the Crisis of Governance in*

Sudan, pp. 406–34. Ithaca, NY and London: Cornell University Press.

Sekyi-Otu, Ato (1996) *Fanon's Dialectic of Experience*. Cambridge, MA: Harvard University Press.

Senate Foreign Relations Committee (2012) Statement of Ambassador Johnnie Carson, Assistant Secretary of State, Bureau of African Affairs 'Economic Statecraft: Embracing Africa's Market Potential' (28 June).

Shabazz, Saeed (2006) 'Annan: U.S. Wrong to Support Warlords in Somalia'; http://www.finalcall.com/artman/publish/world_news_3/article_2716.shtml

Shabazz, Saeed (2012) 'Somalia's Resources Next Target of Western Intervention?', FinalCall.com News; http://www.finalcall.com/artman/publish/printer_8570.shtml

Shay, Shaul (2005) *Red Sea Terror Triangle: Sudan, Somalia, Yemen and Islamic Terror*. London: Transaction Publishers.

Skocpol, Theda and Edwin Amenta (1986) 'States and Social Policies', *Annual Review of Sociology* 12: 131–57.

Small, Melvin, and J. David Singer (1982) *Resort to Arms: International and Civil Wars, 1816–1980*. Beverly Hills, CA: Sage.

Society for International Development (2004) *Pulling Apart: Facts and Figures on Inequality in Kenya*. Washington, DC.

Somali Information Centre (2012) http://wehelmedia.com/2012/02/13/somalia-president-al-qaeda-now-a-colonial-power

Sorbo, Gunnar M. and Siegfried Pausewang (eds) (2004) *Prospects for Peace, Security and Human Rights in Africa's Horn*. Bergen: Fagbokforlaget.

Speech by the Eritrean Permanent Mission to UN Security Council (2008) United Nations Security Council 5924th meeting (Tuesday, 24 June) New York: S/pv.5924; http://www.securitycouncilreport.org/atf/cf/%7B65BFCF9B-6D27-4E9C-8CD3-CF6E4FF96FF9%7D/Erit%20Djibou%20SPV%205924.pdf

Spillmann, Kurt (1995) 'From Environmental Change to Environmental Conflict', in Kurt Spillmann and Gunther Bachler (eds) *International Project on Violence and Conflicts Caused by Environmental Degradation and Peaceful Conflict Resolution*, Environment and Conflicts Project, Occasional Paper No. 14 (September).

Stewart, Frances (1999) 'Civil Wars in Sub-Sahran Africa: Counting the Economic and Social Cost', in D. Ghai (ed.) *Renewing Social and Economic Progress in Africa*. London: Macmillan.

Stewart, Frances (2000) 'Crisis Prevention: Tackling Horizontal Inequalities', *Oxford Development Studies* 28(3): 245–62.

Stewart, Frances (2001) 'Horizontal Inequalities: A Neglected Dimension of Development', Working Paper 1, Queen Elizabeth House, University of Oxford, Centre for Research on Inequality, Human Security and Ethnicity (CRISE).

Stewart, Frances (2009) 'Horizontal Inequalities: Two Types of Trap', *Journal of Human Development* 10(3): 315–40.

Swain, Ashok (1997) 'Ethiopia, the Sudan, and Egypt: The Nile River Dispute', *Journal of Modern African Studies* 35(4): 675–94.

Tadesse Medhane and John Young (2003) 'TPLF: Reform or Decline?', *Review of African Political Economy* 97: 389–403.

Tekeste Negash (1986) *No Medicine for the Bite of a White Snake: Notes on Nationalism and Resistance in Eritrea, 1890–1940.* Uppsala: University of Uppsala.

Tekeste Negash (1997) *Eritrea and Ethiopia: The Federal Experience.* Uppsala: Nordic Institute of African Studies.

Tekeste Negash and Kietil Tronvoll (2001) *Brothers at War: Making Sense of the Eritrean–Ethiopian War.* Athens: Ohio University Press.

Tekie Fessehatzion (2002) *Shattered Illusion, Broken Promise: Essays on Eritrea–Ethiopia War.* Trenton, NJ: Red Sea Press.

Tekie Fessehatzion (2005) 'Eritrea's Remittance-Based Economy: Conjectures and Musings', *Eritrean Studies Review* 4(2): 165–84.

Thornton, Philip, Peter G. Jones, Polly J. Erickson and Andrew J. Challinor (2011) 'Agriculture and Food Systems in Sub-Saharan Africa in a 4°C+ World', *Philosophical Transactions of the Royal Society A* 369(1934): 117–36.

Tilly, Charles (1990) *Coercion, Capital, and European States: AD 990–1990.* Cambridge: Basil Blackwell.

Trevaskis, Gerald (1960) *Eritrea: A Colony in Transition: 1941–1952.* London: Oxford University Press.

Trevill, Richard (1999) 'Background Notes on the Ethiopian–Eritrean War', *Afrika Spektrum* (Fall).

Twentieth Century Atlas Death Tolls for the Multicides of the Twentieth Century (n.d) Alphabetical Index; http://necrometrics.com/warstatx.htm

UCDP (Uppsala Conflict Data Programme) (n.d.) Uppsala University; http://www.pcr.uu.se/research/UCDP/

Uganda Bureau of Statistics (2010) *Uganda National Household Survey, 2009/10* (November). Kampala.

UNCTAD Stat (United Nations Conference on Trade and Development) (n.d.) 'Total Population, Annual, 1950–2050'; http://unctadstat.unctad.org/TableViewer/tableView.aspx?ReportId=97

UNDP (United Nations Development Programme) (2006) *Share The Land or Part the Nation: The Pastoral Land Tenure System in Sudan* (Study 3). Khartoum, Sudan.

UNDP (United Nations Development Programme) (2011, 2012) *Human Development Report*. New York.

UNDP (United Nations Development Programme) (2012) *Africa Human Development Report 2012: Towards a Food Secure Future*. New York.

UNECA (United Nations Economic Commission for Africa) (2009) *African Governance Report II*. Oxford: Oxford University Press.

UNEP (United Nations Environment Programme) (2000) *IPCC Special Report on the Regional Impacts of Climate Change An Assessment of Vulnerability* (November). New York.

UNEP (United Nations Environment Programme) (2005) 'The State of the Environment in Somalia: A Desk Study' (December); http://postconflict.unep.ch/publications/dmb_somalia.pdf

UNHCHR (Office of the United Nations High Commissioner for Human Rights) (2004) 'Report of UNHCHR Mission to Chad' (April).

UNHCR (UN High Commissioner for Refugees) (2012) 'Country Operations Profiles'; http://www.unhcr.org/cgi-bin/texis/vtx/page?page=49e483836&submit=GO

UNICEF (n.d.) 'Information by Country and Programme'; http://www.unicef.org/infobycountry/

United Nations (2010) *Sudan: Beyond Emergency Relief: Longer-Term Trends and Priorities for UN Agencies in Darfur*. Khartoum, Sudan.

United Nations Security Council (2006) *Report of the Monitoring Group on Somalia Pursuant to Security Council Resolution 1676 (2006)*, S/2006/913; http://www.fas.org/asmp/resources/govern/109th/S2006913.pdf

United Nations Security Council (2011) *Report of the Secretary-General on the Protection of Somali Natural Resources and Waters*, S/2011/661 (25 October); http://unpos.unmissions.org/Portals/UNPOS/Repository%20UNPOS/S-2011-661%20%2825Oct%29.pdf

US Department of the Interior US Geological Survey (2012) *2010 Minerals Yearbook Africa* (August). Washington, DC.

US Military Academy (2007) 'Al-Qaida's (Mis)Adventures in the Horn of Africa', Harmony Project, Combating Terrorism Center at West Point; http://www.princeton.edu/ jns/publications/AQ_ HOA.pdf

US State Department (1995–2005) *World Military Expenditures and Arms Transfers*. Washington, DC.

Van Acker, Frank (2010) 'Uganda and the Lord's Resistance Army: The New Order No One Ordered', *African Affairs* 103(412): 335–57.

Vanhanen, Tatu (1999) 'Domestic Ethnic Conflict and Ethnic Nepotism: A Comparative Analysis', *Journal of Peace Research* 36(1): 55–73.

Vidino, Lorenzo (2006) 'The Arrival of Islamic Fundamentalism in Sudan', al Nakhlah, Fletcher School Online Journal for Issues Related to Southwest Asia and Islamic Civilization (Fall); http:// fletcher.tufts.edu/Alakhlah/Archives/ /media/Fletcher/Microsites/ al%20Nakhlah/archives/2006/vidino_fall.ashx

Von Grebmer, Klaus, Marie T. Ruel, Purnima Menon et al. (2010) *Global Hunger Index: The Challenge of Hunger: Focus on the Crisis of Child Undernutrition*. Washington, DC: International Food Policy Research Institute (IFPRI).

Wallis, John Joseph and Douglass C. North (2010) 'Defining the State', Working Paper, No. 10–26, Mercatus Center, George Mason University (June).

Ward, Kevin (2001) ' "The Armies of the Lord": Christianity, Rebels and the State in Northern Uganda, 1986–1999', *Journal of Religion in Africa* 31(2): 187–221.

Weber, Max (1958) 'Politics as Vocation', in H.H. Gerth and C. Wright Mills (eds) *From Max Weber: Essays in Sociology*. New York: Oxford University Press.

Wesseling, H.L. (1996) *Divide and Rule: The Partition of Africa, 1880–1914*. Westport, CT: Praeger.

Whelan, Theresa (2007) 'Why AFRICOM?', US Department of Defense (August); http://no0ilcanarias.files.wordpress.com/2012/ 10/why-africom-whelan-august20071.pdf

Whitlock, Craig and Greg Miller (2011) 'U.S. Assembling Secret Drone Bases in Africa, Arabian Peninsula, Officials Say', *Washington Post* (20 September).

Williams, Paul D. (2007) 'Thinking about Security in Africa', *International Affairs* 83(6): 1021–38.

Williams, Paul (2011) 'Horn of Africa: Webs of Conflict and Pathways to Peace', Wilson Center (October).

Woodward, Peter (2006) *US Foreign Policy and the Horn of Africa*. Farnham: Ashgate.

World Bank (2009, 2010, 2011) *Africa Development Indicators*. Washington, DC.

World Bank (2012) *World Development Indicators*. Washington, DC.

World Bank (2013) *World Development Report 2013*. Washington, DC.

Wulf, Herbert and Tobias Debiel (2009) 'Conflict Early Warning Response Mechanisms: Tools for Enhancing the Effectiveness of Regional Organizations, A Comparative Study of the AU, ECOWAS, IGAD, ASEAN/ARF and PIF', Working Paper, No. 49, Regional and Global Axes of Conflict, Institut Fur Entwicklung und Frieden (INEF), Duisburg.

Yanacopulos, Helen and Joseph Hanlon (eds) (2006) *Civil War, Civil Peace*. Oxford: James Currey.

Young, John (2005a) 'John Garang's Legacy to the Peace Process, the SPLM/A and the South', *Review of African Political Economy* 32(106): 535–48.

Young, John (2005b) 'Sudan: A Flawed Peace Process Leading to a Flawed Peace', *Review of African Political Economy* 32(103): 99–113.

Zartman, I. William (ed.) (1995) *Collapsed States: The Disintegration and Restoration of Legitimate Authority*. Boulder, CO: Lynne Rienner.

Index ———————————————

Page numbers followed by 't' refer to a table.